THE DISARMAMENT CATALOGUE

THE DISARMAMENT CATALOGUE

Edited by
MURRAY POLNER

A Lakeville Press Book

The Pilgrim Press

New York

The Pilgrim Press, 132 West 31 Street, New York, New York 10001

Library of Congress Cataloging in Publication Data
Main entry under title:

The Disarmament catalogue.

   1. Atomic weapons and disarmament—Addresses,
essays, lectures. I. Polner, Murray.
JX1974.7.D568   1982   327.1'74   82-13226
ISBN 0-8298-0627-X

Acknowledgments appear on pp. 209

Designed by Paul Sagsoorian.

I owe a large debt to Carol Miller, a woman of courage who helped organize Mothers (and Others) Against the Draft and who, as a professional librarian, organized my incredibly disorganized files. Robert Polner helped by ransacking the Columbia University library stacks for appropriate material. Richard Chartier, editor of *Fellowship,* took the time to criticize my original outline and to suggest alternatives. I found the Swarthmore College Peace Collection a rich source of information, and its staff consistently helpful. Abraham Kaufman offered many suggestions and several hundred books, most no longer in print. The literature of the National Interreligious Service Committee for Conscientious Objectors offered many insights. Esther Cohen, my editor, offered excellent advice and criticism. Lakeville Press, Inc. kindly agreed to co-publish this book.

I dedicate this book to my family—Louise, Beth, Alex, and Robert, for living lives dedicated to nonviolence— and to the prophetic words which have always inspired and moved us: "Not by power nor by might but by my spirit saith the Lord."

Contents

"War Hath No Fury Like a Non-combatant."
Charles Edwards Montague, *Dramatic Values* (1911)

"Endless money, the sinews of war."
Cicero, *Philippics* V, 2:5

"God is present whenever a Treaty of Peace is signed."
Hasidic saying

"War is not inevitable but proceeds from definite and removable causes."
G.L. Dickinson, *The Choice Before Us* (1917)

Introduction

Although *The Disarmament Catalogue* opens with dismal and depressing revelations, it concludes optimistically, presenting hundreds of alternative courses of action. The book shows ways to find out what is happening, how to become involved with like-minded people and organizations, what to read, where to invest, and much more. You will learn that nuclear war is not inevitable and that practical means exist to halt its momentum.

I first conceived of the *Catalogue* when I realized that influential groups and people both here and abroad—in communist and non-communist countries alike—have a vested interest in stoking the fires of the Cold War, in selling weapons indiscriminately to anyone with sufficient cash, and in insisting that their own nation increase its armaments. All their propaganda and lobbying for more defense spending appears totally absurd when we realize that the five hundred thousand megatons of nuclear weapons now in storage amount to nearly five times the total of explosives used during the Second World War. When is "enough" enough?

And if all this weren't insane enough, politicians have now begun claiming that this country could survive a nuclear war. A typical remark of this genre was made by Eugene Rostow at his June 1981 Senate confirmation hearing for the position of Director of the U.S. Arms Control and Disarmament Agency: "Japan, after all, not only survived but flourished after the nuclear attack. . . . Depending upon certain assumptions, some estimates predict 10 million [dead] on the one side and 100 million on the other but that is not the whole population." Similar statements have also issued occasionally from hardliners in the U.S.S.R.

In spite of Rostow's remark, my judgment—working from the sources reproduced in the *Catalogue*—indicates that in a full-scale nuclear war about one hundred and forty million Americans alone would be killed at once. In addition, millions more would perish from fallout, epidemics, the unavailability of medical care and food, the destruction of the industrial base, etc. Such an event would also entail similar destruction in Europe, as well as in vast portions of Asia, Africa, and South America. Civilization would come to an end.

I have attended lectures beyond number, I have read endless articles and books, and I have listened to countless people discussing complex technological developments about nuclear armaments with hardly a mention of the damage they will do to people. "What is interesting about the discussion that takes place in this city [Washington, D.C.] on these issues is that it is remarkably amoral," said Senator Paul Tsongas (Democrat-Massachusetts) in March 1982. "In fact, it is fashionable in the arms control community not to allow emotion or feelings to intervene in one's analytical process." Nevertheless, we are presently faced with the possibility that few if any children alive today in the western world (at least) will grow to adulthood in the event of such a war.

To me, these are irrefutable facts. Far more important, however, is that the *Catalogue* promotes the conditions and resources which enable people to build coalitions against the warmakers. For we are confronted by a simple choice: either we stop the arms race and proceed to explore techniques of disarmament, or we face annihilation. Ending wars, nuclear and conventional, means decreasing the factors that lead to nuclear war and to war in general. Obviously this goal is vast, and the *Catalogue* can present no easy answers.

The *Catalogue* proceeds from a number of assumptions. A nuclear war cannot be won; surviving so monstrous a calamity may be worse than death; large-standing conscript armies are no alternative to nuclear arsenals. Nor are foreign policies that make nuclear war possible. The *Catalogue* also works from the assumption that both the Americans and the Soviets often accept uncritically the notion that one side is always right and the other always wrong, that one seeks to preserve freedom and the other to maintain slavery, that one fights for peace and the other for war. These shibboleths, wrote Henry Steele Commager, are "rooted in emotion rather than in reason, [they are] negative rather than positive in [their] objectives, [are] inspired by fear rather than confidence, [and are] inconsistent and even contradictory in logic."

Alternatives to war do exist. The time to seek them out is now. Join a group. Get political. Choose life.

How to Use This Book

The eyes that read these words are composed of matter: $E = mc^2$.

Behind the eyes, sits a brain containing the only force on earth greater than the destructive power of nuclear explosions—which unleash all the energy hidden in matter—the creative force of human intelligence and concern.

Although our eyes, our hands, our whole bodies are matter, matter need not be inert. Atomic bombs are here to teach us that.

Either we realize our full power as spirit, hidden in the form of human beings, or we accept annihilation, mesmerized by our own Frankenstein.

The monstrous institution of militarism wins, if we accept its premise of individual helplessness. If we work together, we win.

Vietnam was the first time in history that the people have stopped an insane military effort. It was a rehearsal for the challenge now before us. An atomic holocaust would be total; our response to that challenge must be global.

This DISARMAMENT CATALOGUE is a first attempt to bring together all the ways people can make a start on working toward peace. As we go to press, new disarmanent organizations crop up all around us. We hope to publish new editions every year, as the anti-nuclear movement takes root and flourishes.

In order to make some sense out of the constantly growing material, we have organized the book into three sections: Part I is a portrait of Frankenstein: his dimensions and what fuels him; Part II deals with arms sales throughout the world; Part III offers food for thought from the increasing number of scientists and public figures who seek to control the monster; Part IV tells you what you as an individual, or in concert with others, can do to begin reversing the current momentum of atomic destruction. *It is the point of the book.*

Before you begin reading, we suggest that you leaf through the first section, glancing at the quotes facing each other at the bottom of the left and right-hand pages; this will help focus your basic feeling for the crucial difference between the logic of madness and the voice of sanity. Then you might wish to quiz yourself with a few of the questions printed at the bottom of the resource listings in Part III, in order to see where you stand before reading the catalogue in depth.

We hope that as you read through the CATALOGUE you will become so excited that you will skip some of the longer essays in the middle section; you can always come back to them later. For if we don't all get to the final section—what to do—soon, there will be no "later."

In our personal lifetimes we all have lost a few battles to the forces of greed and violence. In the long run, they have a way of destroying themselves. The present conflict is different.

From the first tribal war parties to the modern national defense establishments, we have developed our capacity to destroy our neighbors until our military arm stretches entirely around the planet, and now—having run full course—we bump our nose on our own back fence. As Pogo said, "We have met the enemy, and he is us." "Us" is our own moral inertia. The only adequate response comes from stepping forward to call the bluff of those who would leave no second chance . . . for anyone.

We hope you will send us your suggestions, thoughts, listings, quotes, etcetera, for the next edition.

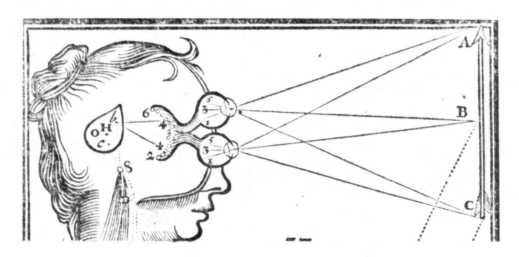

4

The Arms Race

Shalom

- One side says "by mutual assured destruction (to attack would bring equal destruction and self destruction) a stalemate exists."
- Another side says there is "too much overkill in our nuclear stalemate, especially with the superpowers. It is time to dismantle on a barter basis—SS20s for cruise missiles and Pershing-2s, perhaps leading to half your forces for half of ours."
- Another side says we are the target.
- Still another side says we must have the ability to strike first.
- One side condemns the American arsenal.
- Another side condemns the Soviet arsenal.
- Still another side condemns all nuclear arsenals.
- One side wants to increase conventional forces in Europe.
- But another side says "enough is enough.": As of 1982, "64 NATO divisions with 2.8 million troops confronted 68 Warsaw Pact divisions with 2.6 million soldiers."
- And yet another side says there is a stalemate. "There is little to gain by being stronger since we can never be certain that a weaker force will not resort to nuclear war if threatened with defeat."
- One side says that the USSR will attack with nuclear arms and destroy an American city. Then the US will surrender and ask for peace.
- But another side says this scenario is a fantasy, an illusion, a delusion. Why, they ask, would a Soviet leader "count on any President suing for peace when millions of Americans were dying and the US still retained 75 percent of its strategic forces and its entire economic base?"
- And yet another side says that if the Russians attacked they would be counterattacked immediately with air and sea nuclear forces.
- One side says the Soviets are a totalitarian society, "relatively immune from pressures of public opinion or religious conscience that may act as restraints in the west"; and "parallel pressures are needed on Moscow."
- Another side says the Reagan administration is insincere about arms control and reduction of its nuclear arsenal and that it views world events through a gunsight.
- But The Rev. John R. Quinn, archbishop of the San Francisco Catholic Archdiocese, said in October 1981 in a sermon at St. Mary's Cathedral: "At the present time, the U.S. has a stockpile of nuclear weapons equivalent to 615,000 times the explosive force of the bomb dropped at Hiroshima. With that stockpile we can destroy every major Soviet city 40 times over. The Soviet Union, in its turn, can destroy every major American city 17 times over. The Soviet and U.S. stockpiles together contain the equivalent of 12 tons of TNT for every man, woman and child in the entire world.

  "The physical and social destruction which would result from a nuclear blast borders on the unthinkable. . . . I call upon all the Catholic people of the Archdiocese of San Francisco, as well as all people of peace and non-violence, to work for bilateral disarmament and the elimination of nuclear weapons. Let us replace violence and mistrust and hate with confidence and caring."
- And I say what the *Ethics of the Fathers* said: The world rests on three things: "On truth, on justice and on peace." All are related, but the aim of the first two is to bring peace. For Peace is the name of God. And peace is the goal toward which nations and people must aspire.

(Suggested by The Economist, The New York Times, Commonweal, Catholic Worker)

Telling Our Nuclear Stories

Chellis Glendinning

After decades of official silence on the hazards of nuclear technology, Three Mile Island broke the dam. In the months since then, the possibility of meltdown has moved to the forefront of the American consciousness, along with a new awareness of the proliferation of reactors and bombs around the globe, the rise in cancer rates to epidemic proportions and the increasing threat of nuclear war. How can we begin to respond to so many terrifying developments? Apart from numbing ourselves against what is happening, how can we cope?

We can begin by breaking our own personal silence. Everyone has a tale to tell; the total picture includes the stories of each and every person who has lived in this era. How do we respond to the constant threat of death? How does living side by side with nuclear technology affect our sense of ourselves, our survival and our future as a species? After thirty-six years of honoring the taboo against speaking about nuclear weapons, *who have we become?* Apart from the work of a handful of researchers, psychology offers little perspective on these questions; it too has succumbed to the silence surrounding the nuclear problem. We know so little about ourselves in these times, and we will never understand until many, many people have spoken.

Consciousness Raising

In the late sixties, women in many places began to gather in small groups and tell their personal histories of life in sexist society. In leaderless groups, women spoke with each other, telling their secrets, showing their wounds and sharing tales of childhood, puberty, marriage, birthing, birth control, work, aging, roles and relationships. Telling these stories broke the silence and taboo, enabling women to confront their oppressive programming and figure out, as individuals and a class of people, how they could change. Telling their stories served as a basis for understanding, community, personal transformation and political action.

In 1977, psychiatrist Carol Wolman and peace activist Natalie Shiras applied the feminist consciousness-raising model to the Nuclear Age. They conceived a series of questions for exploring people's awareness of nuclear weapons. They used the questions in discussion groups with students, Lockheed engineers, religious organizations and political activists. Some of the questions they asked most frequently were these: How long do you expect life as we know it to survive? How have your personal life choices been affected by the existence of nuclear weapons, including choices about children, work and where you put your energy? If you are actively working against nuclear weapons, how do you feel about people who are not? If not, how do

you feel about people who are? Have you ever discussed your feelings and thoughts about nuclear weapons before? If not, why not?

The goals of consciousness-raising are to help people break out of isolation and despair, to mobilize anger for constructive action, to share sources of hope and strength. But Wolman and Shiras found people in the nuclear discussion groups reacting in a new way. Instead of becoming excited and empowered, as had women in feminist consciousness-raising, they became stiff and unexpressive. Instead of coming together, what emerged were the psychological defense mechanisms that people use to avoid thinking about the Bomb and that prevent them from supporting one another. This development attested to the power of the social taboo against talking or showing feelings about the Bomb. It spoke also of how overwhelmed people feel about nuclear technology. The defenses Wolman and Shiras observed were: personal withdrawal, often with the belief that only those who know about nuclear weapons would be killed in a war; identification with the Bomb as defense ("Our weapons are for peace"); frank denial ("God wouldn't allow a nuclear war"); grandiosity ("If I mobilize the people around me, there won't be a war"); escape into hedonism, and displacement of concern onto other issues that seemed more manageable.

Wolman and Shiras also reported that one's consciousness about the Bomb seems to bear a relationship to one's age. People over forty who remember the Depression, World War II and a world without nuclear weapons tend to experience history as continuous; they see the Bomb as a quantitative, rather than qualitative, addition to a world growing steadily more violent. People younger than forty, including the first post-Bomb generation, were particularly attuned to the horror of nuclear weapons and saw them as a drastic departure from the past. These findings echo the insights of Jeff Nutting in his book, *Bomb Culture* (Delacorte, 1968), who describes the generation gap of the sixties as originating with the Bomb. He sees people who came to puberty before Hiroshima as unable to imagine a world *without* a future and inclined to live their lives as if the threat were insignificant.

People who came to puberty after Hiroshima were unable to imagine a world *with* a future. They directed their anger at what they perceived to be the hypocrisy of their elders by confronting and rebelling aginst their parents' generation.

Degrees of defensiveness varied. The less involved people were in working to rid the world of the nuclear threat, the women found, the more likely they were to avoid talking about it and the more pathological were their defenses. On a larger scale, this might explain the lack of public discussion and debate over nuclear policy. It might also contribute to the widespread nihilism and hedonism of American society.

Theoretically, telling our nuclear stories can provide a first step towards involvement in decisions that affect the future of nuclear technology and at the same time towards healing our own psyches and even physical ills. Everyone who has lived with the nuclear threat offers an essential part of the complete story; in telling the tales, like the feminists who created an entire political movement from their personal stories, each speaker can help to break through the paralysis of responsibility that afflicts most people. But Wolman and Shiras' work has demonstrated that we share a great reluctance to go forward into unknown territory.

Breaking the Taboo

How can we make a transition from silence to expression and involvement if the taboo against speaking and showing feelings about nuclear weapons is so strong? Every day we remind ourselves to "have a nice day," and most people in America can still manage to put on a smiling face because, like radiation, most nuclear technology is invisible to us. We aren't even aware of how firm a hold the nuclear taboo has on us.

Last year, my friend Tom was visiting from Washington State. Tom is a radical lawyer, an organizer of reform in higher education who is dedicated to social change. When I told him of my interest in the nuclear weapons situation, he was surprised. He couldn't understand why. Instead of explaining the facts about the arms race—facts that can inspire a person to look further but can also scare one off—I asked Tom to tell me his earliest experience with the Bomb.

"I was five years old in 1945," he began, thinking aloud. "On August fifth, I learned the alphabet. The next day I sat looking out the window of our first floor New York apartment. I saw a man hawking the newspaper on the street. The headline was so big I could read the letters—my very first word—A-Bomb." From that memory, Tom traced the history of his awareness of nuclear weapons. He remembered that until the middle sixties he had been thinking about nuclear weapons and encouraging others to think about them, too. Then he stopped. He put them out of his mind for some fifteen years. But since he told his story to me, Tom has become a member of his local chapter of the American Friends Service Committee and is actively working for peace.

A setting that potential storytellers view as safe and supportive is essential for making the crossover into prohibited territory. In the case of Tom, we had the trust of a long-term friendship and I had presented the topic inquisitively instead of trying to persuade him to talk. The act of breaking the taboo not only provokes anxiety, it also opens the "transgressor" to whatever pain might lie on the other side of the restriction. Last December, eight peace activists gathered for a four-day retreat in northern California to tell each other what they called their nuclear stories. At first, they debated about how to do this. They decided finally against the more structured format used by Wolman and Shiras in favor of what they felt would be a cozier, safer setting: sitting around a fire, sipping tea and story-telling, one by one. The first night, one man said: "Telling our stories is like passing the pipe. It's like an initiation rite. In a metaphorical way, we are passing the pipe around the circle and going new places together."

To speak of something so anxiety-provoking as our

relationship to nuclear war exposes a vulnerability many people are not accustomed to show. Implicitly, it requires asking to be cared for as a fragile and sensitive being. For many, this admission alone is as scary as the content of the story. Also, just as we tend to live and to die in character, so we tend to respond to the global situation in character and to reveal our relationship to nuclear weapons carries the risk of also revealing the very fiber of our personalities.

Since Three Mile Island, I have asked many people to tell their stories. I have set up formal consciousness-raising groups, conducted workshops, initiated the topic at parties, hosted radio talk shows and spoken with individuals. Everywhere, whether the story tellers were students, corporate directors and their wives, activists or health professionals, I have found people willing to risk extending at least one toe across the line of taboo. A NASA scientist characterized what many others had expressed: "I never would have thought to talk about the Bomb, much less my personal relationship to it, but as soon as you suggested it I knew how important this kind of questioning is. I've wanted to do this for a long time."

When we share our histories, we are indeed passing the pipe around the circle and stepping over into the territory of intimacy. Such a step takes courage. It is an initiation ritual into the Nuclear Age.

Myth Making

In traditional societies, one learned during the course of initiation about the important institutions and customs of the tribe, as well as the names of the gods and goddesses and the "sacred history" of their works. One also learned the perception and values that are reflected in the tribe's mythology. An important outcome of telling our nuclear stories is to provide some very useful material that can help us construct a contemporary mythology. These topics were not ignored in the past. In Australia, for example, where people lived near natural radioactive deposits of uranium, a myth emerged that a great green ant would emerge if the people tampered with the uranium in the mountains.

If we are to create our own "sacred history," we must address the tampering that has taken place and the emergence of the great green ant. Imbuing the history of the Nuclear Age with symbolic dimensions, we must see the nuclear scientists—Einstein, Teller, Oppenheimer, Fermi, Szilard and the others—as god-like men who used their power of mind to meddle with the mysteries of matter and energy. The journey to the underworld was taken by the victims and survivors of Hiroshima and Nagasaki, by American servicemen who were sent to "clean up" the bombed cities, by atomic veterans ordered to witness testing in Nevada and the South Pacific, by the inhabitants of the Islands where testing took place, by Native American uranium miners and the residents of Harrisburg. Each and every human being on the planet who has grappled, consciously or

unconsciously, with the uncertainty of living in the Nuclear Age becomes the hero.

Apart from providing metaphors of universal proportion and so offering guidance in the face of insecurity can viewing our stories as archetypal help us to deal with the times in which we live? The purpose of myth is to find origins, to construct a worldview that begins at the point from which we have come. Wolman and Shiras reported that many people in their groups felt that the newly acquired ability of humans to destroy life on earth brings with it the need for a new philosophy and worldview.

Nuclear weapons, more than any other scientific development, have been shrouded in mystery. The discovery of how to split the atom signaled the beginning of classified research and added to the gap between public knowledge and governmental policy-making in this country. A scarcity of public nuclear events to

serve as common reference points and provide communal memories further obscures the nuclear issue from our minds. At the same time, the existence of nuclear weapons, more than any other single scientific development, alters the foundation upon which we base our lives. The pursuit of nuclear technology penetrates every sector of our society. It affects federal spending, the economy, public safety and the feelings we have about ourselves and our future. To tell our stories is to begin to frame a conscious conception of ourselves and our times.

If a paramount theme of mythology is the rebuilding of a worldview from which we emerge as unique, the re-creation of modern myth from the first explosion on July 16, 1945, or the first use of the Bomb on August 6, 1945, returns us to the point where we were all transformed into something entirely new. To the alchemists, gold ore could be transmuted into gold. To the physicists at Los Alamos, uranium could be changed into plutonium. For those of us who live in the Nuclear Age, our individual stories can become the stuff of the transformation of ourselves and our potential to reshape the world. The mystery discovered in the telling can lead

Francis A. Fitzgerald

us back to the meaning of our lives in this age and to the crucial tasks laid before us in our lifetimes.

At the same time, it leads us back to the basis of our cosmos. The very content of the tale—the splitting of the material from which we are made—takes us to our origins, scientifically and spiritually. Said one storyteller, a dance therapist: "Realizing what has gone wrong in this age helps me return to values of living and loving in my daily life. It is also so terrifying that dealing with it requires that I go beyond the psychological, beyond the political. To speak of these things I *must* draw on the resources of my awareness of the vast and incomprehensible reality of the universe." Said another, an activist: "While we cannot substitute spiritual perspective for action, we also cannot afford to forget the strength that comes from seeing ourselves as part of something bigger."

The Voice of the Nuclear Story

When we speak of our relationship to nuclear weapons, we are inevitably mustering up the material of something far deeper than the relationship of person to bomb, of hero to dragon. Although we may choose to begin our tales in 1945, this relationship was shaped long before the first radioactive cloud mushroomed against the July New Mexico sky. Are we not speaking of the texture of human nature as it has evolved in the last five thousand years in what has been called "the patriarchal age?" Are we not speaking of our discomfort with the one who points the gun, of our discomfort with ourselves and each other in a society that encourages competition, discrimination, rape, and winning, while using the language of justice, self-determination and freedom?

In 1939, when scientists were pursuing the potentials of nuclear physics, Niels Bohr said about the problem of making bomb-grade material: "It can never be done unless you turn the whole United States into one huge factory." Although the process of producing Uranium-235 has since been refined, Bohr's warning was prophetic. Today the nuclear industry extends throughout our economic, social, political and geographic landscape, its operations threatening the lives of Native Americans, scientists, servicemen, people who live near reactors and test sites, and many others, its end product threatening all life on the planet. In many ways, the nuclear industry exists as a microcosm of the system we live in. To tell our nuclear stories is to speak of that system: to reveal all the stories of pain, death, hypocrisy, hope, caring and striving in our society.

The voices that tell their nuclear stories do not tell them in tones of political rhetoric: "I am the victim of your technology." "We owe our freedom to the Bomb." They speak of common experience, common vulnerability, common caring: "When they dropped the Bomb, I felt awe. I didn't understand, but I knew it was something big." "Most of all I feel fascinated with its power." "If it happens, I am terrified I won't be with my children."

Last year I interviewed a mechanical engineer from Lawrence Livermore Lab for an article on how people numb themselves against feelings about nuclear weapons. William Roberts had been involved with nuclear technology for a long time. He had helped build the atomic particle accelerator at the Berkeley Radiation Lab, assembled equipment for atmospheric testing in the fifties, designed containers for radioactive materials at Livermore, worked on the Ram Jet nuclear-powered aircraft, and participated in the Rasmussen Study on the safety of nuclear reactors. Although he knew that our political perspectives were different, he was so elated to have a place to reveal his feelings that he talked for two hours, telling me things he later said he didn't want published or re-told. He readily admitted his detachment from the bombing of Hiroshima and his enthusiasm for gathering equipment for the tests.

"I loved it," he said. "It was a whole different attitude in those days. The word 'ecology' wasn't in vogue. You never thought of the world as a worn-out, second-hand world. It was still a place to be conquered. I was young and my work was exciting.

"I don't know, really, what my reaction to the tests was. I had spent a lot of time preparing for those explosions and damn if I wasn't going to see them! Oh, I appreciated the problems of radiation all right. It's a hazard, like amps and volts are for people in power plants." He called himself not "gung-ho the Bomb", but in favor of reactors.

Six months after the article was published, Roberts wrote me a letter. He said it had taken a long time for the impact of the piece to sink in. He was still for nuclear power, he wrote, but, seeing his interview in the context of a discussion of numbing, he realized he was indeed a "victim of numbing" against nuclear weapons. He wanted to rethink the situation.

Everyone lives with the threat of nuclear holocaust. Everyone has feelings about it and has struggled, whether consciously or unconsciously, with the danger nuclear technology brings to the world. This overwhelming threat is the greatest equalizer of all; as such, its presence offers us the ultimate opportunity to come together for common survival. For the tellers of the nuclear story, there are no clear-cut answers, but there are great opportunities for us to muster our most profound creativity and sense of continuity. Telling our nuclear stories is not an answer or an attempt to doc-ument a political position. Rather, it is an exploration, a step towards that mustering. If the word "nuclear" refers to the core of that from which we are made, it also refers to the seed of our transformation. To tell about our lives in the Nuclear Age is to become the heroic bearers of kernels of the truth of our times. It is to sit in a circle and, at last, pass a pipe for peace.

Chellis Glendinning is a therapist, teacher and writer who has been conducting Waking Up in the Nuclear Age workshops. For information on the workshops, write to Waking Up in the Nuclear Age, Box 23, Fort Mason Center, San Francisco, CA 94123.

Guidelines for Telling Your Story

What is needed to begin is permission, focus and support. If you want to initiate a group discussion, you might start with the group closest to you: your family, political organization, church, associates at work, or circle of friends. Then, if you wish, you can reach out to other groups or even offer a workshop to the public.

I have encouraged nuclear story-telling in many situations: in buses, at a large conference, in university classrooms, in cafes, at dinner parties, with individuals, with groups. The most important foundation for the experience is that the focus and methods be clearly drawn and agreed upon by all participants. This consensus provides the basis for safety. The focus is to share experience and feelings of living in the Nuclear Age. Methods may vary. If members of the group are accustomed to expressing deep feelings, they may want to cry or hit pillows as part of the telling. Or they may prefer to sit in straight-backed chairs and talk. They might like to make a special trip to the country for the sharing, or simply do it on their lunch hour at work.

Sitting in a circle is wise. As the tales come forth and we face their content and the feelings they elicit, we need the support that a circle seems to provide. It is much easier to pass the pipe around a circle than down the straight lines of chairs in a classroom. It is easier to hold hands in a circle.

You may want to choose a facilitator and structure the group as Wolman and Shiras did, asking specific questions, one at a time, for group discussion. Or you may want to do what the eight peace activists in California did: have each person tell her/his own tale, one at a time.

The stories themselves are an intertwining of events, feelings and thoughts. Some important points to cover are:

History of Awareness: *What are my earliest memories of nuclear weapons? What is the history of my awareness? When has it been greatest? When least? What important emotional experiences have I had that relate to nuclear weapons?*

Psychic Numbing: *How do I numb myself against the reality of nuclear weapons?*

Coping: *When I am not numbing myself, how do I cope with what I know?*

Acknowledgement: *If I have never explored my relationship to the nuclear situation, what have I learned by weaving this thread into my life story?*

The Future: *Where do I find support, strength and hope? Do I need more? Where can I find more?*

Chellis Glendinning
Fellowship, *December 1981*

Anyone can goof up—even a nuclear missile technician. American or Russian. That's why nuclear war is a growing danger in today's tension-ridden world.

But there is a way out of this mess.

It's called the Freeze. With the Freeze, the United States and Russia would stop making nuclear weapons. Period. We've got 30,000; they've got 20,000.* That's more than enough.

The bottom line is survival. That's why neither country has broken any of the 14 nuclear weapons agreements they've signed.† To help prevent cheating, each side **watches** the other with high-powered sensors and satellites (ours can read a license plate in Moscow). Of course, the Freeze won't solve everything; but it would be a strong first step toward a safer tomorrow.

The Freeze is our best hope for preventing nuclear war. And that's no accident.

☐ I support the Freeze.

☐ Please send me more information about the Freeze.

☐ Here's _____ $20 _____ $50 _____ $100 _____other
to support this important work.

Name _____

Address _____

City _____ State _____ Zip _____

THE FREEZE

Because Nobody Wants A Nuclear War

THE WEAPONS BEHIND AMERICA'S DEFENSE SYSTEM GET WHERE THEY'RE GOING BEHIND A LOCOMOTIVE.

Much of the freight transported by the Department of Defense couldn't be moved in any other way.

Take the M-60 tank, for example, a behemoth that weighs in at a tidy sixty tons. With 6400 railroad-owned flatcars augmented by another 1000 owned by the Department of Defense, getting such heavy equipment where it's needed is easy. Even if it were feasible for trucks to do the job, the result would be great highway damage and an expenditure of more than three times as much fuel.

So, when it comes to meeting America's military transportation needs, the railroads are irreplaceable. They've proved themselves so both in peacetime and in war for more than one hundred years. And today they're in a better position than ever to meet a national emergency, should one ever occur.

This message is from the American Railroad Foundation, an organization of companies supplying and servicing the railroad industry. An industry that's carrying the lion's share of the load.

AMERICAN RAILROAD FOUNDATION
1920 L St., N.W., Washington, D.C. 20036

To the Rulers

(to lay down arms)

M.L. Rosenthal

I

This imperial day the dawn sun calls,
quick shadow like the meridian line unseen,
calls with unheard voice through afternoon's
bright arcade, calls after the bright lord
whose golden, purposed path leads down
to voluptuous dark boudoirs in the dead man's
  land.

II

Do not speak of Auschwitz, or even Vietnam.
The ass's skull is braying again:
Some day, science will put everything right.
Slam the face shut, quick-freeze the heart;
our true loves have all died in our arms.

III

Lay down arms.
  What bomb unmakes
  the unblinking past?
  What honor (say
  what you will) awakes
  the napalmed babe?

Consider the dead
  of the East, of the West.
  Rulers,
  fear ye not?

He who is right
  stays his hand.
  Lo, the poor addict
  fears withdrawal.
  Fear ye not.

M.L. Rosenthal. Poems 1964-1980. N.Y.: Oxford University Press, 1981.

Comparison of U.S. and U.S.S.R. Strategic Systems and Warheads

	1967		1972 (SALT I)		1979 (SALT II)		1985 (With SALT)		1985 (No SALT)	
	US	USSR	US	USSR	US	USSR	US	USSR	US	USSR
Intercontinental Ballistic Missiles	1054	500	1054	1500	1054	1398	1054	1250	1054	1400
Submarine-Launched Missiles	656	100	656	500	656	950	624	900	688	1100
Heavy Bombers	690	150	449	150	348	156	348	100	368	150
TOTAL SYSTEMS	*2400*	*750*	*2159*	*2150*	*2058*	*2504*	*2026*	*2250*	*2110*	*2650*
TOTAL WARHEADS	*5000*	*900*	*6000*	*2300*	*9200*	*5000*	*11,500*	*10,000*	*14,000*	*12,000*

Unclassified estimates assembled by the staff of Senator Daniel Patrick Moynihan from various documents.

TIT-for-TAT

We must anticipate what the Soviet response will be to our massive arms buildup, however misplanned or misdirected that buildup is. Clearly the Soviets will view it as a grave threat. Clearly they will view our prospective sale of "lethal" weapons to the People's Republic of China as a grave threat. Clearly they will respond both to our massive arms buildup and to our "playing of the China card" as compelling reasons to augment even further their already escalating arms buildup.

The Soviet response will surely take into account their growing alarm about the direction of American policy. According to Soviet Defense Minister Marshal Ustinov, the current U.S. policy will "undo whatever good was done in Soviet–American relations during the 1970s and break the rough military parity between the Soviet Union and the United States." Mr. Ustinov claims that the United States hopes to undermine the Soviet bloc economies by drawing them into a heated arms race. He wrote recently: "It is already being calculated by some men in Washington how many of the Soviet Union's economic programs would thereby be frustrated and how much less the people in the Socialist countries would get of food and medical care."

Five years from now, after the expenditure of $1.6 trillion, and with the People's Republic of China armed with modern American equipment, we may find ourselves no better off vis-à-vis the Soviets than we are today. The Soviets will not benignly sit by and watch us attain dominance or overwhelming superiority in armaments. As we dare them, they fear us. As we build, so will they.

Senator Thomas F. Eagleton (D-Mo.)
December, 1981

These are the facts:

The U.S. and its NATO allies have outspent the Soviet/Warsaw Pact military forces for many years—$215 billion to $175 billion in one year alone.

The cost of new and often unnecessary weapons continues to escalate. This year the Pentagon says the cost of 47 weapon systems will be $50 billion higher than its estimate for the same weapons in 1980.

The massive U.S. Navy exceeds the Soviets in warship tonnage and nuclear-powered submarines and ships, and outnumbers the Soviets in aircraft carriers by 13 to 0. Now we are building 110 new warships.

Our submarines carry 5,000 nuclear weapons—3,000 of which are always aimed and ready to fire at the U.S.S.R. The Soviets keep 400 nuclear weapons at sea, ready to fire at the U.S.

The United States has 410 strategic bombers, compared to the Soviet's 145. More than half of the Soviet bombers are still propeller-driven.

We have *always* had more strategic nuclear weapons than the Soviets. Today we can explode 12,000 nuclear weapons on the Soviet Union, while they can explode 7,000 on us.

The United States will build 17,000 new nuclear weapons in the 1980's, if we continue to move forward with current plans for the MX, Cruise, Trident, Pershing II, and other weapons.

Center for Defense Information

The Truth and Nothing But . . .

. . . while the era of U.S. superiority is long past, parity—not U.S. inferiority—has replaced it, and the United States and the Soviet Union are roughly equal in strategic nuclear power.

Defense Department report for the fiscal year 1982, page 43

GLOBAL OVERKILL:
A Guide
to Nuclear Weapons

Paul Rogers

The remarkable resurgence of the nuclear disarmament movement has led to an increased demand for information about nuclear weapons. Few people have the time or energy to sort out the information that is available, so to help meet the demand the two most recent Peace Studies Papers from the Bradford University School of Peace Studies have been devoted to aspects of nuclear weapons and the nuclear arms race. Paper No 4 by Frank Barnaby is entitled The Nuclear Arms Race *and gives general information on the nature of that race, the weapons developments now going on, nuclear proliferation and possible ways of curbing the race. Paper No 5,* A Guide to Nuclear Weapons *by Paul Rogers, attempts to describe the huge range of nuclear armaments now available in many countries. Copies of both papers are available from* School of Peace Studies, Bradford University, Bradford 7, West Yorkshire, England, *at 80 pence each plus 17 pence postage; and also from* Housmans Bookshop, 5 Caledonian Road, London N1. *Housmans are joint publishers of all the Peace Studies Papers: all trade orders and bulk orders for peace movement groups should be sent to them.*

The following notes on nuclear weapons by Paul Rogers are drawn largely from his A Guide to Nuclear Weapons *but are less than a fifth of the length of that paper and inevitably represent rather a brief summary. The greatest emphasis here is placed on the major new nuclear weapons such as Trident and the SS-20.*

United States of America

The United States has around 9,000 nuclear warheads intended for strategic use and well over 20,000 smaller weapons for tactical and theatre use. The strategic weapons are delivered either by intercontinental ballistic missiles (ICBMs), submarine-launched ballistic missiles (SLBMs) or long range bombers. These three components make up the so-called "strategic triad" and major new developments of all three kinds of delivery system are under way with the US being around four to five years ahead of the Soviet Union in most forms of weapons technology.

Intercontinental Ballistic Missiles

Minuteman. There are 1,000 Minuteman missiles, all made by Boeing and all deployed in silos protected by blast resistant concrete. The 450 Mark I missiles have single 1.5 megaton (million tons of TNT equivalent) warheads and a range of 7,000 miles. The 550 Minuteman Mark II missiles are much more advanced and most carry a multiple independently-targetable re-entry vehicle (MIRV) system containing three weapons each of 200 kilotons (thousand tons of TNT equivalent). These Mark 12 warheads are rapidly being replaced by the Mark 12A, the most formidably accurate nuclear weapon available and the first one to form a significant threat to opposing missiles in their protective silos. The 12A warhead has a 350 kiloton yield and has a 50% chance of landing within 200 yards of the target at a range of 8,000 miles (200 yards is therefore the missile's circular error probability or CEP).

Titan. This is a very large ICBM first deployed in 1963 and carrying a massive 9 megaton warhead, 750 times the size of the Hiroshima bomb. The United States has 52 of them but they are difficult to maintain and have a tendency to blow-up (the fuel tanks that is, not the warheads so far!).

M-X. This is the "missile-experimental" now being developed by Martin Marietta and due to be ready in the mid-1980s. Not much bigger than the Minuteman but capable of carrying weapons weighing four times as much, the initial M-Xs will probably have a MIRV system of ten warheads rated at 350 kilotons and with CEPs of 100 yards, coming down eventually to as low as 20 yards. The M-X system may be deployed in a phenomenally expensive mobile form to limit its vulnerability to Soviet ICBMs. Even now the United States is spending around three billion dollars a year on it.

Submarine-launched Ballistic Missiles

Polaris. This was the first SLBM and was built by Lockheed. Very few are left in service (160 missiles on ten submarines) and each carries three warheads of 200 kilotons with a low accuracy.

Poseidon. Considerably more advanced and carrying ten 40 kiloton warheads, the Poseidon was first test-fired in 1970 and still makes up the bulk of the US SLBM force with over 20 submarines in service. Ex-President Carter claimed that one submarine with 16 missiles and 160 warheads could destroy every major city in the Soviet Union.

Trident. This third-generation SLBM is, like the other two, a product of Lockheed. It has a much longer range (4,600 miles compared with 2,875 miles) and carries eight 100 kiloton warheads. Twelve of the Poseidon-carrying submarines are being re-fitted with the Trident missile and a number of huge new Trident submarines are also being built, each taking 24 missiles. Two (*Ohio* and *Michigan*) have been launched and eight boats are on order at two billion dollars each. These boats will also be able to take the Mark II Trident, due in 1987 with greater range, payload and accuracy. This missile will probably be a first-strike countersilo weapon.

Strategic Bombers and Associated Missiles

Boeing B52. This is a massive eight-engined long-ranged jet bomber which first became operational in

1955. About a third of the 750 built between then and 1962 are still in service, mostly equipped with four large free-fall H-bombs and 20 Short Range Attack Missiles (SRAM) each. The SRAM carries a 200 kiloton warhead and can travel 100 miles so that the B52 does not need to fly over the target. B52s are going to be equipped with the Boeing Air-Launched Cruise Missile (ALCM) also capable of carrying a 200 kiloton warhead, but over a distance of 1,500 miles with considerable accuracy. Each B52 can carry six ALCMs under each wing and eight more in a rotating rack in the bomb bay. By combining ALCMs with B52s, the USAF has ensured that the B52 will remain a formidable nuclear delivery aircraft until around the turn of the century. More advanced cruise missiles are under development.

General Dynamics F-111. This swing-wing bomber exists in several versions including the FB111A based in the United States and capable of carrying six SRAMS or ALCMs. In addition, 156 medium-range variants are based in Europe, mainly Britain, and can carry any of seven different kinds of nuclear weapon.

Rockwell International B1. The United States is likely to proceed with a new strategic bomber, either based on a stretched version of the F-111 or else a revamped version of the much larger B1, originally developed in the early 1970s but cancelled in 1977. Although full development was halted, the prototypes were kept flying and the B1 could easily be produced as a long-range supersonic cruise missile launcher, carrying up to 32 missiles.

Stealth. The so-called stealth aircraft is, in reality, a general term for several costly new developments, all designed to produce aircraft which are difficult to detect by radar.

Anti-Ballistic Missiles

The United States developed a pair of anti-ballistic missiles, Spartan and Sprint, which used nuclear warheads exploded in the vicinity of incoming missiles to try and destroy them. The system proved very costly and of dubious accuracy and most anti-ballistic defences in the future are likely to be based on particle beam, laser or mini-missile concepts. The United States is currently spending many hundreds of millions of dollars a year on such developments.

Theater and Tactical Weapons

There are many different examples including atomic demolition munitions, mines, nuclear depth bombs, nuclear shells and even nuclear-tipped air-to-air missiles. There are also many different kinds of land-based and carrier-based aircraft which can carry nuclear weapons. Three of the most important missiles are listed here as examples of many.

Tomahawk Cruise Missile. Developed by General Dynamics, this is the missile due to come to Europe shortly. It has a similar range and warhead to the ALCM but is launched from a large lorry, a surface

ship, a submarine or even a hovercraft. Its ability to hug the ground makes it difficult to detect and its accuracy could make it a first-strike weapon.

Lance. This is a surface-to-surface artillery missile which can deliver a conventional, nuclear or neutron bomb warhead over a distance of 75 miles. Its launcher is mobile and it has been in service since 1973.

Pershing. 72 of the Pershing 1A are in service in Germany and can deliver a 400 kiloton warhead over 460 miles. The new Pershing 2 is very much more accurate, being fitted with the RADAG terminal guidance system. It has double the range yet, because of its accuracy, it can destroy small targets using a much smaller warhead than the earlier version. The Pershing 2 is potentially a first-strike weapon.

Union of Soviet Socialist Republics

The Soviet Union has fewer warheads in its strategic arsenal than the United States but they tend to be bigger, although less accurate. It relies more heavily on ICBMs and SLBMs and has few long range bombers. In addition to its strategic forces it has a huge range of tactical and theater weapons.

Intercontinental Ballistic Missiles

SCARP (SS-9). This was a huge missile, larger than any of the American ICBMs and capable of carrying a single 25 megaton warhead. Such an H-bomb could, for example, destroy London and most of the Home Counties in a single explosion. Scarps appear to have been replaced by the newer SS-18 but could be redeployed as a threat to cruise missile deployment areas in Western Europe (such as most of Britain . . .).

SS-11 (SEGO). A rather old missile first deployed in 1966 but still making up a large part of the Soviet ICBM inventory with 580 currently deployed. It has a range of over 6,500 miles and can carry a 1 to 2 megaton warhead or three 100 to 300 kiloton warheads.

SS-13. Sixty of this rather shorter-range missile are deployed, each with a single 1 megaton warhead.

SS-17. This much newer missile is much more accurate than earlier Soviet ICBMs with a CEP of 500 yards. It is fitted either with a single 5 megaton warhead or a MIRVed system of four 900 kiloton weapons.

SS-18. This is the most formidable of the current Soviet ICBMs, a huge missile capable of carrying many different kinds of warhead including massive 25 megaton weapons and MIRVed systems of eight 2 megaton weapons. Even so, most analysts do not believe that the SS-18 is yet accurate enough to threaten American missiles in their silos. Over 300 SS-18s are now deployed.

SS-19. This is slightly smaller than the SS-18 and 300 have so far been deployed. Various warheads may be fitted and some are as accurate as all but the most recent American systems.

Experimental ICBMs. The Soviet Union is developing new warheads for existing missiles and is also developing several new ICBMs although some may be little more than modifications of existing missiles. Even so, the accuracy of Soviet ICBMs is increasing to the point where they may threaten protected American missiles within five to eight years. Nuclear warfighting then becomes steadily more likely.

Submarine-launched Ballistic Missiles

The Soviet Union has considerably more ballistic missile-carrying submarines than the United States but manages to keep far fewer of them at sea at any one time. They also tend to be noisier and therefore easier to detect and destroy. Even so, the Soviet submarines are formidable nuclear systems, involving a wide range of missiles.

SS-N-6 (Sawfly). 470 of these are deployed in 29 submarines and each is roughly similar to the American Poseidon missile but with just three warheads per missile.

SS-N-8. This much longer range missile (up to 5,700 miles) is carried in Delta class submarines and over 300 missiles are deployed. Several kinds of warhead may be carried but most are fitted with a single 1 to 2 megaton warhead.

New SLBMs. These include the SS-NX-17, the SS-N-18 and the SS-NX-20, all under development as replacements for existing SLBMs. The most significant development is probably the use of the SS-N-18 in the huge new Typhoon class submarines, even bigger than the American Trident boats and carrying 24 missiles each. The Soviet Union also has a range of several hundred older submarine-launched cruise missiles which are intended for antiship attacks but could be used against land targets. The new nuclear-powered battlecruiser Kirov has twenty SS-NX-19 nuclear missiles, each with a range of over 200 miles.

Strategic Bombers

The Tupolev Tu-95 Bear and Myasischev M-4 Bison are the two old long-range Soviet bombers of which

120 are still available for this role. They are obviously capable of causing immense destruction but are far less significant than, for example, the B52.

Intermediate-range Ballistic Missiles

The Soviet Union does have a range of IRBMs designed to travel 2 to 3,000 miles or thereabouts and intended for use in Europe and Asia against, for example, China, Japan and some NATO countries. The SS-4 (Sandal) and SS-5 (Skean) are two significant examples, each capable of delivering 1 megaton warheads. Over 400 are deployed but they are now being replaced by the SS-20.

SS-20. This is a mobile IRBM, 52 feet long, 6 feet in diameter and with a range of up to 3,000 miles carrying three 150 kiloton warheads with considerable accuracy. As many as 200 may now be deployed, 40% of them being targeted on China and elsewhere in Asia.

Anti-Ballistic Missiles

The Soviet Union has a rather old antiballistic missiles system, the Galosh system, involving 64 missiles "protecting" Moscow and surrounding ICBM bases. Half of these are reported to be withdrawn from service at present but while the Galosh system may be rather primitive, there is little doubt that the Soviet Union is investing heavily in antiballistic missile developments.

Theater and Tactical Nuclear Weapons Systems

As is true of the United States, the Soviet Union has a very wide range of smaller missiles and aircraft together with mines, nuclear-capable artillery and depth bombs. These include the FROG 7 (Free Rocket Over Ground!) and SS-12 missiles and the Medium range Tupolev Tu-16 (Badger) and supersonic Tupolev Tu-22 (Blinder) bombers.

Tupolev Tu-26 (Backfire). The Backfire bomber is a swing-wing supersonic bomber which has been under development for around fifteen years and is currently being deployed at the rate of around 36 a year. It is smaller and has a shorter range than the American B1 but can be fitted with the medium range Kingfish missile which can carry a large warhead.

United Kingdom

The UK has a strategic "deterrent" of four Polaris submarines, each carrying 16 missiles with three warheads. New Chevaline warheads are now being fitted and the government now plans to replace the complete fleet with four or five Trident missile-carrying submarines in the 1990s. This programme will be hugely expensive and could involve an increase in the number of warheads to over 2000. Britain also has many other nuclear weapons including free-fall nuclear bombs carried by around 170 Vulcan, Buccaneer and Jaguar aircraft. There are also nuclear depth bombs carried by the Nimrod long-range antisubmarine aircraft and by various helicopters.

In addition to this variety of weapons the UK has

nuclear-capable artillery and Lance missiles in North Germany together with atomic demolition munitions.

The Vulcan and Buccaneer aircraft are going to be replaced with around double their number of Tornado supersonic aircraft during the 1980s. It is possible that the Trident SLBM program may get cancelled, in which case a highly likely alternative could be a British-built cruise missile fitted to the Tornado.

France

France has long maintained an independent nuclear force and long continues to spend heavily on developing it further. The main component is currently the fleet of five submarines equipped with a total of 80 MSBS (M-20) missiles each with a single 1 megaton warhead. These are now being replaced with the new MSBS (M-4) missile which is a MIRVed system. France also has 18 intermediate range ballistic missiles housed in silos and capable of reaching most parts of European Russia. The old version is the S-2 with a 150 kiloton warhead but this is now being replaced with the S-3 with a 1 megaton warhead.

The Dassault Mirage IVA is the main nuclear bomber and each plane can deliver a 70 kiloton bomb over a range of 3300 miles. France also has 140 land-based and carrier-based nuclear-capable strike aircraft together with 30 Pluton artillery missiles with a range of 75 miles. Future developments include a Super-Pluton and probable deployment of neutron bombs.

China

China has a nuclear arsenal running to many hundreds of bombs. It has 400 short-range bombers and 80 medium-range bombers. It also has around 130 CSS-1 and CSS-2 IRBMs, the latter carrying large 1 to 3 megaton H-bomb warheads. The CSS-2 can reach most of the Soviet Union east of the Urals.

China developed a multi-stage ICBM which was first tested in 1976. Only four are deployed at present and no more are likely to be built. Instead the CSS-X-4 has now been tested and is believed to be a longrange ICBM carrying a large 5 to 10 megaton warhead and capable of reaching any part of Europe, Asia or the United States. It is now reported to be in production. China is also developing a two-stage SLBM similar to an early Polaris missile and a newly-built nuclear-powered ballistic-missile carrying submarine is now undergoing trials.

Other Nuclear Powers

India exploded a small atom bomb in 1974. The government claims it is not actively developing nuclear weapons but many analysts find this difficult to accept. Certainly India has nuclear-capable aircraft such as the Canberra and the home-built HF-24 Marut. India also has a considerable civil space research pro-

gramme with rockets capable of putting satellites into earth-orbit.

Israel probably has a nuclear arsenal of 20 to 30 atom bombs together with a wide range of potential delivery systems such as Phantom, Mirage and Kfir strike aircraft. The Gabriel ship-to-ship missile could most probably be adapted to carry a nuclear warhead. Israel has also been reported to have developed the Jericho (MD-600) ramp-launched two-stage missile with a range of over 250 miles and the potential to carry a nuclear warhead.

South Africa has close military ties with Israel and those might even extend to nuclear technology. A consensus of informed opinion is that South Africa either has nuclear weapons or could produce them at very short notice. It has a range of strike aircraft capable of delivering them but may also be interested (like Israel) in developing low-yield nuclear shells for long range artillery.

Potential Nuclear Powers

Many countries could develop nuclear weapons. These include Canada, Sweden, Australia, New Zealand and as many as twenty others who have decided not to do so yet. Other countries may have active nuclear weapons development programs and might become nuclear powers in the next decade. The most likely candidates are probably Argentina, Brazil, Egypt, Iraq, Libya, Pakistan, South Korea and Taiwan.

Peace News, May 15, 1981 (Nottingham, England)

Quote, Unquote

Henry Kissinger, to a Moscow audience in 1974:

"One of the questions which we have to ask ourselves as a country is what in the name of God is strategic superiority. What is the significance of it—politically, militarily, operationally—at these levels of numbers? What do you do with it?"

Kissinger explained later why he thought the Soviets would not cheat on SALT:

"It can be said with some assurance that any country which contemplates a rupture of the agreement or a circumvention of its letter and spirit must now face the fact that it will be placing in jeopardy not only a limited arms control agreement, but a broad political relationship."

Robert McNamara, in 1965, said that the Soviets ". . . have decided that they lost the quantitative race and they are not seeking to engage us in that contest. It means there is no indication that the Soviets are seeking to develop a strategic nuclear force as large as ours . . . [and] their rate of expansion today is not such as to allow them even to equal, much less exceed, our own 1970 force."

In his San Francisco speech in 1967, he asked: "Is the Soviet Union seriously attempting to acquire a first-strike capability against the United States?

"Although this is a question we cannot answer with absolute certainty, we believe the answer is no."

Kissinger statement in Moscow: Statement made July 3, 1974; quoted in October 29, 1979, *Congressional Record*, p. S 15334.
1st Kissinger quote: From *Shall America Be Defended? SALT II and Beyond,* by Daniel O. Graham, Arlington House Publishers, p. 145.
McNamara: From *SALT II Shall America Be Defended? SALT II and Beyond,* by Daniel O. Graham, published by Arlington House, p. 81.

Conservative Digest, April 1980

How Large a Use of Neutron Bombs?

Warsaw Pact forces in Central Europe have some 20,000 tanks and a single Warsaw Pact breakthrough operation on that front could involve some 600 tanks and 500 armored fighting vehicles with as many as six major breakthough efforts proceeding simultaneously. This would come to 6600 Warsaw Pact armored vehicles. If each neutron bomb could destroy three, on the average, this would still require 2,200 enhanced radiation weapons. This could irradiate 28,000 square kilometers or roughly 11% of the total land area of the Federal Republic.

Warsaw Pact forces fearing neutron bomb attack could be expected to hug the Western forces and populated areas so as to discourage use of the atomic weapons on allied forces. If we assume for the radiated areas only the average population density for the country as a whole (247 persons per square kilometer), more than 5 million West German civilians would be potentially affected by the neutron flux with millions dying promptly or within a few months.

Military use could not be very precise because a tank moving cross country at 30 miles per hour would move from the target point to a location 900 meters away within a minute and this is about the lethal radius of a one kiloton neutron warhead (for immediate incapacitation of the crew). Because forward observers could not secure release of atomic weapons anywhere near so quickly, tanks would have to be barraged to compensate for outdated intelligence and delays in the command and control system. Efforts to streamline delegation of authority of release would lead to still more collateral damage of civilians and Western forces.

Federation of American Scientists Public Interest Report October 1981

Nations Possessing Nuclear Arms

USA	Great Britain	China
USSR	France	India

Nations Capable of Building a Nuclear Weapon

Canada	West Germany	South Africa
Switzerland	Italy	Japan
Sweden	Israel	Pakistan

Nations That Could Possess Nuclear Arms by 1990

Holland	Spain	Australia	Iraq
Norway	Libya	Finland	Egypt
Denmark	Brazil	Austria	South Korea
Belgium	Argentina	Yugoslavia	Taiwan

Welcome to the Nuclear Club

The More Things Change

In November 1981 the French [Socialist] government announced that they would develop a new tactical missile system and construct a nuclear submarine, the country's seventh. They will also increase spending for war by 17.8 per cent.

The Madness Goes On

According to the 1981 edition of *World Military and Social Expenditures*, edited by Ruth Leger Sivard, an ex-official of the U.A. Arms Control and Disarmament Agency, the amount of money spent on the manufacture of weapons is $550 billion annually, a sum equal to the combined income of the poorest half of the world's population. The amount spent on arms includes $100 billion for nuclear weapons.

The SIPRI* Yearbook 1980 shows, with facts and figures, that:

- World military expenditure is predicted to run by 1980 to over $500,000 million per year. NATO and the Warsaw Treaty Organization together account for about 70% of this total. The Third World accounts for about 15%.
- The level and trend of military spending in the two great-power blocs are most disturbing because experience has shown that increases by either side are used as rationalization for increases by the other.
- Other groups of states have during the 1970s increased their military spending particularly rapidly. The Organization of Petroleum-Exporting Countries (OPEC) group has increased its military expenditures by 15% and Southern Africa by 16% a year.
- Official development aid to Third World countries—only one-twentieth of the value of military expenditures—has lagged far behind this upward trend in resources devoted to military purposes.
- The total value of imports of major arms during the decade of the seventies was about three and a half times as much as in the previous decade. The yearly rate of increase ran at 25% for the latter half of the decade, as compared to 15% for the first half.
- Two-thirds of the global arms trade involves transfers of weapons to the Third World, a good part of which suffers from underdevelopment, starvation and disease. The largest arms-importing regions in the 1970s were the Middle East, the Far East and Africa.
- The nuclear arsenals of the world today contain more than 60,000 nuclear weapons. The threat that these weapons may be used through accident, miscalculation or just folly is increasing with the continual accumulation of these weapons.
- Most ominous are the sophisticated weapon systems emerging with distinct nuclear war-fighting capabilities, such as the US land-based MX missile and the Trident II submarine-based missile, as

*Stockholm International Peace Research Institute

well as the new Soviet intercontinental ballistic missiles.

- The SALT II Treaty was signed in 1979, but is still not in force, a deplorable fact in light of the pledge by the USA and the USSR to continue efforts towards significant reductions and qualitative limitations of strategic offensive arms.
- The risk of a nuclear war breaking out in Europe is becoming greater due to the development of new types of "Eurostrategic weapons"—aircraft and missiles located in or targeted on Europe and not covered in any of the current international arms control negotiations.
- By the end of 1979, 75% of all satellites orbited were for military purposes. In 1979, 84 military satellites were launched by the USSR and 10 by the USA. Satellites capable of "killing" other satellites are being developed.
- Nuclear weapon testing also continues unabated. In 1979, 53 nuclear weapon test explosions were carried out—28 by the USSR, 15 by the USA, 9 by France and 1 by the UK.
- The world community relies on the Non-Proliferation Treaty to prevent the further spread of nuclear weapons. But the continuing arms race poses a great threat to the existing non-proliferation régime.

Sveavägen 166, S-113 46 Stockholm, Sweden or
Crane, Russak and Company, 3 East 44th Street, N.Y., N.Y. 10017.

The $39.5 Billion Boondoggle

When it was first conceived, the B-1 bomber was designed to be a manned bomber that would penetrate Soviet air defenses by flying low enough so as to escape radar detection. But three things have since overtaken the B-1's theoretical superiority:

1. The Reagan version of the B-1 will not be supersonic.
2. The Soviets will shortly develop a look-down, shoot-down airborne radar which would sight the B-1 long before it reaches its target.
3. With the coming of air-launched missiles which penetrate air defenses, why the need for a manned bomber?

The original estimate for 100 planes was $20 billion. The independent Congressional Budget Office now estimates that the ultimate price tag will be $39.5 billion.

"To Increase the Efficiency of the Defense Dept., You Have to Abolish It."

The U.S. already has enough nuclear submarines to "sink everything on the ocean . . . We must expect that when war breaks out again, we will use the weapons available. I think we'll probably destroy ourselves. I'm not proud of the part I played."

Admiral Hyman G. Rickover, founder of the U.S. nuclear navy, delivering his farewell remarks to the congressional Joint Economic Committee, January 27, 1982

We're Number One

Dr. Carl Johnson of the Department of Preventive Medicine at the University of Colorado Medical School told the yearly session of the American Association for the Advancement of Science that people living near three of the country's nuclear arms factories have abnormally high cancer rates. Excessive rates of cancer have been detected near the Savannah River nuclear weapons reactors in South Carolina, near the Rocky Flats plant not far from Denver, and near the Los Alamos operation in New Mexico. —January 4, 1982

First Publicly Funded Military High School to Open

A plan to create a publicly funded military academy for high school age problem students has been approved by the Richmond, VA school board. The Franklin Military Institute, scheduled to open, will be the first of its kind in the U.S.

The students will be required to wear uniforms, receive weapons training, and attend courses in military science from Army officers, in addition to taking traditional academic subjects.

According to James Hunter, Richmond school superintendent, enrollment in the academy will be voluntary and students must have written parental consent. Rev. Leontine Kelley however, the lone dissenter on the school board said: "I don't think the young people will really have much choice . . . Usually in this situation, the parent is not very informed.

"These kids will be largely poor and largely black, and so many poor young people have no alternative other than military service anyway," said Kelley. "To begin them on this route at age 14 just further limits them . . . I don't think civilian public schools should delegate discipline and character building to the Army."

Supporters of the plan regard the availability of strict military discipline at a military academy as simply another educational alternative on par with open classrooms and vocational training.

"This is not a military program designed to teach students to fight and kill but to develop leadership potential and make good citizens out of these kids," said ROTC instructor, Col. James Norwood, a major supporter of the plan. Pentagon spokesperson Maj. Anthony Caggiano said, "This academy . . . is seen by the Army as a way to get young men and women interested in the military."

Some opponents of the plan are concerned that the school may become a "dumping ground" for difficult students, while others are concerned over the military's influence. Phyllis Conklin, who directed a tutoring program in Richmond said, "This plan is particularly appalling because psychologists say that this age (high school) is the time to teach kids to open their minds. That does not happen in a military school."

The city has recommended that the "scope of the academy's curriculum be given flexibility to interrelate military instruction with required academic subjects," said Conklin. "The official proposal says that these kids would receive an hour a day of military training all through the day with academic subjects."

"Basically those opposed to it seem to be the conscientious objector type who are opposed to anything military," said school board vice-president Charles Pugh, a Navy veteran.

Nomlac *(CCCO pub.)*

No hiding place

Too many people are unaware that an estimated 50,000 nuclear weapons are in the hands of United States and Soviet forces alone, some 16,000 of them installed and operational on intercontinental weapons. Since about 7,000 . . . are on Soviet missiles and bombers, aimed at targets in the United States, it takes little imagination to realize that these targets *must* include many military and industrial targets in or near cities, and almost certainly include many population centers themselves.

This is not, therefore, a problem for "scientists" or "experts" or military men somewhere else—it's a problem for the average citizen who happens to be sitting in that target city.

Thomas A. Halsted, Director, Physicians for Social Responsibility

The Manhasset Project:
Report jeopardizes MX Missile option

Columbia's physics department, which pioneered in the development of the atomic bomb with the "Manhattan Project," is now continuing its research in weaponry with the "Manhasset Project," in which MX missiles will be carried around on the Long Island Railroad.

Pentagon planners originally believed that the LIRR's covert scheduling and routing procedures might offer an acceptable alternative to the wholesale excavation of Nevada and Utah. However, a recent risk analysis simulation conducted jointly by the Columbia scientists and the Defense Department has raised serious questions about the project. *CCT* has obtained a portion of the secret document, which describes a possible red-alert scenario:

Scene: The office of R. J. Bigelow, president of the LIRR. The telephone rings. He puts down his highball, extinguishes his cigar, brushes his secretary off his lap, straightens his tie, and answers it.

Voice: Mr. Bigelow? This is Ronald Reagan. The Russians have attacked. Fire the MX missile immediately.

Bigelow: Sorry, Mr. President, there's a dead cat on the tracks at Woodside and we're expecting half-hour to 45-minute delays.

Reagan: But you don't understand, this is Armageddon!

Bigelow: Amagansett? Sorry, no stops after Patchogue.

Reagan: Look, we don't have any time to waste — fire those missiles now!

Bigelow: Oh, in a hurry? Tell you what. I'll send a bus out there and drive the passengers to Port Jeff. You can take the ferry to New Haven, use Conrail to get to Penn Station, then hop the next train out.

Reagan: For God's sake, the Russian missiles will strike in 15 minutes!

Bigelow: Omigod! Not another strike! — my conductors went out just last week! No one tells me anything — where's my pen? (Makes note: "Remember to fire entire staff and hire more relatives.")

Reagan: Hurry up and fire those missiles — the world is coming to an end!

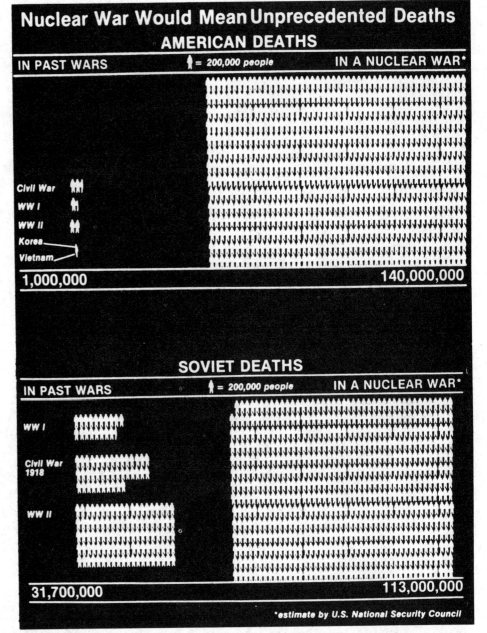

Bigelow: All right, all right, don't get hot under the collar. Look, just hold on to your ticket stub. Send it in to our main office in Jamaica when you get to your stop, and we'll refund the purchase price. Enjoy your ride, and thank you for taking the Long Island Railroad.   *S.O.S.*

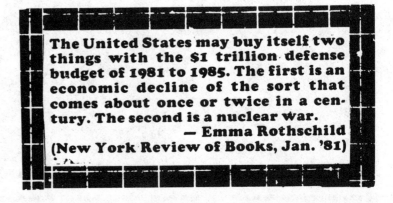

The United States may buy itself two things with the $1 trillion defense budget of 1981 to 1985. The first is an economic decline of the sort that comes about once or twice in a century. The second is a nuclear war.
— Emma Rothschild
(New York Review of Books, Jan. '81)

Of several minds: *Thomas Powers*

ON NUCLEAR DISBELIEF
'MAYBE IT JUST WON'T HAPPEN'

I HAVE NEVER seen a nuclear weapon. But last spring I visited the Atomic Museum at Kirtland Air Force Base on the edge of Albuquerque, New Mexico, and saw a great many bomb casings. When you look at them your eye says *bomb!* but your mind says they are just hollow shells. The bomb guts are missing. Still, you get the idea. Some match your idea of what a bomb ought to look like—Fat Boy, for example, the 9000-pound bulbous monster which destroyed Hiroshima. The one in the Kirtland Atomic Museum is painted olive drab. The one at the Bradbury museum at Los Alamos is painted white. Both are grossly fat and thoroughly lethal in aspect.

But scariest of all is the Mark 17 bomb casing. According to the sign this was the first hydrogen or fusion or thermonuclear bomb which could actually be dropped from an aircraft, but it's hard to credit. It's hard to imagine anything could get it off the ground, short of a derrick. It is 21 feet long and five in diameter and it weighs 24 tons. But the numbers don't suggest the impression. The designer of the Atomic Museum had talent and a flair for the dramatic. The displays are in a great cavernlike hall, dramatically lit from below, and the Mark 17 looms up in the gloom like a . . . well, quite a lot like the great blue whale which hangs from the ceiling in the American Museum of Natural History. The thing is *so* huge, the casing is *so* massive you simply can't believe it could get off the ground. But like all the others it's hollow. It's not really a bomb at all, just a suggestion of the bomb, nothing more than a teaching aid.

At Vandenberg Air Force Base a year ago I saw a Mark 12-A re-entry vehicle, a black cone-shaped object, perhaps three feet high, with a carbon-carbon skin and a polished nose cone of specially heat-resistant alloys which erode away in the terrible heat and wind of re-entry at ten thousand miles an hour. It was sitting in a classroom where Air Force officers take an introductory course in ballistic missiles. One of the instructors began to rattle off statistics and then stopped abruptly. "Sir," he said, "what is your clearance?" I said I was a journalist and didn't have any sort of clearance. That was the end of the lecture. But I marveled at the RV all the same. It was so small, light and sleek. Is there any limit to human genius? Somehow the guts of the Mark 17 leviathan had been refined and reduced and squeezed into this neat package a couple of men might cart off in a wheelbarrow.

So I've never really seen a bomb—just drawings, photographs, and the outer skins of bombs. Most people haven't seen the skins. For us the bomb is a purely mental thing, an abstract concept, a kind of pocket of anxiety in the mind. I *know* the New York City subway system is going through hard times because I ride it every day. I *know* the price of gasoline is up. The sting in my eyes tells me Los Angeles has an air pollution problem. No one has to tell me that blacks and Puerto Ricans live in a different world because I brush their alien shoulders on the city's streets. Things physically present announce themselves unmistakably, but the bomb is like the knowledge of death. It comes and goes, a kind of mood. A story in the paper, or a siren late at night, can bring it heaving up out of the unconscious part of the mind. But then it sinks back, like other things we know but can't bear to think about.

In the last two years I've talked to a lot of military people about nuclear weapons, strategic policy, what the Russians are up to, and the like. For the most part, they have been an impressive group of men—sober, intelligent, knowledgeable, and orderly in their habits of mind. They did not seem at all warlike. Nothing they said suggests that the defense of the United States is in careless or reckless hands. The motto of the Strategic Air Command, which has authority over bombers and land-based intercontinental ballistic missiles, is "Peace is our Profession." As I remember it's carved on the lintel over the main entrance to SAC headquarters at Offut Air Force Base near Omaha. This is the sort of thing to invite a bitter smile, everything considered, but so far as I could tell, SAC people take it seriously. I asked a colonel at Offut if he thought the ICBMs would ever be launched, and he said no—they *all* say no—and added, "If that happened we would have failed in our job." It's tempting to poke ironic fun at such earnest remarks, but it wouldn't be fair. The officer wasn't being smarmy. He really meant it. His job was preventing wars, not winning them.

The military men involved in nuclear weapons policy—and their civilian colleagues, too, for that matter—don't believe it's ever going to happen. For them, I suspect, no belief is deeper and stronger. Their assurances on this point have none of the tinny quality of budget officials, say, telling you the federal deficit will disappear in 1984, when they know full well this barely qualifies as even an honest hope.

When you think about it, the equanimity of military people makes perfect sense. They know the United States and the Soviet Union have got 15,000 strategic nuclear weapons between them. They've been trying to figure out a way to fight a genuinely limited nuclear war for thirty years, and haven't come up with anything convincing yet. They know the Pentagon periodically tries to plan for the post-attack world but always throws up its hands in despair because there is simply no way of projecting how bad it would be. The destruction would be too general. The normal means of recovery and reconstruction would be threatened in too many ways to calculate.

Take transportation. Airfields, ports, railway marshaling yards, and major highway intersections would be destroyed. Aircraft, ships, rolling stock and large numbers of busses, trucks, and cars would be destroyed. Many of the factories which might build more would be destroyed. If factories remained, the workers might be dead or too sick to work. The breakdown in transportation would make it hard to feed or care for them. Power lines would be out. Most petroleum refineries would have been destroyed, fuel would be in short supply, and the little remaining would be hard to distribute. And so on and so forth. How can you predict how long it would take to get things·moving again when so many factors are involved, which overlap in so many ways? The answer is you can't. The government goes on churning out civil defense and reconstruction plans, but the Pentagon has never made a serious official guess how well they would work—or even if they would work at all—because the computers can't factor in all the variables.

This is the sort of thing military men know, generally in great detail, and none of it is encouraging where the subject of nuclear war is concerned. On top of that, they *know* we shall never get rid of nuclear weapons. Arms agreements *may*—even that is in doubt—limit their number and type, but disarmament is not on the horizon. It is not *over* the horizon. When you put these two things together—knowledge of what nuclear weapons can do, and a conviction we shall always have them—you can see why military men tell themselves, and everybody else, the bombs will never be used. They are flesh and blood, after all. Their wives and children all live in target areas. They can't *bear* to think anything else.

I'T'S DIFFICULT to remember how I thought about things a couple of years ago, when I first started to read seriously about nuclear weapons. A lot of things came as a shock then which seem familiar now. I made lots of errors in writing about the subject. Once, for example, I wrote that the bomb dropped on Nagasaki was the last one in the American inventory. In late August, 1945, I thought, there were no bombs in the world at all. But later the man who assembled the core for the fourth bomb told me I was wrong.

After two or three months of reading I went through a period of intense sadness. At first I didn't know what it was. I thought the source might be worry about my father, who is 89, or a friend whose marriage was breaking up, or chronic financial anxiety, or something else of the kind. Then I told myself I was an idiot. Of *course* I was sad. I had finally schooled myself in the numbers and knew for the first time that we *really had* built weapons enough to break the back of our civilization. I'd gotten the details straight about radiation sickness, theories of war-fighting which all imply any nuclear war will go the limit, the steady march of technical improvement in weapons design which makes military people so jumpy, and so on and so forth. I had read or been told *nothing* which suggested we were going to learn to get along without these weapons. It was quite clear, in fact, that we were going to go on pointing them at enemies until we used them or the world came to an end. Since the news on the geological front is all good, and the planet can expect to survive another couple of billion years, that meant, as a practical matter, we would go on as we were until we used them. In short, it seemed to me as clear as night follows day that it is going to happen.

But everybody I talked to took the contrary view. Everybody, that is, profes-

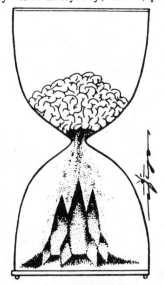

sionally involved in defense matters. Ordinary citizens often entertain foreboding of the darkest sort. In a quite matter of fact way they will say, ''What else were they built for?'' Defense community people *never* say that. What they say is, ''It doesn't make sense. There is nothing to be gained. No rational man would ever use nuclear weapons. They can serve no useful purpose in war.''

That, of course, is true enough. But does that mean they won't be used? You might have said all those things about the great armies of Europe in 1914. Indeed, people did say them. Reasons for not using nuclear weapons are also reasons for not having them. Citing the litany of their horrors is an argument against their possession or use, not an argument we won't use them—given we have them. Such arguments are really an expression of hope, and we depend on hope because there is nothing else. I have heard dozens of defense people explain why nuclear weapons will bever be used. I have *never* heard a note of fear or despair. Their confidence is sunny and unshakable. If we just stick to our guns and make sure we've got a weapon for every weapon they've got, then there's nothing to worry about. There is a soothing quality to these reassurances, as if we were being told that airplanes really do work, and it's safe to fly.

But now comes the curious thing. After a year or two of seeing things in this light, for the first time I feel the tug the other way. I find myself wondering if perhaps the military men aren't right after all. They say it would be crazy, and are absolutely right. We worry about so many things that fail to come to pass. Two hundred years ago Malthus was worrying that the world's population had already stretched the planet's resources to the groaning limit. Maybe fear of nuclear weapons is enough to keep everyone sober and cautious. Maybe the only danger is falling behind, just as the Pentagon says. Maybe all those people in Washington are right, and I'm wrong. I devoutly hope they are right. Maybe it just won't happen.

This is a mood I'm describing, not really an argument. I don't believe it for a minute.

The problem is disbelief. An argument is the ephemeral stuff of the mind. It has no solidity. It surrenders to the world, over time, and the world tells us tomorrow will be much like today. It is a considerable undertaking to go out and see the Air Force bases and atomic laboratories and missile-launching centers. But even there the note of the lethal is missing. The bomb casings are all hollow. The missiles are all mock-ups used as teaching aids. The military men work eight to four and go home to their families. Nobody shows any sign of fear. Everything suggests tomorrow will be much like today.

We know we are mortal but we don't feel mortal and we live, generally, as if there were plenty of time for everything. The moments of recognition are few and they fade. We know that nothing lasts, nations die, the continents move, atmosphere whirls off into space, suns burn out—but not here, now, to us. These things we can't believe. It is the same with the missiles in their silos. We know what they will do. Most people don't even have to be told. They *know*. But knowing and believing are very different things. The world has its disconcerting way of going on from day to day, just as if nothing were ever to change. Belief is frail and fades away.

The people in the defense community have all had their ghastly moments, from the president on down to the missile-launch control officers reading paperback novels in their steel cubicles suspended on springs forty feet beneath the Great Plains. Every last one of them, I am convinced, has looked it in the eye at one time or another. Even Nikita Khrushchev had his dark moment. He once told the Egyptian journalist, Mohammed Heikal, "When I was appointed First Secretary of the Central Committee and learned all the facts about nuclear power I couldn't sleep for several days. Then I became convinced that we could never possibly use these weapons, and when I realized that I was able to sleep again." Thus we all go on, sustained by disbelief.

THOMAS POWERS

NO COMMENT DEPT.

" . . . the fact of the matter is that if we used all our nuclear weapons and the Russians used all of their nuclear weapons, about 10 per cent of humanity would be killed. Now this is a disaster beyond the range of human comprehension. It is a disaster which is not morally justifiable in whatever fashion. But descriptically and analytically, it's not the end of humanity. It's not the destruction of humanity. People like to use slogans . . . "
—Zbigniew Brzezinski
October 9, 1977

"...We must guard against the acquisition of unwarranted influence, whether sought or unsought, by the military-industrial complex. The potential for the disastrous rise of misplaced power exists and will persist."

President Eisenhower

NEW WAR PLANS FOR U.S. HOSPITALS

The Department of Defense is now asking for voluntary agreement from civilian health administrators in 17 U.S. cities to allocate beds and staff to military casualties of "a future large scale war overseas" which will probably "begin and end very rapidly and produce casualties at a higher rate than any other war in history". By the end of 1981, a national capacity for 50,000 beds will be "reserved" for such casualities. While agreement is technically between hospitals and the DOD, hospitals are expected to insure participation of their own staff.

In the fall of 1980 this military plan, called the Civilian-Military Contingency Hospital System (CMCHS), was quietly endorsed by the American Medical Association, the American Hospital Association, and the Joint Commission on Accreditation of Hospitals. Not until early 1981 has the plan begun to be unveiled to a broader public and press. Still sketchy, the story has been leaked principally through materials provided hospital staff at conferences sponsored by the military. Information packets given out at these meetings have included the following: a wounded patient profile, billing procedures, bed availability estimate forms, memo of understanding agreement with DOD, map of sites for the program in the U.S., and a sample letter for hospitals to provide the DOD with hospital personnel employee profiles (age, sex, and military status). Yearly drills with the military are already planned, with West Coast hospitals among the first to be targeted.

According to the packet materials, the preparations are being made for a major conflict outside the United States where the "forward military medical units will concentrate on quickly stabilizing patients and moving the more severely wounded and sick" to U.S. hospitals. Hospitals with 150 beds would be expected to commit 50 to CMCHS, and civilian health workers may be required to assist "sorting teams" which meet planes carrying the wounded. The plan could become operative upon declaration of a national emergency by the President.

Already health care service workers are organizing against CMCHS in general opposition to war preparations and to the "racist impact" this plan may have for minorities now seeking health services. For more information contact: Committee to Defend the People's Health, Room 24, 4170 E. Piedmont Ave., Oakland, CA 94611; or Committee Against CMCHS, 3240 21st Street, San Francisco, CA 94110.

ARMS RACE?

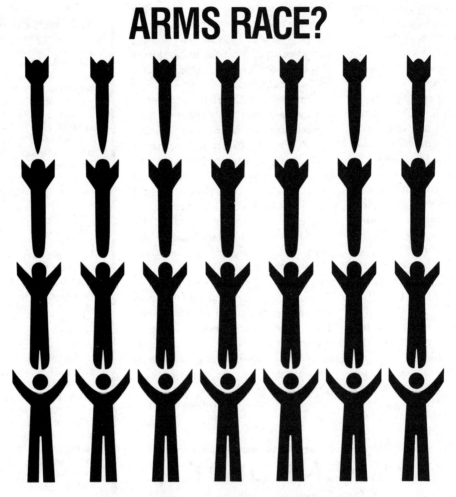

OR HUMAN RACE?

Estimated Deaths in a Nuclear War*

 = 200,000 people

*estimate by U.S. National Security Council, Presidential Review Memorandum #10, June 1977.

In past wars:

Civil War

WW I

WW II

Korea

Vietnam

140,000,000

1,000,000

Verification of a Nuclear Weapons Freeze

by Mark Niedergang
Institute for Defense
and Disarmament Studies

A common objection to the proposal for a US-USSR nuclear weapons Freeze is: 'You can't trust the Russians. The Freeze is a nice idea, but this is a nasty world and they would take advantage of us. The USSR is a closed society, so we wouldn't know if they cheated.' This article is about how we would know if the USSR cheated. It also discusses past Soviet treaty adherence.

Challenges to the verifiability of a bilateral Freeze must not be avoided, deflected or minimized. As Congressman Les Aspin wrote in Scientific American, "The keystone of any international arms control agreement is the ability of each side to make sure the other side abides by it."[1]

One can assert with confidence that a Freeze agreement could be made adequately verifiable. Potential obstacles exist, but the problems could be worked out, for they are more political than technical. This is the case for most major arms control proposals. The Stockholm International Peace Research Institute states, "Verification is said to be the main stumbling block,...but history shows that, once political will to obtain an agreement exists, verification problems are easily dealt with."[2]

This article attempts to give basic answers to most questions about the verifiability of the Freeze. But some verification issues, especially those relating to production of nuclear weapons, have not been thought about much. Experts disagree on several key points. More research is needed in order to know what provisions and agreements between the US and the USSR would be necessary to verify some parts of the Freeze proposal.

More important than detailed answers, at the moment, is the perspective, the framework, for approaching issues of verification.

I. A FRAMEWORK FOR APPROACHING VERIFICATION

The Meaning of 'Verifiable'

Verification is not an open-and-shut proposition. Experts are almost unanimous in saying that verifiability is a relative concept. We do not need to be 100 percent certain that the Soviets are observing an agreement. The critical questions are: How much might they cheat before we detected it? Could they gain any advantage without our noticing it? And could we respond in time to protect ourselves?

In a New York Times Magazine article of November 29, 1981, Leslie Gelb, former head of the State Department's Bureau of Political-Military Affairs, observed:

The basic test of a verification technique is whether it can catch militarily significant treaty violations in time to put together a comparable weapon or to take defensive action. But as Paul H. Nitze, a leading defence expert and an arms negotiator for the Reagan Administration, has testified, verifiability is not "an absolute requirement; it is a means toward the end of a good agreement. If those provisions of an agreement which are strategically significant to us are adequately verifiable, the agreement might be a good agreement, even if its less important provisions are not confidently verifiable."[3]

How Are Arms Control Agreements Verified?

Most arms control agreements are now policed by what are called 'national technical means.' These are spy satellites (reconnaissance satellites), aircraft, and ship- and shore-based listening posts, equipped with photographic, infrared, radar, radio and other electronic sensors. The satellite-based cameras, which cover every inch of the USSR, are said to be "accurate enough to capture an automobile license plate on film."[4] Close-look cameras can zoom in on anything suspicious and snap ultra-detailed photos. "Missile silos, launch-control systems, airbases, bombers on the ground, naval bases and submarines in port are all visible. Factories, submarine-construction yards, highways, and railroads stand in clear view."[5]

'Cooperative' verification measures are negotiated and can take many forms, such as seismic installations, restrictions on concealment practices, on-site inspection and data exchanges.

The Soviet Record of Treaty Compliance

The Soviet record of adherence to arms-control agreements is clear. In the past 21 years, the USA and the USSR have signed 15 agreements. None has been violated by the Soviets.[6] These agreements include the 1963 Partial Test Ban Treaty, the 1967 ban on nuclear weapons in outer space, the 1972 SALT I Agreement and Anti-Ballistic Missile Treaty. The SALT II Treaty, signed in 1979 but not formally ratified or legally binding, has been upheld by both parties by informal agreement.

Despite this good record, "officials involved in monitoring SALT compliance in the Nixon, Ford and Carter Administrations acknowledge that the Soviets have tried to exploit ambiguities and have disregarded US views on the spirit of the accords. But they argue that little basis exists for the charge that actual violations have been committed."[7]

SALT I established a US-Soviet Standing Consultive Commission, a forum in which the USA and the USSR can question or challenge each other about compliance with strategic arms agreements. As of June 1979, eight issues had been raised by the USA and five by the Soviet Union. "In each case the United States has raised, the activity in question has either ceased or additional information has allayed our concern."[8]

Cheating: Small Gains, Great Risks

The greatest fear that people have is that the Soviets, after agreeing to a Freeze, will secretly develop a super weapon and spring it on us. Such a development is totally implausible, for it takes nearly 10 years for a significant new development in the nuclear arms race to come to fruition. Congressman Les Aspin, commenting on the steps in this process, has said: "The introduction of a new strategic weapon involves at least five stages: research, development, testing, production and deployment. At any one of these stages the present ability of the US to detect clandestine activity on the part of the USSR ranges from fair to excellent. The key point, however, is that the Russians would have to disguise all five stages, and that the odds against their successfully doing so are extremely high."[9]

It should be emphasized that the testing of a new strategic weapon generally takes 1-3 years while the deployment of significant numbers of a new weapon usually takes 3-5 years and sometimes even longer. These two stages, which are easily detected, offer highly-reliable evidence of new developments well in advance of the time when they might tip the military balance.

Perhaps more important, in an age of enormous nuclear overkill, with nuclear arsenals numbering in the tens of thousands, the clandestine production by one side of a few tens or even some hundreds of new nuclear missiles would not diminish the nuclear deterrent of the other side much, if at all.

Government leaders would have to weigh the marginal advantage that might be offered by concealed production against the great risks and penalties of discovery. The larger the transgression, the greater would be the risk of detection. The price in the event of exposure, in terms of international prestige, future international relations, and future agreements, would be terrible. "The Soviets...know that, rather than tolerate cheating, the US would scrap the new agreement and take countermeasures before any threat to our national security could develop."[10] In addition, the Soviets would recognize that relations generally—not only with the United States but also with other countries—would be impaired for years, possibly decades.

Soviet Position on On-Site Inspection

The most reliable way to check that cheating is not occuring is to go in and check in person, on the ground. This is called 'on-site inspection.'

While most parts of the Freeze proposal can be verified without on-site inspection, some parts would clearly benefit from this form of control. However, in the past, excessive demands for on-site inspection have been advanced by those who wanted to continue the arms race, in order to block arms control agreements. Thus, it is important to insure that the independently-verifiable parts of the Freeze not be held hostage to those which are more difficult to verify without on-site inspection.

The USSR has been reluctant to allow any sort of on-site inspection in the past. But in recent years, as Leslie Gelb has observed, "there have been signs of a softening in the Soviet position. In the Threshold Test Ban Treaty, signed in 1974 but still unratified, for the first time, Moscow and Washington agreed to exchange data on their nuclear weapons programs and to limit testing to specific areas to assist verification. In the related treaty on Peaceful Nuclear Explosions, signed in 1976 and also unratified, the two parties agreed not only to exchange information to enhance confidence,...but also to allow for observers and for access to the sites of the explosions."[11] (The two treaties in question, like the SALT II treaty, have been supported by the USSR but not brought to a vote in the US Senate.)

A breakthrough came during the negotiations for a Comprehensive Test Ban Treaty in 1978. "American and British negotiators extracted a significant concession from the Soviet Union. This was an agreement to allow the employment of ten seismic stations—black boxes that would accurately record every Soviet test of nuclear weapons—on Russian soil."[12] "At the same time, the USSR also agreed to on-site inspections to buttress the data provided by the seismic stations in particular circumstances."[13]

One would think that the more stringent the US demands for on-site inspection, the less likely the USSR would be to agree to an arms control proposal. However, according to Yuri Kapralov, First Secretary at the Soviet Embassy in Washington DC, "...the more comprehensive the substance of the treaty in question, the greater degree of on-site inspection we would agree to."[14] Thus the Freeze proposal may win greater Soviet cooperation on verification than might be expected.

II. THE FREEZE PROPOSAL

The Freeze proposal, as described in the "Call to Halt the Nuclear Arms Race,"[15] covers all types of nuclear weapons, short-range as well as strategic, intercontinental systems. It applies to three activities: testing, production and deployment. (Research and development, including design, "breadboard" and theoretical studies of new weapons, are not included in the proposal because they are not reliably verifiable.) The proposal covers nuclear warheads, weapon-grade material used in making nuclear warheads, and aircraft and missile systems designed to deliver nuclear warheads.

Verification of Non-Testing

Tests of nuclear warheads:

The Soviet concession on seismic sensors and on-site verification was not enough to secure agreement to a Comprehensive Test Ban Treaty by the US government. (Underground testing continues.) The United States says that tests of very small nuclear warheads can escape detection. Actually, "[t]here is considerable military interest in the further development of low-yield nuclear weapons, particularly for tactical purposes."[16] The failure to conclude a CTB Treaty has little to do with verification and a great deal to do with the political power of the military in the USA.

Testing of missiles and aircraft:

US satellites, ground stations and mobile 'collection platforms' (ships and aircraft) could verify a ban on tests of ballistic missiles. Verification of limits on the number of nuclear warheads in any given missile test is included in SALT II, as is a ban on 'encryption' (coding) of electronic data sent back from missile tests. Naturally, checking a complete halt in ballistic-missile tests would be easier than checking limits on the number of warheads in each individual test conducted.

In the case of small cruise missiles, designed to fly close to the ground (a type currently developed only by the USA and not yet available in the USSR), independent verification of non-testing would be more difficult and less reliable, though still possible. This area needs further investigation to determine the adequacy of national means of verification.

Testing of new bomber aircraft designed to deliver nuclear weapons could be observed. More difficult would be to check that patrol and test flights of existing aircraft are not used to test advances in aircraft component technology.

Verification of Non-Production

Whether a ban on the production of nuclear warheads and of nuclear-capable aircraft and missiles could be adaquately verified is among the most controversial aspects of the Freeze proposal. Some analysts have suggested that the scope of the Freeze should exclude production. But, *"if the Freeze is limited to the testing and deployment of missiles and aircraft, leaving out the production activities that take place in factories under a closed roof, the most likely result is that the military on one or both sides will insist on taking the ban literally. They will continue to produce additional missiles and aircraft, and warheads for them, and will either store them in warehouses indefinitely or else treat the Freeze as a temporary, two-or-three year moratorium ... Either course would totally undermine the concept and the purposes of the Freeze."*[17]

The comprehensiveness of the Freeze proposal means that verification of the whole package would be significantly easier than verification of the separate parts. High-confidence verification of one link of the production chain could compensate for weaknesses in other links. Each of the three aspects of production of nuclear weapon systems constitutes a potential bottleneck for a cheater.

Production of weapon-grade fissionable material:

The International Atomic Energy Agency (IAEA) uses on-site inspection and tamper-proof cameras to verify that plutonium (a waste product of nuclear reactors) and enriched uranium are not being removed and clandestinely reprocessed to provide nuclear-bomb fuel by non-nuclear nations which have signed the Non-Proliferation Treaty (NPT). The IAEA safeguards could be extended to the USA and USSR. This would not only verify their non-production of weapon-grade fissionable material, but also make the NPT and its safeguards more attractive to countries which do not yet have nuclear weapons, thereby helping to halt the spread of nuclear weapons. The United States and the United Kingdom have already agreed in principle to allow IAEA inspection of civilian reactors; and the USSR has agreed to some demonstration checks. The United States could, as part of the Freeze proposal, require the USSR to permit IAEA inspection.

As a supplement or alternative, non-production of weapon-grade fissionable material could be verified by checking that the small number of plants which make weapons from the raw material are completely shut down. Non-activity in these few, large, highly-specialized plants could be checked by the infrared sensors on satellites, which detect the heat in active plants. Assurance of non-production would also be offered by (1) the lack of demand for new weapon-grade material, given non-production of new nuclear-capable aircraft and missiles; and (2) the military uselessness of small stocks of fissionable material, in the context of the enormous existing stocks of spare bombs and of surplus fissionable material from retired bombs.

Production of nuclear warheads:

There are only three plants central to the manufacture of nuclear warheads in the United States: the Rocky Flats plant near Denver, Colorado, where the plutonium 'triggers' for the fission part of bombs are made; the Oak Ridge, Tennessee, plant, where the lithium-deuteride fuel for the fusion part of bombs is fabricated; and the Pantex plant in Amarillo, Texas, which assembles the fission, fusion and non-nuclear components of bombs. It is likely that an equally small number of weapon-producing plants and component-producing facilities exist in the Soviet Union and that they are known and monitored by US satellites. Since the Freeze would be a complete ban, any activity at these plants—trucks or railroad cars leaving or entering—would immediately be suspect.

Production of nuclear-capable missiles and aircraft:

A freeze on the production of missiles and aircraft designed to deliver nuclear weapons can be checked by surveillance satellites. There are three reasons for this: (1) the large size and known location of existing production plants; (2) the known transportation location of existing routes of major components being brought together for assembly; and (3) the small scale and known location of existing non-deployed stocks of missiles and aircraft.

US intelligence information about Soviet military production facilities is extremely detailed. A report to Congress by the Defence Intelligence Agency on July 8, 1981 states: "There are 134 major final assemby plants involved in producing Soviet weapons and end products. In addition, we have identified over 3500 individual installations that provide support to these final assembly plants."[18] The report asserts that 37 plants produce aircraft materiel and 49 produce missile materiel. A lengthy table gives figures for Soviet production of missiles, aircraft, and even small items such as field artillery and rocket launchers.

Referring specifically to strategic nuclear missiles, the US Department of Defense October 1981 pamphlet "Soviet Military Power" states:

Four major Soviet design bureaus specialize in strategic missiles development. These bureaus are supported by activities at main assembly plants, at hundreds of component production plants, at test ranges, and at launch complexes. The Soviet missile development program shows no signs of slackening. We expect improvements leading to new missiles and to the modification of existing missile systems ... It is anticipated that the Soviets will develop solid-propellant ICBMs to supplement or replace some of the current liquid propellant systems.[19]

The February 1982 "Posture Statement" of the US Joint Chiefs of Staffs adds: "[T]he Soviets are apparently ready to begin flight testing of two new solid propellant ICBMs; either or both could reach IOC [initial operational capability] by the mid-1980s."[20]

These statements indicate that Soviet missile design, development and production facilities are so well known that activities in the early stages of development prior to flight testing can be identified with considerable precision. Large-scale production of the same items should be even easier to detect.

Deployment

A significant advantage of the Freeze is that a complete ban on new weapon deployments should be much easier to verify than the intricate limits on deployment of various categories of new weapon systems that were established in the SALT I and SALT II agreements. The bombers, land-based missiles and submarine-launched missiles covered in SALT II are large and readily visible to satellites. What about smaller intermediate- and short-range nuclear missiles and new, small cruise missiles? Intermediate-range missiles, such as the Soviet's SS-4, SS-5 and new, mobile SS-20 are large enough to be identified by satellites. This is confirmed by the precise numbers of such missiles included in Western estimates and by President Reagan's proposal to ban such missiles.

Deployment of cruise missiles may not be independently verifiable directly, but can be checked through controls on the number and loading capacity of air-, naval- and ground-platforms and launching systems. This was the procedure followed in SALT II, where the numbers of Air-Launched Cruise Missiles are controlled through limits on the numbers of bombers permitted to be fitted with cruise missile launchers and through limits on the numbers of cruise missiles to be carried by each bomber.

Conclusion

When opponents of a Freeze speak about the difficulties of verification, a political response may be more helpful than a technical one. There are risks in any nuclear-weapon policy. The absolute certainty in verifying each separate part of a Freeze package that some people demand is unreasonable. A more reasonable approach is to weigh the risks of violation of a Freeze against the risks of the alternative: an expensive and destabilizing nuclear arms race which will increase the likelihood of nuclear war.

Footnotes

1. Les Aspin, "The Verification of the SALT II Agreement", Scientific American, February 1979, p.38.

2. Frank Barnaby and Ronald Huisken, Arms Uncontrolled, Cambridge, MA: Harvard University Press, 1975, p.202.

3. Leslie Gelb, "Keeping An Eye on Russia", New York Times Magazine Section, November 29, 1980, p.148.

4. Ibid.

5. Union of Concerned Scientists, "Strategic Surveillance: How America Checks Soviet Compliance With SALT", Cambridge, MA, 1979, p.3.

6. Stockholm International Peace Research Institute, "Armament or Disarmament", Stockholm, June 1980.

7. Robert J. Einhorn, "Treaty Compliance", Foreign Policy, Winter 1981-82, p.30.

8. US Department of State, "SALT and American Security: Questions Americans Are Asking", US Government Printing Office, November 1979.

9. Aspin, op.cit.

10. Union of Concerned Scientists, op.cit.

11. Leslie Gelb, "US Tells Soviet Any Arms Pacts Must Include On-Site Verification", New York Times, September 2, 1981, p.9.

12. Dale Van Atta, "Inside a US-Soviet Arms Negotiation", The Nation, December 19, 1981, p.666.

13. Barry M. Blechman, "The Comprehensive Test Ban Negotiations: Can They Be Revived?", Arms Control Today, Washington DC: Arms Control Association, June 1981, p.3.

14. Telephone conversation, 1982.

15. "Call to Halt the Nuclear Arms Race", St. Louis: Nuclear Weapons Freeze Campaign National Clearinghouse, 1981.

16. Barnaby and Huisken, op.cit.

17. Randall Forsberg, "Is a US-Soviet Nuclear-Weapon Freeze Possible?", CALC Report, New York: Clergy and Laity Concerned, October 1980.

18. Statement of Major General Richard X. Larkin, Deputy Director, and Edward M. Collins, Vice Director for Foreign Intelligence of the Defence Intelligence Agency before the Joint Economic Committee, Subcommittee on International Trade, Finance, and Security Economics, "Allocation of Resources in the Soviet Union and China—1981, July 8, 1981.

19. Washington DC: US Government Printing Office, pp.56-57.

20. Washington DC: US Government Printing Office, p. 106.

Other Sources:

William Epstein, "A Ban on the Production of Fissionable Material for Weapons", Scientific American, July 1980.

Herbert Scoville, Jr, "SALT Verification and Iran", Arms Control Today, Washington DC: Arms Control Association, February 1979.

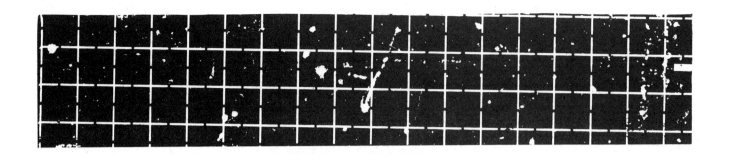

choose life

so that you
and your children
will live

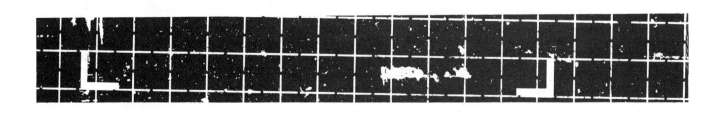

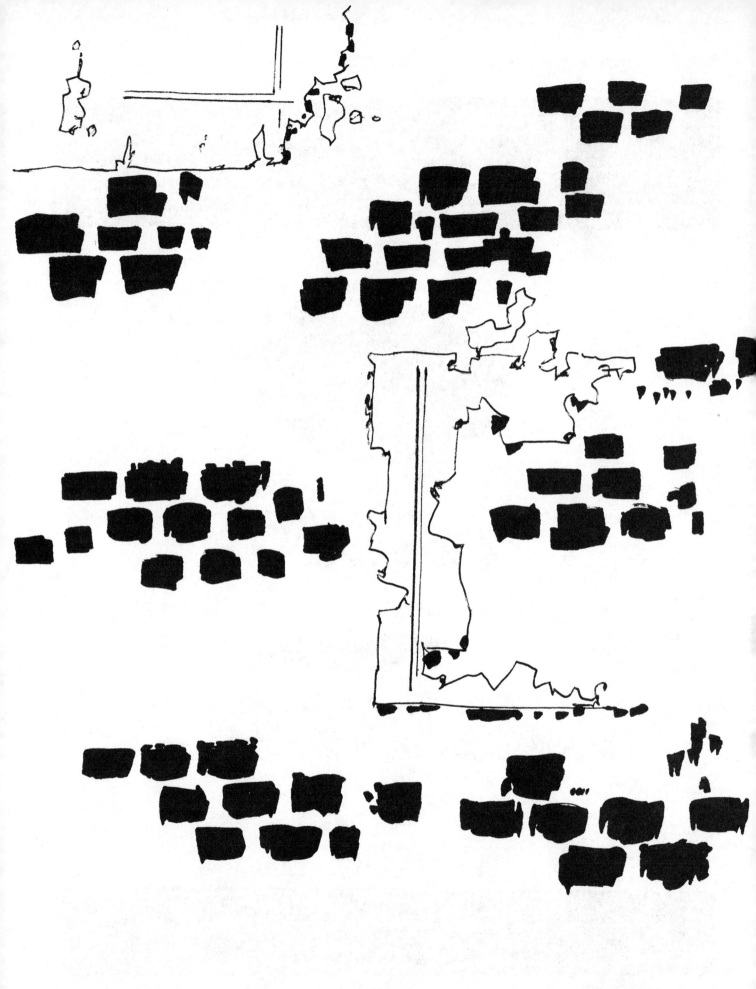

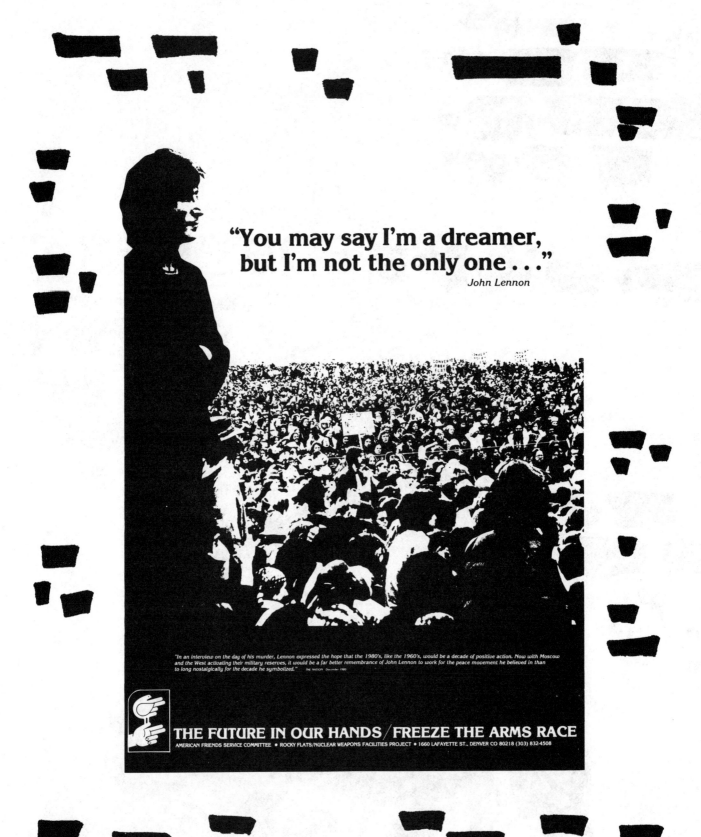

"You may say I'm a dreamer,
but I'm not the only one . . ."

John Lennon

"In an interview on the day of his murder, Lennon expressed the hope that the 1980's, like the 1960's, would be a decade of positive action. Now with Moscow and the West activating their military reserves, it would be a far better remembrance of John Lennon to work for the peace movement he believed in than to long nostalgically for the decade he symbolized." THE NATION December 1980

THE FUTURE IN OUR HANDS / FREEZE THE ARMS RACE

AMERICAN FRIENDS SERVICE COMMITTEE ● ROCKY FLATS/NUCLEAR WEAPONS FACILITIES PROJECT ● 1660 LAFAYETTE ST., DENVER CO 80218 (303) 832-4508

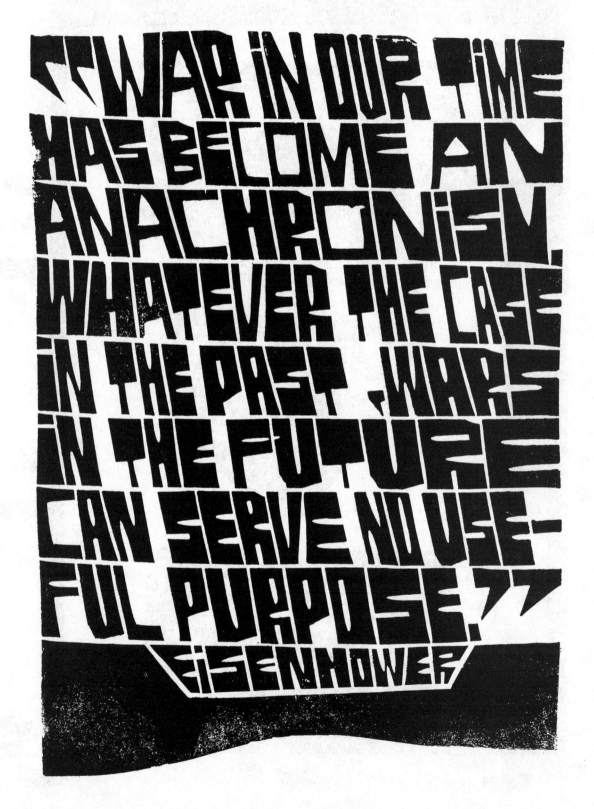

"WAR IN OUR TIME HAS BECOME AN ANACHRONISM. WHATEVER THE CASE IN THE PAST, WARS IN THE FUTURE CAN SERVE NO USEFUL PURPOSE."

EISENHOWER

TO THE PEOPLE
OF THE USA
AND THE SOVIET UNION

ОБРАЩЕНИЕ К НАРОДАМ СССР И США

The nuclear armaments race between the USA and the USSR is a race towards death. Peace will not be secured by a balance of power on a still higher level. The vicious escalation of nuclear arms inevitably leads to a common Holocaust. By irresponsibility, miscalculation or accident

We only have one world and to save it we must have courage to face the danger - we must have courage to be afraid - courage to act

Hundreds of thousands are demonstrating in London, in Bonn, in Paris, in Brussels, in Rome to show their fear. The European peace-movements refuse to accept a Europe saturated with nuclear warheads, - more than 10.000 tactical ones, thousands of intermediate range rockets

We protest against the planned deployment of even more nuclear weapons, the Pershing-II and the cruise missiles, - against the dangerous illusion that a nuclear war can be limited to Europe, - against the latest leads from the Reagan administration: the neutron bomb, and the plan for firing a nuclear device for demonstrative purposes

We protest against the massive build up of SS-20 missiles, - against the sending of a Soviet submarine, possibly armed with nuclear weapons, into Swedish territory, hampering efforts to establish nuclear free zones

We believe that after the first nuclear bomb has been fired, nothing can stop the destruction of the world

We do not believe that we have to arm to be able to disarm

We do not accept the insane logic which says that a nuclear bomb in the East justifies one in the West, or vice versa Massmurder can never be justified

We demand sincere negotiations and disarmaments NOW!

We protest against the enormous waste of resources for military purposes, when millions of people all over the world are starving

The survival of mankind is too important to be left to the politicians alone. Support your local peace-movement, or start one!

Express your demands for nuclear disarmament to your neighbours, your church, your union, your representative in Congress or in the Supreme Soviet

Гонка ядерных вооружении - гонка к смерти. Мир не обеспечивается балансом сил на растущем уровне. Безумное наращивание вооружения ядерного оружия обязательно ведет к общей гибели. Из за неответственности, неправиль ного расчета или случайности

Есть только одна Земля, чтобы спасти ее требуется мужество осознать опасность - требуется мужество показать свою боязнь - требуется мужество приступить к действию

Сотни тысяч демонстрируют в Лондоне, в Бонне, в Париже, в Брюсселе, в Риме и тем самым показывают свою боязнь. Европейское движение мира отвергает насыщение Европы атомными боеголовками - более 10 000 тактических тысячами ракет среднего радиуса действия

Мы протестуем против запланированного размещения большего количества атомного оружия Першинг-2, крылатых ракет - против опасной иллюзии о возможности о граничивать атомную воину в пределах Европы - против последних инициатив администрации Рейгана. Решение о производстве нейтронной бомбы и план о предупреждающем ударе атомной боеголовкой

Мы протестуем против размещения в широком масштабе ракет типа СС-20, против пребывания советской подводной лодки, возможно, вооруженной ядерным оружием, в швед ской морской территории, что препятствует усилия установить безъядерные зоны

Мы считаем, что как только первая атомная бомба запущена, ничего не сможет остановить истребления Земли

Мы считаем неправильным положение о том, будто надо вооружаться прежде чем возможно разоружаться

Мы отвергаем абсурдную логику о приемлемости запад ного удара в ответ на удар с Востока и наоборот. Массовое убийство никогда не может быть оправдано

Мы требуем серьезных переговоров и разоружения СЕЙ ЧАС!

Мы протестуем против огромной затраты ресурсов на во енные нужды в то время, как миллионы населения Земли го лодают

Будущее человечества является слишком важным делом чтобы его предоставить одним лишь политическим деятелям Поддерживайте местную организацию мира - или основы ваите сами организацию мира! Выражайте ваши требования о ядерном разоружении соседям, профсоюзу, конгрессмену или депутату в Верховный Совет СССР

НЕТ! АТОМНОМУ ОРУЖИЮ!

NO/NJET
TO NUCLEAR WEAPONS

From 7.006 people in Denmark, who signed and paid for this advertisement.
Вао приветствуют 7.006 датчан, подписавших и заплативших за это обращение.

This message will be given to the Soviet and the American embassy in Copenhagen, Denmark.
Обращение передано Советскому и Американскому посолтству в Копенгагене, Дания.

WITHOUT DISARMAMENT..

...WHO WILL HAVE GRANDCHILDREN?

Women's International League for Peace and Freedom 1213 Race Street   Philadelphia, Pa. 19107

SOME TRUST IN CHARIOTS
AND SOME TRUST IN HORSES
BUT WE TRUST IN THE LORD OUR GOD
PSALM 20

PEACE SABBATH 1981

Clergy and Laity Concerned • Fellowship of Reconciliation • Religous Task Force/Mobilization For Survival • Riverside Church Disarmament Program
198 Broadway • New York • N.Y. 10038   Box 271· Nyack · N.Y. 10960   198 Broadway · New York · N.Y. 10038   490 Riverside Drive · New York· N.Y. 10027

Maryknoll photo

"What do I now see as the way out for the underdeveloped world? Not violence. Today established violence keeps millions of people in a subhuman situation. For the Third World to turn to violence would be to declare that no alternative exists...I dream about the day when there will dawn for mankind a new civilization with justice and peace recognized as the essential values. For me that dream has validity because I believe in the power of truth and love. I believe in the work of God, who will not allow falsehood and hate to prevail among men for all time. So I shall continue my attempts to carry out concrete action looking toward justice and peace, confident that those values will prevail — perhaps tomorrow, perhaps the day after tomorrow."

Archbishop Dom Helder Camara

The Fellowship of Reconciliation, Nyack, New York

44

Arms Sales

The New Merchants of Death

In the opening scene of the motion picture "Reds" (1981), John Reed (Warren Beatty) addresses a Portland, Oregon Chamber of Commerce luncheon. It is 1916, and he is responding to the question why there is a war in Europe. Reed stands, pauses, and then answers, "Profits." The same answer largely applies to the contemporary arms trade. Other factors play a role in determining who gets whose weapons. But overall, it is a very lucrative business for the United States, the Soviet Union, the French, the West Germans, the British, and others.

Top 100 Defense Contractors Awarded Prime Contracts in FY 1980

Rank	Companies	Thousands of Dollars
1.	General Dynamics Corp.	$3,517,906
2.	McDonnell Douglas Corp.	3,246,557
3.	United Technologies Corp.	3,108,901
4.	Boeing Co.	2,385,459
5.	General Electric Co.	2,202,042
6.	Lockheed Corp.	2,037,044
7.	Hughes Aircraft Co.	1,819,058
8.	Raytheon Co.	1,745,107
9.	Tenneco, Inc.	1,524,414
10.	Grumman Corp.	1,322,023
11.	Northrop Corp.	1,227,339
12.	Motor Oil Hellas	1,058,646
13.	Chrysler Corp.	970,881
14.	Rockwell Intern'l Corp.	969,234
15.	Westinghouse Elec. Corp.	932,053
16.	Sperry Corp.	844,977
17.	F.M.C.	834,640
18.	Martin Marietta Corp.	808,681
19.	Honeywell Inc.	687,018
20.	Litton Industries, Inc.	652,383
21.	American Tel. & Tel. Co.	597,074
22.	R.C.A. Corp.	588,935
23.	Textron Inc.	578,738
24.	Fairchild Industries, Inc.	559,277
25.	L.T.V. Corp.	510,902
26.	General Motors Corp.	508,803
27.	T.R.W. Inc.	508,084
28.	Int'l Bus. Mach. Co. (IBM)	496,953
29.	Exxon Corp.	479,637
30.	Standard Oil Co. of Calif.	474,954
31.	Singer Co.	435,426
32.	Texas Instruments, Inc.	431,428
33.	Teledyne, Inc.	396,237
34.	Ford Motor Co.	395,777
35.	Todd Shipyards Corp.	394,298
36.	Congoleum Corp.	377,879
37.	Int'l Tel & Tel Corp. (ITT)	335,107
38.	Amerada Hess Corp.	331,699
39.	Bendix Corp.	322,485
40.	General Tire & Rubber Co.	317,893
41.	Gen. Telephone & Elec. (GTE)	309,970
42.	Avco Corp.	286,665
43.	Atlantic Richfield Co.	285,673
44.	Harsco Corp.	280,256
45.	Mobil Corp.	276,244
46.	Sam Whan Corp.	266,340
47.	Goodyear Tire & Rubber Co.	264,156
48.	North American Philips Corp.	260,518
49.	Coastal Corp.	250,432
50.	Gould, Inc.	244,184
51.	Sun Co., Inc.	230,065
52.	Royal Dutch Shell Group	225,090
53.	Agip Spa.	223,660
54.	Texaco Inc.	221,123
55.	Hercules, Inc.	220,302
56.	Hanil Dev. Co. & Mabani	217,558
57.	Standard Oil of Ind.	202,129
58.	Reynolds Industries, Inc.	202,003
59.	Motorola Inc.	199,291
60.	Emerson Electric Co.	190,278
61.	Mi Ryung Construction	172,125
62.	G.K. Technologies, Inc.	168,331
63.	Johns Hopkins Univ.	163,684
64.	Harris Corp.	163,052
65.	Signal Companies Inc.	162,922
66.	Aerospace Corp.	160,394
67.	E-Systems, Inc.	157,639
68.	Mass. Inst. of Tech.	155,953
69.	Summa Corp.	153,979
70.	Sverdrup Corp.	151,666
71.	Pacific Resources, Inc.	147,523
72.	Gen. Agencies & Whan	144,306
73.	American Motors Corp.	142,180
74.	Control Data Corp.	139,481
75.	Saudi Maint. Co., Ltd.	128,834
76.	Pan Am. World Air., Inc.	126,565
77.	Xerox Corp.	120,706
78.	Guam Oil & Refin. Co.	118,382
79.	Chamberlain Mfg. Corp.	113,254
80.	Mitre, Corp.	110,919
81.	Sun Chemical Corp.	110,874
82.	Getty Oil Co.	110,256
83.	Groves Kiewit Granite	109,040
84.	Kasler Cont. Heller	103,925
85.	Thiokol Corp.	103,217
86.	Eastman Kodak Co.	103,130
87.	Sanders Associates, Inc.	102,227
88.	Lear Siegler, Inc.	101,656
89.	Loral Corp.	100,276
90.	Felec Services, Inc.	99,328
91.	First Colony Farms, Inc.	97,156
92.	Pride Refining Co.	95,840
93.	Imperial Chem. Ind., Ltd.	94,966
94.	Centex Corp.	94,464
95.	Computer Sciences Corp.	92,955
96.	Montedison Spa.	92,248
97.	City Investing Co.	91,696
98.	Ashland Oil Inc.	90,562
99.	Gulf Oil Corp.	90,262
100.	Hewlett Packard Co.	85,579

NARMIC, September 1981

Big Business

The American military establishment is the largest, richest, most powerful institutional complex in the United States—perhaps in the world. So large is it and so extensive are its operations that it dwarfs all other institutions in American society. It is the biggest spender in the U.S. economy as well as the largest purchaser of goods, accounting for more than two-thirds of the government's purchases and almost three-fourths of its expenditures. It owns thirty million acres of land, about forty-five thousand square miles, an area almost the size of New York, and an additional ten million acres under control of the Army's Civil Works Division, altogether valued at over two hundred billion dollars. In addition it operates over two thousand bases in almost one hundred different countries employing over two million military and civilian personnel and expending hundreds of millions annually. Its budget varies from year to year, ranging between seventy and eighty billion. And to this amount must be added the cost of various international programs, space research and technology carried on for military purposes, the Veterans Administration, and programs that, exclusive of the CIA, bring the total cost of the military establishment to between ninety and one hundred billion, almost ten percent of the gross national product. In short, war has become the nation's leading industry.

Prof. Louis Morton, in ''The Military and American Society,'' (Reviews in American History, *Vol 1, Number 1, March 1973*) (Redgrave Info Resources Corp., 53 Wilton Rd-Westport, Ct. 06880)

The British Love to Sell Arms, Too: How to Fight the Traffic

Campaign Against Arms Trade, 5 Caledonian Road, King's Cross, London N1 9DX, England

Lorna Lloyd and Nicholas A. Sims, *British Writing on Disarmament, 1914-1978: a bibliography* (London: Francis A. Pinter, 1979)

J. Stanley and M. Pearton, *The International Trade in Arms* (London: Chatto & Windus, 1972)

Bernt Engelman, *The Weapons Merchants* (London: Paladin, 1969)

Who's on Welfare?

General Dynamics is. Without taxpayer handouts, it could not survive.

In 1980, with sales of $4.74 billion, General Dynamics received 74% of its total income from the U.S. government:

Military aircraft	37%
Submarines	19%
Missiles and gun systems	14%
Space systems	2%
Telecommunications and data processing	2%
Total	74%

GO AHEAD, I DARE YOU!

Francis A. Fitzgerald

The Way It Really Works—
Part 1

Clark MacGregor, Washington lobbyist for United Technologies Corporation, tells how he influences Washington politicians and bureaucrats to buy weapons made by UTC.

> I see high-ranking people at the White House, in the Congress and at the Defense Department. I see (White House Chief of Staff) Jim Baker and his wife a lot. . . . I might find myself sitting next to Ursula Meese (the wife of White House power broker Edwin Meese) at a concert at Wolf Trap. . . .

P.S.

MacGregor also directs UTC's political action committee, which handed out $140,200 to candidates for the 1980 elections—most of it to Republicans. He also played a crucial role in lobbying for the sale of AWACS aircraft—made by Pratt and Whitney, a UTC division—to Saudi Arabia.

P.P.S.

Secretary of State Alexander Haig was the president of United Technologies before President Reagan appointed him to the State Department. Will he return to UTC after he leaves Washington?

Information gleaned from The Wall Street Journal

The Way It Really Works—
Part 2

The Defense Contract Audit Agency, responsible for auditing contractors' costs on defense projects, audited ten such contractors in Washington. After four years of court delay resulting from Pentagon challenges, *Common Cause* printed the audit results in August 1981. They revealed how the American taxpayer had paid for the following:

- $8,516 was given to the Raytheon Company for lodging and guides at goose hunts in Maryland
- $12,032 was paid to Lockheed Aircraft for first-class air tickets and travel expenses of executives and their wives attending the air shows in Paris and Farnborough, England.
- $42,976 was paid to Hughes Aircraft for a condominium in Washington.
- $181,861 went to Martin Marietta for creating "rapport" with congressional representatives from 35 states in which the corporation has divisions.

Hard at Work

Ex-CIA deputy director Vernon Walters was paid $300,000 in 1981 from a firm that manufactures military technology and sells it to foreign nations. One year after he left the CIA (he served from 1972 to 1976), he got in touch with Moroccan authorities on behalf of Environmental Energy Systems, Inc. of Alexandria, a company wishing to upgrade Morocco's tank corps. Walters described his primary job as "putting them (company officials) in touch with the right people."

AP (NY Daily News—9/23/81)

Southern Fried Porkbarrel

Ever wonder why all those Southern Democrats in Washington are submitting draft bills and supporting Reagan's military spending proposals? A private research group may have come across the answer. According to Employment Research Associates (ERA) of Lansing, Michigan, the Sunbelt region will gain the most from increased military spending at the expense of the Northeast. The study done by ERA (in 1981) concluded that the military budget is by far "the most important factor accounting for the massive shift of resources from the Northeast and Midwest to the South and West."

The study, entitled "The Pentagon Tax: where it comes from, where it goes," reached its conclusions by figuring out how much of the defense budget is allocated to individual states and comparing those figures with the tax funds the states provide for defense. "Military outlays in the Northeast and Midwest totaled about $44 billion in 1980, but their share of the Pentagon tax burden totaled more than $70 billion for a net drain of more than $27 billion," the study said.

Marian Anderson of ERA criticized statements by David Stockman, OMB Director, that all states and regions benefit equally from defense spending as "irresponsible." She added that "The states which provide the industrial core of the United States are being drained."

The Objector, 7-25-81

The Global Trade in Arms

In dealing with the international trade in arms, one major problem is the impossibility of forming a mental conception of what the arms trade *is*. Arms exports are now running at a value of approximately $20 billion annually, of which about three-quarters go to developing nations. How much is $20 billion? What does this scale of expenditure mean to the world?

For the Third World, we must consider not only the "opportunity costs"—the medical, educational, agricultural, and social benefits which could be provided if these huge sums were not spent on armaments—but also the effects of increasing militarization within these countries, including the entrenchment of military governments, and the acceptance of military values and norms.

During the 1970s, supplies of major weapons (aircraft, missiles, armoured vehicles and warships) to Third World countries rose at a yearly average of 15%. From 1974–78, this growth accelerated to 25% per year. Over the decade, the Middle East was by far the largest importing region in the Third World.

The major arms exporters—the United States, Soviet Union, France, and Great Britain—accounted for nearly 90% of these weapons transfers, with the remaining arms coming from West Germany, Italy, China, and a host of other countries.

The quantitative growth in arms transfers has been accompanied by a qualitative change in the sophistication of the weaponry. While the arms-producing countries once supplied primarily second-hand or obsolete weapons to Third World countries, they have in recent years transferred many of the most advanced conventional arms. Very sophisticated weapons can often be purchased on the arms market even before they enter the arsenals of the producer countries. The number of weapons stockpiled around the world heightens the risk of armed conflict or war; the sophistication of the weapons means that the wars, when they do happen, are increasingly destructive to combatants, civilians, and the environment.

Within the exporting countries, continued reliance on military exports, and government support for military research and development, mean that other areas of export are ignored. Little attention is given to possibilities for conversion of arms industries and redeployment of people employed in these industries. Funds are not available for research and development of medical or agricultural or transport equipment. A mythology about the "need" for arms exports is encouraged in the press and other media, and the defence ministers of foreign countries are fêted when they come to view each exporter's wares.

Purchasers unwilling to spend so much of their foreign currency reserves can arrange for indigenous production under license, and they in turn become exporters too, justifying the need for exports to keep down unit costs at home . . . and the arms spiral continues. And licensed production creates new patterns of dependency, with the licensee forced to rely on the licenser for technical advice, spare parts, etc.

Annual studies of the arms race, such as the Stockholm International Peace Research Institute's *Yearbook*, the U.S. Arms Control and Disarmament Agency's *World Military Expenditures and Arms Transfers*, and the excellent *World Military and Social Expenditures*, edited by Ruth Leger Sivard, provide information on transfers of major weapons systems.

But the international trade in arms is far wider. It includes small arms and ammunition, which are virtually impossible to monitor; electronic and communications equipment, which is sometimes included as part of a major weapons system or is, more often, sold as non-military equipment; equipment for surveillance or other use within the country, which is considered as police rather than military equipment; and training, maintenance and servicing, the total value of which often amounts to far more than the cost of the original item of equipment.

The international trade in arms also encompasses spare parts and second-hand equipment—a part of the trade which is even more underhanded than the more open sale by governments and manufacturers, and which doesn't even pretend to abide by embargoes and other limitations on the transfer of arms. And by extension the international trade in arms also includes the transfer of nuclear technology and equipment, for these transfers allow an increasing number of countries to develop and produce their own nuclear weaponry.

Campaign Against Arms Trade

Getting Us Ready

"How will we keep this island [the U.S.] functioning without ships" reads a Todd Shipyards Corporation full page ad in November 1980.

"That's an advocacy ad," Robert J. Daniels, Todd's public relations director, told the press. "We're trying to influence the administration and the Congress to beef up the merchant marine and the Navy." Todd manufactures cargo ships and Navy vessels.

Commented George C. Wilson, military affairs writer of the *Washington Post*, on November 25, 1980: "One side effect of all the advertising could be to condition the public and federal decision-makers to the idea that intervening militarily in such distant areas would be an acceptable use of American power, despite the U.S. experience in Vietnam."

Canadian Uranium: Fueling the Arms Race

In 1979, Canada exported $170 million worth of uranium to the Soviet Union for enrichment in that nation's nuclear fuel plants. Each year since, this quantity has increased, although accurate figures have not yet been tabulated.

Despite the hostility that prompted a boycott of the Olympics, a halt to wheat shipments and a slew of equally ineffectual retaliation strategies, the uranium trade between Canada and the U.S.S.R. has gone on since 1976. Greenpeace Canada has been investigating this trade, as well as that between Canada and other members of the nuclear club such as the United States, West Germany, Argentina, Japan, Britain and France. The investigation has led conclusively to one point: although Canada righteously denies participation in the arms race, the uranium mined in her provinces is contributing to the proliferation of nuclear weapons throughout the world.

Uranium is mined in Ontario and, to a much larger extent, in Saskatchewan. At peak production in 1958, the Saskatchewan mines supplied 6 million pounds of uranium to the United States alone. At this time there were very few nuclear power reactors in the United States, the primary use for uranium being nuclear weapons production triggered by the Cold War.

During the 1960s, uranium production fell to insignificant levels. In the early 70s, however, Canada and other uranium-producing countries formed a secret cartel to boost prices. Today, Saskatchewan's production exceeds that of the 50s boom and is forecast to continue rapid growth. By the end of the decade, Canada may be producing 20 percent of the western world's uranium supply.

Questioned with increasing frequency over Canada's ties to the nuclear weapons producing countries, the government has resorted to passing the buck. Saskatchewan and Ontario provincial leaders renounce any responsibility over what becomes of the uranium once it leaves their borders, asserting that this sort of "policy question" should be addressed to the federal government. In a sadly naive response to "waste disposal, proliferation, terrorism and moral and ethical" criticisms of Saskatchewan's uranium policies, the provincial government states that "political will," and not the trade in implements of destruction is to blame for war.

"Proliferation has acquired a momentum of such force that it will not be stopped or even fractionally reduced by Saskatchewan withholding her uranium from the world market . . . the real answer to proliferation is for all people to work to create the political will for disarmament."

The federal government's answers are no better. It doggedly refers to the Non-Proliferation Treaty and to the assurances of its fellow signers that only good will come of Canada's participation in the trade in nuclear materials.

Unfortunately, at least one of Canada's importers, France, has not signed the Non-Proliferation Treaty. In this case, therefore, there is not even the pretense that Canadian uranium will not go into the processing of nuclear weapons. The French connection becomes even more suspect when one looks behind the scenes at a recently opened mine in northern Saskatchewan.

The Cluff Lake mine is 80 percent owned by Amok Limited, a subsidiary of the French Amok Consortium. The Amok Consortium, in turn, is 30 percent owned by the French atomic energy agency, Commissariat de l'Energie Atomique, the authority responsible for the French weapons and nuclear testing programs. At this time, 300 thousand pounds of uranium from Cluff Lake are waiting to be processed at the Port Hope, Ontario uranium refinery for shipment to France. Because France has refused to sign the Non-Proliferation Treaty, it is illegal for Canada to export uranium for end-use in that country. However, "interim" agreements have been made to allow trade pending permanent negotiations over the matter.

Even in countries that have signed the Non-Proliferation Treaty, there are no real assurances that Canadian uranium will not be put to military use. A country can back out of the treaty after a 90-day notice, and there are no sanctions for a signer who violates the rules.

In some countries, the Soviet Union for example, the only check on whether the same amount of enriched uranium leaves the country as is imported from Canada comes in the form of occasional inspections by the International Atomic Energy Agency, an organization that has no enforcement powers. Inspectors for the I.A.E.A. report not to the Canadian government but to the governments of the enriching countries, so there is rarely if ever any investigation of suspected treaty violators.

For these reasons and many others, Greenpeace Canada is calling for a moratorium on uranium mining in Saskatchewan and Ontario. Canada must either stop pretending to be blind to what is happening with the uranium it is exporting, or it must stop proclaiming itself a peace-loving, non-proliferating country.

The Greenpeace Examiner—*Box 6677, Portland, Oregon 97228. Summer 1981.*

The money required
to provide adequate
food, water, education,
health and housing
for everyone in the world
has been estimated
at $17 billion a year.
It is a huge sum of money

...about as
much as
the world
spends on
arms every
two weeks.

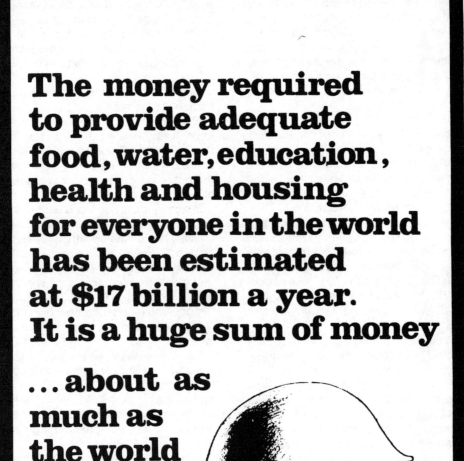

HOW MUCH IS ENOUGH?

INX © 1981 BOB GALE

Boomerang!
Winning Hearts and Minds Through Arms Trade

Military powers have made large military investments in developing countries, giving lavishly of weapons ($60 billion in military gifts since 1946 by the US alone), and providing training for hundreds of thousands of foreign soldiers (44,000 in the USSR alone). Unfortunately few of these investments have paid off handsomely. Most have boomeranged, many on the receiving countries, even more on the generous donors. Herewith a few examples from the press records of the military aid rendered by the major powers:

Egypt received $4 billion in Soviet military aid before switching to the US as principal arms supplier. In 1979-80, Soviet arms previously supplied to Egypt turned up in Afghanistan in the hands of rebels fighting Soviet forces.

Argentina, long a major military client of the US (including $88 million in military gifts), rejected further aid in 1977 on grounds that US criticism of its massive violations of human rights represented interference in its internal affairs.

Yemen received $400 million in emergency western arms aid during its 1979 war with communist South Yemen. In 1980 Yemen turned to the USSR for Mig fighters and tanks, and edged toward a merger with its communist neighbor.

Nicaragua, after years of dependency on US aid (and $24 million in military gifts), ousted dictator Somoza in 1979 and emphasized its intention to diversify suppliers by signing cooperation agreements with USSR and Eastern Europe.

Mozambique, recipient of communist arms aid since 1975, rejected Soviet requests for a naval base and is now turning to the west for military and development assistance.

Iran, whose Shah had been the best customer of all for US arms (including $900 million in military gifts), toppled his regime in a revolution armed with 300,000 weapons looted from government arsenals.

China and the USSR had a falling-out in mid-1960 and Soviet technicians were abruptly withdrawn. Among other forms of aid, USSR had supplied China with nuclear information. The two communist giants now face each other with nuclear missiles over a tense border.

Laos, a favorite recipient of US aid ($2.7 billion in military gifts), consolidated ties with the Soviet Union in 1976.

Sudan, after years of Soviet support, broke off relations in 1977, expelling all Soviet military advisors.

South Korea, recipient of $7.6 billion in US military gifts and with more than 30,000 US troops on its soil, lost a brief flirtation with democracy in 1979 when Korean officers of the joint US-Korean command took power in a surprise coup.

Indonesia, major Soviet military client in the early 1960's, broke ties with the USSR in 1965.

Vietnam received China's military aid until 1978, when it became a member of Comecon and heavily dependent on Soviet aid. In 1979 China invaded Vietnam, facing some of its own arms in a short but bloody war.

Ethiopia, the largest recipient of US arms in Africa ($244 million in gifts) and thanks to them a modern military power despite an abysmally low level of national income, staged a revolution in 1974 which brought a Marxist government to power. Ethiopia became a Soviet ally.

Iraq received most of its military equipment from the USSR (over $3 billion from 1960-1977) but recently has reestablished ties with conservative Arab states and sharply increased arms purchases from France.

And more musical chairs . . .

USSR is now making use of the large naval bases in Vietnam constructed by the US during the Vietnam War.

US is negotiating with Somalia to occupy the Berbera base which the USSR constructed before Somalia and USSR parted company in 1977.

—so it goes

Ruth Sivard, World Military and Social Expenditures. *Copyright © 1980 by World Priorities, Inc.*

South Africa and Chile Get U.S. Arms Despite Cutoffs

In the midst of the panic, of the cries of the wounded, other aircraft were heard approaching. This time it was four gigantic American C-130 Hercules transport planes, which dropped their cargos of parachutists, armed to the teeth, around the village . . . Terrified, the Namibians tried to break through the infernal circle, and the small group of guerrillas protecting the village held on to their defensive positions. But how were they to stop this force of half a thousand parachutists, with three thousand civilians on hand? . . . Of the 3,608 Namibians living there, more than 600 were killed; some 350 were wounded, 160 of them severely. —Jane Bergerol, reporting on the South African attack May 4, 1978 on Kassinga, a Namibian refugee camp in Angola (Afrique-Asie magazine, May 29, 1978)

The cases of South Africa and Chile illustrate the variety of loopholes that can be found in arms embargoes. Both countries are well known as human rights violators. Both are officially the object of arms embargoes. Both have continued to receive U.S. weaponry.

In 1963 the United Nations adopted an arms embargo against South Africa, whose hated *apartheid* system denies basic human rights to the black majority. The U.S. government accepted the embargo but undermined it by allowing **LOCKHEED** to sell South Africa a "civilian" version of the C-130 troop-carrying transport plane. **CESSNA** was allowed to sell Model 185 light planes to South Africa, where they are used for border patrol. South Africa has acquired numerous other

planes which have U.S. engines or are built according to U.S. designs. Some 40% of the front-line aircraft listed in South African Air Force hands by the authoritative *Military Balance* for 1977-78 are partly or fully of U.S. origin.

On November 4, 1977, following the death in prison of black leader Steven Biko, the U.N. Security Council adopted a new, mandatory arms embargo. Implementing it, the State Department issued formal guidelines which U.S. firms are now seeking to overturn, claiming that the new restrictions will hurt the U.S. balance of trade. The guidelines do not affect sales to civilians of "military capable" goods such as light aircraft, which can easily be used for military purposes in the hands of South Africa's all-white civilian "Air Commandos."

Several U.S. firms have engaged in illegal gun-running to South Africa. **OLIN CORPORATION** was fined $510,000 in March 1978 for selling South Africa 3,200 firearms and 20 million rounds of ammunition. **SPACE RESEARCH CORPORATION,** a U.S.-Canadian firm on the Vermont-Canada border, is under investigation for allegedly shipping artillery shells to South Africa by way of Montreal, Antigua, and Barcelona.

In Chile, public outrage over atrocities following the fall of the democratically elected, socialist government of President Salvador Allende in 1973 prompted Congress in late 1974 to end U.S. military aid and arms sales programs to the country. *Commercial* sales by private companies were still allowed, however, and thus Chile was able to buy riot control agents and 1.2 million rounds of ammunition through commercial channels before this loophole was plugged by Congress in 1976.

The 1976 Congressional action barred all new arms orders but left untouched the $120 million backlog of orders placed before June 30, 1976. Through this loophole Chile received more than $50 million worth of U.S. arms in fiscal 1977, including 18 **CESSNA** A-37 counterinsurgency aircraft, and more than $10 million of arms in fiscal 1978.

NARMIC, 1979

Arms Sales to the Third World

The U.S. is selling weapons to some of the most repressive governments in the world. Arms sales by the U.S. and other industrialized countries are turning the Third World into an armed camp.

The Stockholm International Peace Research Institute's 1978 Yearbook estimates that three quarters of the current world trade in weapons is with the Third World nations of Africa, Asia, Latin America, and the Middle East. For these countries, costly arms purchases are a diversion of resources badly needed for social and economic development. And the arms bought by Third World countries are often used against their own citizens, or against their neighbors. As the level of lethality and sophistication of weaponry increases, so does the violence and bloodshed inflicted when fighting breaks out.

As the world's number one arms merchant, the United States bears heavy responsibility for the militarization of the Third World. The U.S. had 52% of the share of arms transfers to the Third World between 1967 and 1976, according to U.S. Arms Control and Disarmament Agency figures; the Soviet Union had 27% during the same period.

In the 1950's and '60's, U.S. foreign military sales to the Third World were relatively small, averaging $230 million a year. But under the Nixon Administration, key restraints were dropped, and arms sales shot up. U.S. foreign military sales to the Middle East and south Asia jumped from $265.5 million in the fiscal year 1970 to $857.3 million in fiscal 1971 and $1.3 billion the following year; other Third World regions experienced similar increases. U.S. foreign military sales to the Third World totalled $351.8 million* in fiscal 1970; in fiscal 1978 they amounted to $11 *billion*,* or 81% of America's worldwide total of $13.5 billion.

The increase in arms sales under President Nixon was connected to a growing balance of payments problem and to the need of arms makers to offset the drop in weapons orders for Vietnam. Arms sales also fit in with the Nixon Doctrine, a new foreign policy emphasis of sending weapons and equipment rather than American troops to protect U.S. interests abroad.

Jimmy Carter campaigned on a pledge "to increase the emphasis on peace and to reduce the commerce in weapons," and on May 19, 1977 President Carter issued a series of guidelines aimed at curbing arms sales. But Carter's new controls do not cover "commercial" exports (direct sales by U.S. companies to foreign governments, as opposed to "foreign military sales" which are arranged through the Pentagon). Nor

*These figures are for foreign military sales agreements (as opposed to actual deliveries) to the countries of Latin America, Africa, the Middle East, and Asia (excluding Japan). They do not include commercial (company-to-government) sales.
NARMIC, 1979*

do they include military construction work and other technical services, which for Saudi Arabia alone will amount to an estimated $3 billion in fiscal 1979. Carter's policy also allows exceptions for "extraordinary circumstances" and for countries with which the United States has "major defense treaties."

The official rationale for arms exports, as stated in the Carter Administration's fiscal 1979 presentation to Congress, is that "by assisting friendly and allied nations to acquire and maintain the capability to defend themselves, we serve our worldwide interests in collective security and peace." But the Third World dictatorships that receive U.S. arms are more likely to have to defend themselves against their own people than against foreign aggressors, and security can hardly be found in countries where large numbers of people are malnourished and out of work. As recent events show, even the most "stable" dictatorship can erupt without warning. Iran and Nicaragua may represent the war-torn future for Argentina, South Korea, or other U.S. arms recipients described in this pamphlet.

M-16 rifles for Nicaragua, Chemical MACE for South Korea, tear gas for Indonesia—U.S. arms have been used by repressive dictatorships to stifle change. Now is the time for our country to press for international restraints on the arms trade, in a spirit of genuine disarmament. Now is the time for a humane foreign policy that genuinely fosters human rights around the world.

Good Friends

Africa's arms race is one of the world's best-kept and most dangerous secrets. Since 1963, military outlays by the African states have doubled every five years (after inflation). While the French and Americans have recently trimmed weapons sales, the Soviets are filling the gap.

"U.S. National Interests in Africa," by William J. Foltz, The Wilson Quarterly, *Summer 1981*

Stoking the Fires of War

The intended sale of 200 West German Leopard tanks, the last word in European armor, to Saudi Arabia has again raised the troublesome question of the supply of arms by the industrialized nations of both West and East to the Arab countries. (The arms sold to the Arabs account for the bulk of the weapons trade with the Third World today.)

These exports of the instruments of war to often backward lands whose true passion is war-making, or at least war-mongering, have been shrouded in a very thin veil of secrecy. They are in fact regularly reported in the literature, notably by the Stockholm International Peace Research Institute (SIPRI).

Such publication is frequently inconvenient, mainly to the sellers, but not even the Soviet Union has been able to keep its weapons deals under wraps for any long periods of time. In lieu of suppression, great effort has been invested in drawing attention away from the facts, and in rationalizing them. Attention is diverted, for example, by focussing it on one small country, whose arms trade is less than one per cent of the global total, and in any case is but a direct function of manufacturing for home defence.

It should come as no great surprise to anyone that that particular country is the State of Israel.

Selling arms to the Arabs is however also presented, especially in the West, as a means of obtaining political leverage over the buying country, and denying entry to the rival power—and as an indispensable aid in recycling petrodollars and assuring a regular supply of oil for the domestic economy. Marketing the agents of death to the Arab world thus becomes a legitimate way of providing a livelihood for tens of thousands of otherwise idle workers.

When couched in such starkly "realistic" terms, these arguments are virtually immune to rebuttal on moral grounds. But the wily and impious weapons traders are also anxious to sell to the masses of peace-loving people that their grubby occupation is also a pious service to the cause of world peace and security.

Sometimes, indeed, it is, but much more often it achieves the exact opposite result, and its long-run consequences, in the Middle East, may fairly be described as potentially most dire.

According to a reliable report, there is a French military mission in Khartoum right now, whose purpose may easily be divined: it is to assist President Jaafar Numeiry to defend the Sudan against the megalomaniac expansionist ambitions of Libya's tinpot dictator, Col. Muammar Qaddafi. For once the French appear to be in the right place, planning to do the right thing. Has the lesson of Chad been learned?

Yet who is it that in fact nurtured in the little Libyan Caesar the crazy notion that he could one day be supreme ruler of all Africa, but the French?

To be sure, they have not been alone. A recent list of Libya's western arms suppliers includes the U.S., Britain and Italy as well. But it is France's Mirage fighters, Gazelle helicopters, Matra antiaircraft missiles and Combatante missile boats that have largely helped convert Col. Qaddafi's ragtag, illiterate army into a military force that today, under suitable Soviet instruction, and with Soviet-made tanks, is threatening France's, and the West's, position in a major part of the black continent.

Apparently the lesson of Chad has not been learned. Unbowed by the frustration of their grand design in Libya, the French are now rushing to completion a grandiose plan for the rearmament of another "peace-loving" Arab nation—Iraq.

A squadron of Mirages has just been hastily moved, under tight security, through Cyprus to Iraq. This may be a way of making good on a commercial transaction, but are the French really so anxious to ensure Iraq's victory in its war of aggression against Iran? French—and Italian—technicians are back in Baghdad, seeking to make operational the French-made Osirac nuclear reactor, which President Saddam Hussein has just conceded is designed to produce atomic weapons.

Are the French willing to barter a few barrels of Iraqi oil for a nuclear club in Iraq's hand over Israel?

Paris would be horrified by the suggestion. French statesmen are rather prone to view President Hussein, on the basis of a vague statement he has recently made in Kuwait, as a "man of peace." The West Germans, for their part, are persuaded that King Khaled, too, is essentially a "man of peace"—and a reliable ally to boot. Therefore, Chancellor Helmut Schmidt is willing to waive a long-standing ban on the sale of arms to "areas of tension" by supplying Saudi Arabia with the 200 Leopards.

The formal argument is that Saudi Arabia, contrary to manifest reality, is not located in an "area of tension." The German "national interest" has thus fathered a great invention.

What these unthinking arms deals—to which the U.S. has unfortunately been a full partner—do is stoke the fires of war in the region and not damp them down, as is sometimes contended. The Gulf war has shown again, that the problem is not Israel's alone, but it is Israel's all the same, and very much so.

Let those who consider themselves its friends be duly warned, therefore: Western arms supplies to the Arab states, whether avowedly "extremist" or reputedly "moderate," compound and do not neutralize Soviet weapons deliveries—and they slowly but inexorably turn the balance of power against Israel. Too broke to exercise even all its most vital arms options, faced with a new order of sophisticated weaponry that tends to blunt its traditional qualitative edge, Israel may slowly be pushed to a strategy of desperation in defence of its very existence.

Wishful thinking will not avert this terrible danger.

Jerusalem Post *editorial 2/81*

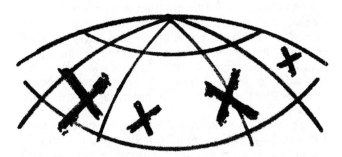

How to Control Arms Sales

First, priority should be placed upon arrangements between the West European suppliers and the U.S. rather than the negotiation of Soviet-American accords.

1. Major arms sellers should begin foreign policy consultations on specific nations or regions.
2. The adoption of a "market-sharing" technique regarding sales of weapons to Third World states. For example, the largest Western seller and producer might be persuaded to limit its portion of the market while France, which leans heavily on arms sales for economic reasons, might also reduce sales.

Second, at the point when the international atmosphere has become considerably more propitious than today, and after consultations have been held with the West, a new attempt should be made to discuss arms sales with the Soviet Union.

Third, the suppliers should seek to involve the recipients in planning for restraints. The political and psychological dimensions are important. Proposals for restraint should not be seen as inherently discriminatory.

Source: Andrew J. Pierre, The Global Politics of Arms Sales (Princeton, N.J., 1982)

Merchants of Death

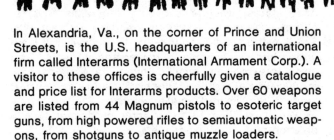

In Alexandria, Va., on the corner of Prince and Union Streets, is the U.S. headquarters of an international firm called Interarms (International Armament Corp.). A visitor to these offices is cheerfully given a catalogue and price list for Interarms products. Over 60 weapons are listed from 44 Magnum pistols to esoteric target guns, from high powered rifles to semiautomatic weapons, from shotguns to antique muzzle loaders.

But the catalogue does not mention other products—M-16 rifles, heavy machine guns, even tanks and jet fighters. Interarms is the largest independent arms dealer in the world. With headquarters in Monaco and regional offices in Britain, Argentina, Finland and Singapore, it does an annual business estimated at $80 million.

Richard S. Winter, the executive vice-president in charge of North American operations, flatly refused to discuss Interarms involvement in international arms trade. But Samuel Cummings, 51-year-old president and sole stockholder of Interarms, has not been reluctant to discuss his business over the years. The self-made millionaire currently lives in Monte Carlo for tax purposes and is proud of his success. He sees little difference between his business and the automotive industry. Guns and automobiles. Both are weapons. Both can kill.

Arms dealers are often able to purchase yesterday's weapons for pennies. After a little oiling and reconditioning, these are sold to less technically advanced nations. Interarms also picks up surplus weapons at the end of a conflict.

Cummings claims that his business is severely restricted by governments competing for his clients and by all the red tape he must go through before a deal can be closed. But the fact is that the annual global arms trade is estimated at $30 billion. In that kind of high finance, even a small chunk is a monumental fortune.

In the United States, the export of every kind of weapon from a pistol through a tank or war vessel must be approved for sale by the Arms Control and Disarmament Agency at the State Department. Big ticket items like fighter planes must be approved through the Defense Department.

How difficult is it to get approval? It seems that as long as the dealer is licensed and the country is neither communist nor specifically embargoed by Congress, i.e., Chile or Argentina, the sale of less sensitive items is almost automatic. The State Department merely registers serial numbers. (Sensitive items include fighter planes, rockets, etc.)

Who gets the weapons? One report says the Costa Rican civil war in the 1950's and the Bay of Pigs invasion in 1961 were just two examples of conflicts in

which Cummings supplied arms to both sides. He reportedly worked out a $2.5 million arms deal in 1975 with a militia group in Lebanon.

How much could Cummings hope to make on such a deal? One report cited M-16 automatic rifles, normally selling wholesale for $85, but priced at 10 to 12 times that much on the black market. A single M-16 bullet, which usually sells for ten cents, was going for a half dollar or more. A heavy mortar was quoted at $10,000.

Cummings has demonstrated his lack of concern for causes by selling to both sides in a conflict. He also boasts that his warehouses in Alexandria and in Britain contain the finest selection of firearms available from one source in the world, more than 500,000 light arms and over 100 million rounds of ammunition. This has been estimated as more than twice the firepower the U.S. military has in active service.

Munitions makers, balance of power theorists and militarists insist that every country should have a right to defend itself. They contend that it is better to provide weapons for self-defense than soldiers, that foreign countries will not stop buying arms if we stop providing them, that a favorable arms trade with foreign countries is one way of cementing friendly relations.

However, according to a 1970 study, there were more than 85 million military rifles scattered throughout the world. This does not include the M-16, the standard U.S. military weapon, nor the estimated 300,000 new M-16s being produced each year by just one manufacturer, Colt Industries. These facts alone suggest that there are far more military firearms in circulation than there are soldiers or police to use them.

Back in 1921 the League of Nations inquired into the private manufacture of arms and laid the most devastating blame directly on munitions dealers. The report said that armament firms: 1. Actively fomented war scares and persuaded their own countries to increase their armaments. 2. Attempted to bribe government officials at home and abroad. 3. Spread false reports concerning the military and naval programs of various countries in order to stimulate armament expenditures in others. 4. Sought to influence public opinion through the control of newspapers in their own country and others. 5. Organized international armament rings to accelerate the arms race by playing one country against another.

Is the situation better today?

Albert Schweitzer once said, "Reverence for life affords me my fundamental principle of morality." He believed that good consists in the preservation, the savoring of life and the desire to raise it to its highest value, its greatest development. He also understood that evil consists in the destruction of life, in its repression and in the repudiation of its values. It is unlikely that arms dealers and manufacturers will turn to Albert Schweitzer for guidance.

Source: "Merchants of Death," Charles R. Greer, Jr., Maryknoll *Magazine, August 1979.*

Makers of the Nuclear Holocaust

A Guide to the Nuclear Weapons Complex and Citizen Action

COMBAT NON-VIOLENT - 130 - HEBDOMADAIRE - 5 au 11 MAI 1977 - 4 F.

The Rocky Flats/Nuclear Weapons Facilities Project has produced an authoritative guide to America's nuclear weapons complex and how we can go about dismantling it. The laboratories, factories, transportation routes and deployment systems are all here—with maps, charts and photographs. Facts and figures on the corporate connections and on the local hazards of nuclear weapons production are included, and a directory of organizations actively working for conversion of the nuclear weapons complex.

This is an attractive, highly readable, 24-page booklet. Price: $1.25 (10-100 copies, 75¢ each; over 100 copies, 60¢ each. Add 15% for postage or UPS on bulk orders). Order from FOR, Box 271, Nyack, NY 10960.

Edited by: Samuel H. Day Jr.

Prepared by:
Nuclear Weapons Facilities Task Force, American Friends Service Committee, and The Fellowship of Reconciliation

THE RIDDLE OF THE PEACEABLE KINGDOM
according to the prophet Isaiah
1976

Man is a riddle made of many elements
which must harmoniously blend into each other
in order to fulfill our Lord's command
to live in peace with our fellowman.

There is the little child in us who plays
in blissful innocence with creatures of the wild,
with wolf and lion, asp and cockatrice,
protected by its faith in God, our Creator.

I have a dream, said Martin Luther King,
that we shall overcome hatred with love.
If we could only master our passions,
greed, lust for power, envy, callousness,
perhaps we might deserve to enter
into that Kingdom of Utopia — Peace —
where we make plowshares out of swords.

F.E.

ISAIAH II ✡ FRITZ EICHENBERG 1976

THE RIDDLE OF THE PEACEABLE KINGDOM

THE COMPLAINT OF PEACE
1970

"Let us look at the past ten years.
What land and sea did not witness warfare?
What region was not soaked in Christian blood?
The cruelty of Christians surpasses that of pagans and beasts.
Christians attack Christians with the very weapons of Hell.
Remember the battles fought during the last 10 years?
You will find that they were fought for causes
that did not concern the common man.
In most wars the safety of the heads of government
is assured and the generals stand to gain.
It is the poor farmer and the common people
who bear the brunt of the destruction.
Skilled labor, art and commerce rapidly decay,
banks are closing down.
And at the same time consider earnestly the moral degeneration
and absence of public discipline
whose restauration will be a difficult matter.
There are times when peace must be purchased.
Considering the tremendous destruction of men and property,
it is cheap at any price.
We must look for peace by purging the very sources of war —
false ambitions and evil desires.
As long as individuals serve their own personal interests,
the common good will suffer.
Let them examine the self-evident fact that this world of ours
is the Fatherland of the entire human race."

Desiderius Erasmus (1465 — 1536)
Excerpt from "Querela Pacis," 1517 AD

The Complaint of Peace

"We must look for peace by purging the very sources of war – false ambitions and evil desires. As long as individuals serve their own personal interests, the common good will suffer. Let them examine the self-evident fact that this world of ours is the Fatherland of the entire human race."

Desiderius Erasmus
from
Querela Pacis
A.D. 1517

Fritz Eichenberg
A.D. 1970

Erasmus 1469-1569

THE COMPLAINT OF PEACE

WAR AND PEACE UNDER THE CROSS
1954

"All must realize that there is no hope
of putting an end to the building up of armaments,
nor reducing the present stocks, nor, still less,
of abolishing them altogether,
unless the process is complete and thorough,
and unless it proceeds from inner convictions:
Unless, that is, everyone sincerely cooperates to banish fear
and anxious expectations of War with which men are oppressed.
If this is to come about,
the fundamental principle on which our present peace depends
must be replaced by another which declares
that the true and solid peace of nations consists not in equality of arms,
but in mutual trust alone.
We believe that this can be brought to pass,
and we consider, that this is something which reasons requires,
that it is eminently desirable in itself,
and it will prove to be the source of many benefits."

Pope John XXIII
"Pacem in Terris"
issued April 10, 1963

WAR AND PEACE UNDER THE CROSS

Food For Thought

Layle Silbert

The Mutual Hostages

In the United States, the hatred and fear of communism has always taken on an aura of obsession and paranoia. Sordid little men such as Richard Nixon made a career out of anti-communism. The 1919-20 Palmer raids, the unjust electrocution of Sacco and Vanzetti, the execution of the Rosenbergs, the rise of Senator Joseph McCarthy and his minions have always depended on arousing fear of "communists." Whenever the Pentagon, the arms manufacturers, and their propagandists wanted some more billions of dollars, the "Russians are Coming" scare was dusted off and presented anew. Repeatedly, the American people have fallen for this strategy.

Ironically, there *is* a Soviet threat, but it is not the one the warhawks and witch-hunters see. Thus, during the 1960s, when Lyndon B. Johnson convinced himself that Americans opposed the war in Vietnam largely because of foreign—read Communist—influence, he turned the CIA and FBI against peaceful American citizens and organizations, until finally there were in all probability more CIA and FBI agents than American communists in the American Communist Party.

All the same, there is a real danger from the Soviets. Their obsessions about foreign encirclement and attack and their completely closed society leave little room for internal questioning of their own positions and dangerously little flexibility in their nuclear policies, Compounding these dangerous tendencies are the factors of their enormous military power, their aging leadership, and the possible future rise to power of ultra-nationalistic reactionaries.

We must find ways to alleviate our mutual distrust. We must learn to avoid the trap of seeing every confrontation and every revolution through gun sights and basically as Soviet-American rivalries. We must, finally, outgrow the myopic fear of many Americans and Europeans that the Soviets are twenty feet tall; that view concedes far too much to the Soviets. They have been defeated in Yugoslavia, China, Somalia and Egypt to name but a few of their former allies. The old men in the Kremlin, their Chinese nightmare in the east, their unreliable client states in the west (especially Poland), their failing economic system, their increasingly restive nationalities, their harsh governing system are the realities—not hawkish chatter that the Soviets are poised to strike this year, next year, or the year after that.

Above all, the Soviet Union possesses a huge nuclear arsenal. Both the U.S. and the U.S.S.R. are mutual hostages of one another's overwhelming might. Care must be taken. Great care.

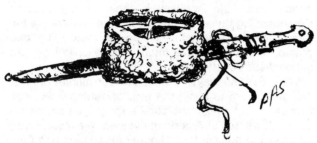 

If We Could Talk with Leonid

If by some remarkable feat we could walk into the Kremlin and have a heart to heart talk with Leonid Brezhnev, this is what we would like to say: Leonid Ilyich! We in the West are very troubled by the events in Poland. We know you are too, though for different reasons, and we wonder how deeply you and your colleagues have thought through the future. Your country stands at a crossroads. For it must decide whether it will continue to hold together its alliance by military power alone, or whether it will take the risk of a posture of restraint and begin to build the kind of solidarity and friendship with allies that rests on mutual confidence and respect.

You could move into Poland now—by whatever subtle means—and bolster the Communist Party's control there. But aren't you, then, merely postponing the problem? Will not the Poles' yearning for greater freedom continue to burn within, and explode again—if not now then tomorrow or the day after? It is no accomplishment at all to influence at the point of a gun. But to influence by force of example—that is much harder and, yet, the only effective and rewarding influence.

Can you seriously think that you can solve the problems of your system (and you admit that there are many) without making some changes? Without trying new things, experimenting a little? And, above all, without giving the Poles (and others) the leeway to experiment? In the long run, it may be riskier *not* to let the Poles work out their own way of doing things. For, if we're certain of anything, it's that the spirit of independence and pursuit of national freedom is a force no tank or missile can ever extinguish. Russians, who so passionately love their homeland, should understand this above all peoples.

If you decide to intervene in Poland, our hearts will be heavy. Not only for the Poles, who seek no threat to the powerful Soviet Union, but also for the Russian people who, despite a capacity for good as boundless as the Siberian expanses, will have turned to instincts ignoble. They too will be the losers. Hatred is the worst enemy to face, and when it comes from within the family fold, it is even harder to live with, and conquer.

If We Could Talk with Ronald

While the threat of Soviet intervention in Poland has not passed, headlines are filled with equally ominous signs that the United States is contemplating for El Salvador something very similar to what we deplored of the Soviets in Afghanistan and feared in Poland. Substituting "El Salvador" for "Poland," this is how we might begin if we could talk with President Reagan:

> *You could move into El Salvador now, by whatever subtle means, and bolster the junta's control there. But aren't you, then, merely postponing the problem? Will not the people's yearning for greater freedom continue to burn within, and explode again—if not now then tomorrow or the day after? It is no accomplishment at all to influence at the point of a gun. But to influence by example—that is much harder, and yet, the only effective and rewarding influence.*

Military intervention will never be the way to settle what are basically political problems, and as we enter the 1980's, it becomes increasingly crucial that we employ and strengthen political, social, and judicial means of international conflict resolution. Those who claim that military muscle is the only answer must recognize the potential consequences of that sentiment in an increasingly well armed, interdependent, nuclear world. As Robert Johansen notes in "How to Avoid Death and Taxes," "war was never a good idea. But in the past we could live with it. Now we can only live without it."

Source: AFSC

60 Minutes

And so we await the Geneva [nuclear arms control] talks, which begin a week from now, and bid Godspeed to Paul H. Nitze, who will head our delegation. A great public man, somehow not inured to the subject he has dealt with so long.

For many of us I wonder if the difficulty is not somehow different: of not really grasping how much has changed. I joined the Navy in 1944 and rose to be a gunnery officer and loved every moment. The sea and the ships and the guns and crew were all one could ask. This was before the fleet became a weapons system. You were part of a long history. On the midwatch, I would read T. S. Eliot: "Phoebus the Phoenician, a fortnight dead. . . ." Perry could have commanded our flotillas, as Nimitz could have commanded his.

We forget how slowly mass destruction came upon us. Twenty Americans died at Yorktown. In all of the quarter century of Napoleonic Wars, including the War of 1812, the British Navy lost scarcely 6,000 men. How are we to think of civilization disappearing in an hour's time? Hard and carefully, that is how.

Senator Daniel Patrick Moynihan, November 23, 1981

Guns and Butter

With the [Reagan] administration cutting domestic spending, pushing long-term growth in military expenditures, and proclaiming that global war can be won, perhaps it's time to recall comments from two who cannot be dismissed as "mindless pacifists"—former President Harry S. Truman and General Douglas MacArthur.

In his oral biography of Truman, Merle Miller quotes Truman on budgeting and defense spending as follows:

"It is an amazing thing. Every 10 cents that was spent for those work-relief projects, the W.P.A. and the P.W.A. and those, every dime was looked into, and somebody was always against spending a nickel that would help poor people and give jobs . . . to the men that didn't have any. But the minute we started spending all that defense money, the sky was the limit and no questions were ever asked. The 'economy boys' never opened their mouths about that, and I don't understand it. . . . All through history it's the nations that have given most to the generals and the least to the people that have been the first to fall."

To which, General Douglas MacArthur added, when addressing a Michigan State University graduation, that accelerating the arms race might itself spark a global war of extermination.

"No longer can global warfare be a successful weapon of international adventure," he concluded. "If you lose, you are annihilated. If you win, you stand only to lose. No longer does it possess even the chance of the winner of a duel. It contains now only the germs of double suicide."

Harry Fleishman, 1981

Why War?

The development of weapons is of considerable psychological interest, since there is a vast difference emotionally between slaughtering an enemy at a distance, and attempting to kill him at close quarters. If human fights were confined to fisticuffs, an appreciable number of human beings would still be killed; for, as we have seen, man's paranoid potential overrides the operation of the natural inhibitions which prevent most animals from dispatching their defeated opponents. Moreover, as Konrad Lorenz has pointed out, it is just because human beings are so ill-equipped with natural weapons that they lack strong inhibitions against injuring their own species. Better-armed animals are better protected by inhibitions against intra-specific aggression; and if men had tusks or horns they would be less, rather than more, likely to kill one another. The artificial weapon is too cerebral a device for nature to have provided adequate safeguards against it. Nevertheless, traces of inhibiting mechanisms do remain in that many humans recoil at kicking an enemy when he is down, or will even feel pity for, and extend help to, a wounded opponent. All traces of this "decent" behaviour disappear, however, as soon as a moderate distance is interposed between contestants. It is obviously true that most bomber pilots are no better and no worse than other men. The majority of them, given a can of petrol and told to pour it over a child of three and ignite it, would probably disobey the order. Yet, put a decent man in an aeroplane a few hundred feet above a village, and he will, without compunction, drop high explosives and napalm and inflict appalling pain and injury on men, women and children. The distance between him and the people he is bombing makes them into an impersonal target, no longer human beings like himself with whom he can identify.

Anthony Storr, Human Aggression (Atheneum, 1968)

Resisting War

An essay by BOB SEELEY

Bob Seeley is editor of CCCO News Notes, *the quarterly newsletter of the Central Committee for Conscientious Objectors in Philadelphia. He is now at work on a revision of the* Committee's Handbook for Conscientious Objectors.

> Action from principle, the perception and the performance of right, changes things and relations. It is essentially revolutionary, and does not consist wholly with anything which was.
> —Henry David Thoreau

In 1944 the Allied strategic bombing campaign against Germany was at its height. At first because they could not bomb accurately, but later as part of a "morale-breaking" strategy, Allied bombers poured tons of high explosives not only on military targets, but on cities of no military importance. The destruction, as at Dresden, was frightful; the campaign itself, controversial. Britons and Americans from the Fellowship of Reconciliation and the pacifist Vera Brittain to the military theorist B. H. Liddell Hart protested. But the campaign went on, destroying one or even two German cities each week.

George Wilson was part of an American bomber crew in 1944. One night the pilot called the crew together and told them he planned to refuse to fly missions against non-military targets. He would do this, he said, even at the risk of court-martial. After a discussion which lasted almost until dawn, the crew decided to join their pilot in his refusal.

For George Wilson, and probably for the others, it was a new experience. Deliberate bombing of civilians had confronted his pilot, and now confronted him, with a choice. He had followed his conscience rather than the order. He had become—though he would put it this way only later on—a war resister. Then he rejected an order. Later he rejected all war.

War resistance today has its roots in the great religious and ethical traditions of the East and West. These have had a vision of peace which inspired some of their followers to renounce war entirely. The "peace churches" like the Society of Friends (Quakers), the Mennonites, and the Church of the Brethren have been the best-known, but virtually all churches have a pacifist tradition within them. Others, while not pacifist, have joined with pacifists to seek peaceful solutions to conflicts and reconciliation among the world's peoples. These goals have become more urgent as war has become more and more terrible, threatening the end of humanity itself.

But for George Wilson, alone with his conscience, religion and ethics at first meant less than natural human impulse. Psychologists and anthropologists argue incessantly over whether people are natural killers. Military planners know better. They speak of war only in euphemisms (one "cleans out a bunker"; one does not methodically kill its inhabitants), as if they feared what would happen if we began to speak plainly about it. They drill recruits endlessly in the mechanics of the bayonet, the rifle, the cannon, until killing becomes automatic and one hardly realizes what one is doing. This keeps soldiers from losing their nerve, but it does more: it makes them able to kill.

In a world which has seen the trenches of World War I and the concentration camps of World War II, and may see the mutual suicide of World War III, such training seems superfluous. But it does not always work. Surveying U.S. troops after World War II, Brig. Gen. S.L.A. Marshall found that in some units up to seventy-five percent of the soldiers on the line did not fire their weapons as ordered. In the last year of the active

IMAGINE
A WORLD
WITHOUT
WEAPONS

Francis A. Fitzgerald

draft, 1972, more people applied for conscientious objector status than were drafted into the military; and thousands of others refused to cooperate with the draft at all. From our traditions, and from natural impulse, comes a reluctance to kill. It is small, but it gives some hope for a peaceful world.

War resistance is not in essence a mass movement. Each resister, even one from a "peace church," confronts first the demands of conscience, and then the war system. When enough people are outraged by a war, they become a movement, and they can, as in Vietnam, help to stop the carnage. But men and women like George Wilson stand against war because they cannot do otherwise and live with themselves. They do not stop war. They undercut its moral basis. They become, as Einstein called them, "the pioneers of a warless world."

Modern war is neither simple nor one-dimensional. A shooting war like World War II is a "total" war: it mobilizes all, or nearly all, of the population; its target is more the enemy's country than the enemy's troops. Even in peacetime there is Cold War, and the institutions of war penetrate the institutions of society until, at times, it is difficult to see where civilian work begins and military work ends. Taxes in the United States, for example, support a military establishment whose cost is in the hundreds of billions, and nearly half of each tax dollar goes for war.

One major effect of this new complexity has been to blur the lines between traditional pacifism and the non-pacifist peace movement. The overwhelming danger of nuclear war has made such distinctions less important. Both sides can make common cause in the common emergency.

For the individual, modern war has made moral choice both easier and harder. War is now so destructive that the hypothetical questions beloved of draft boards seem foolish. One Navy man told me that he had become a conscientious objector to war in one morning when he saw nuclear missiles being loaded aboard his submarine. He had known they were there, but actually seeing them was moral shock. "I realized that I'd been sitting on this stuff for a year, and it could actually destroy the world," he said. "I packed my bag and went UA (absent without leave)." He had found, as most resisters do, that an objection to war is a gut-feeling which cuts through rationalizations and doubts to the truth of what one is.

Stuart, who awoke to nightmares when he saw what he was part of, had realized that he could not support war. But what was he to do? How could he stop being part of an all-pervading system? His first solution was simple and direct: leave the Navy at once, regardless of consequences. Later he applied for discharge as a conscientious objector and gained his freedom. Others find the path less clear. There are no untouched woods to withdraw to, and most resisters want to stop the system as well as divorce themselves from it. This has led to a variety of actions—all of them, in one way or another, compromises, but all actions against war.

It is action which distinguishes war resisters from others who merely deplore war or lament over its tragedy. Men and women like Stuart or George Wilson put themselves on the line. They oppose war with their lives and their bodies, often at great personal cost. Because war uses the young, most of them are young. But older people often resist war by refusing to pay taxes or by practicing civil disobedience during demonstrations.

Not all war resistance is illegal, though we usually think of it that way. When thousands of men in the early 1970s exercised their rights under the draft law, the system broke down under its own paperwork. Following the law became, in effect, a kind of draft resistance. And by stifling a ready source of manpower, it became war resistance on a large scale.

The mass refusal of the draft during the Vietnam era is now thought of as a classic form of war resistance. It has become relevant again because of the Administration's use of draft registration as a geopolitical tool. Many young people—certainly more than Selective Service is willing to admit—see that the distinction between registration and an actual draft is less important than Administration rhetoric has made it sound. Thousands of letters to the Central Committee for Conscientious Objectors, a major national draft counseling group, repeat the same themes: registration is the first step toward the draft; and the draft, in the context of a more and more bellicose American foreign policy, is one more step toward war and disaster. These people would not—could not—be part of it.

So they refused to register. Or, if they chose to register, they tried to file for conscientious objector status despite Selective Service's current refusal to consider such claims. Some non-registrants took public stands, thus increasing their risk of arrest. Others simply stayed home.

There are many reasons for draft refusal. Some resisters oppose not only war, but conscription. They believe that, if they apply for conscientious objector status, they will actually help the system to operate. Some argue that the system is so unjust that they cannot accept what they deem a privileged status. Others object only to particular wars and could not gain conscientious objector status in any case.

The consequences of draft resistance are unpredictable. The law provides a maximum penalty of five years in prison and $10,000 fine for draft offenses. Much, however, depends on fate: where one lives, where one is when the offense takes place, and the attitudes of federal prosecutors and judges in one's district. Selective Service has said that it intends to report non-registrants for prosecution.

Most "public" draft resisters are not deterred by threats of prosecution. They see what they have done as a public statement which will be all the stronger if they end in court or even prison.

One way to renounce war is by refusing to pay for it. As the defense budget has grown, the issues raised by war taxes have become more and more significant.

The number of war tax resisters is small, but their witness has been one of the most dramatic in recent years, when the draft was inactive and the military less visible than during the Vietnam era.

There is no legal way to refuse war taxes. One can claim many dependents or, as some resisters do, claim a "war crimes" deduction. Though Internal Revenue will occasionally allow these deductions and conclude that a resister owes no taxes, this is rare. More likely, IRS will disallow the deductions and inform the resister that he or she owes taxes, usually with interest and penalty.

If the resister does not pay IRS's bill, he or she could face prison, but probably will not. U.S. tax laws give Internal Revenue broad powers to collect money owed them—by taking it from the resister's bank accounts, by placing levies against the resister's salary, or even by confiscating the resister's property and selling it at auction.

In this sense, war tax resistance can be an exercise in futility. The government gets its money despite the resister's best efforts. If a resister simply withholds part of his or her taxes (the part which goes for war), Internal Revenue can still get the balance. And there is no guarantee that the "civilian" part-payment sent in by the resister will not go to the military. This may be why tax resistance has never been as popular as draft resistance or resistance from within the military. Many war resisters consider it ineffective.

Effectiveness as we usually think of it, however, is a criterion that hardly applies to war resistance. Resistance can stop a war, and it has. But the individual's act in refusing to be drafted or pay for war is effective primarily on a different level. It is a witness: it raises the issue of war and makes clear that the issue is moral, not merely strategic or political. By putting the war resister on firm ground morally, it makes possible further actions against war. Considered in this light, war tax resistance may be the most effective of all.

Even war tax resistance involves compromise. The nature of our society makes it impossible to be morally pure. Men and women in the military who decide to renounce war face this dilemma in its strongest form. By being where they are, they automatically compromise themselves. Yet if they leave or refuse orders, they not only risk penalties, but may make resolving their problems even more difficult.

Stuart, who went AWOL from the Navy, found that upon his return he could not simply apply for discharge. The Navy would not consider a claim for discharge until they had decided whether to court-martial him. It was even possible that he could be returned to duty.

All this mattered little to him on the morning when he saw the missiles. Then the overwhelming need was to get away. During the Vietnam era, half a million GIs shared this need. Even today, an average of 300 GIs a day go AWOL. The military, which finds such figures embarrassing, attributes them to "poor-quality" recruits. But if 300 East Berliners a day crossed into West Berlin, the government would say that they were "voting with their feet."

Only a small number of AWOLs—though no one will ever know how small—is consciously anti-war. But AWOL, by its very size as a problem, has become a kind of mass war resistance. It is at least a statement about conditions in the military, where pay is low by civilian standards, promises are not kept, and training is often meaningless.

AWOL is an unsatisfactory approach to discharge. It leaves the problem unresolved and may lead to stockade or brig time. The legal channels for discharge are few and difficult, but in the long run they are a resister's only choice. Some seek discharge as conscientious objectors; the military finds others unsuitable; still others qualify for other discharges.

For resisters who oppose only some aspects of the military, such as nuclear war, but are willing to remain "inside," there are few options. The Army allows soldiers to refuse a transfer to work with nuclear weapons, but other military branches do not. The courts have held that military personnel can speak against bombing of civilians or other acts which they oppose. But a discharge is usually the best solution for these people as well.

War resistance in its many forms is an individual act, but *en masse* it has accomplished astonishing things. The French Army ground to a halt in 1917 when soldiers refused to take part in further pointless, bloody offensives. Draft resistance, both legal and illegal, made the Selective Service System unworkable during the early 1970s; and resistance within the military at the same time made withdrawal from Vietnam necessary if the military was to survive.

Local draft boards are fond of asking war resisters what would happen if everyone followed their example. Some resisters regard their stand as theirs alone, without implications for others. They find the question meaningless. But an answer to the question is implicit in the actions of even these "nonpolitical" resisters.

By "everyone," the draft board usually means "everyone on our side." Thus they talk past the war resister, who, by his or her action, invites everyone *in every country* to refuse to be part of war. Be responsible first for the evils which are done in your name, says the resister, and you will help others to stop the evils done in their names. The Vietnam War was a problem first for the Americans in whose name it was fought. They resisted it in large numbers, and it could not go on. Hitler was first a problem for the Germans themselves. They did not resist, but followed, and helped bring the world and themselves tragedy.

The responsibility for any war—including World War II—is far more complex than this. But resisters, the ones I have known at least, believe in personal responsibility: it is no good blaming history. That kind of analysis has its place, but the moral choice remains.

Source: Confrontation, *Winter 1981*

Sanity

What I would like to see the President do, after due consultation with the Congress, would be to propose to the Soviet government an immediate across-the-boards reduction by 50% of the nuclear arsenals now being maintained by the two superpowers—a reduction affecting in equal measure all forms of the weapon, strategic, medium-range and tactical, as well as all means of their delivery—all this to be implemented at once and without further wrangling among the experts, and to be subject to such national means of verification as now lie at the disposal of the two powers.

George F. Kennan, upon receiving the Albert Einstein Peace Prize, 1981

What Have We Learned? Is a World Without War Possible?

Robert C. Johansen

Do you believe that a world without war is an achievable goal?

Achievable, yes; but it will be extremely difficult. U.S. citizens have deliberately established themselves as the world's most powerful military group, and the Soviet Union now strongly contends for that position. History offers few examples of such entrenched power being given up voluntarily. Also, old myths, pride in military might, and the logic of competition have fueled public support for high levels of military preparedness.

What force are you counting on to overcome these formidable obstacles to demilitarization?

We know that hundreds of millions of people with different languages, religions, and ethnic backgrounds, in some cases spanning an entire continent, live together without resorting to war even though they often experience deep conflicts with one another. If such diverse multitudes can live in domestic peace in China, India, the United States, and the Soviet Union, cannot four billion people also resolve disputes without use of collective violence? We must refuse to confine our imaginations about what the world can become to prevailing perceptions of what is possible.

Today we are puzzled that people could for centuries believe in the efficacy of human sacrifice and the divine right of kings. If humanity survives, our descendants will think it equally baffling that millions of people could live in national and regional tranquility and still believe that global tranquility was not possible.

A warless world *is* possible; but given present trends, it is not probable. To make the possible become probable requires one missing ingredient: firm, persistent action by citizens to demilitarize their own societies within a carefully planned strategy to demilitarize world society and establish a more dependable and humane security system.

"Transition" Nov. 1979, Institute for World Order, 777 UN Plaza, N.Y., N.Y. 10017

Lord Louis Mountbatten on Nuclear War

Speech by Admiral of the Fleet the Earl Mountbatten of Burma on the occasion of the award of the Louise Weiss Foundation Prize to the Stockholm International Peace Research Institute at Strasbourg on the 11th May 1979

Do the frightening facts about the arms race, which show that we are rushing headlong towards a precipice, make any of those responsible for this disastrous course pull themselves together and reach for the brakes?

The answer is "no" and I only wish that I could be the bearer of the glad tidings that there has been a change of attitude and we are beginning to see a steady rate of disarmament. Alas, that is not the case.

I am deeply saddened when I reflect on how little has been achieved in spite of all the talk there has been particularly about nuclear disarmament. There have been numerous international conferences and negotiations on the subject and we have all nursed dreams of a world at peace but to no avail. Since the end of the Second World War, 34 years ago, we have had war after war. There is still armed conflict going on in several parts of the world. We live in an age of extreme peril because every war today carries the danger that it could spread and involve the super powers.

And here lies the greatest danger of all. A military confrontation between the nuclear powers could entail the horrifying risk of nuclear warfare. The Western powers and the USSR started by producing and stockpiling nuclear weapons as a deterrent to general war. The idea seemed simple enough. Because of the enormous amount of destruction that could be wreaked by a single nuclear explosion, the idea was that both sides in what we still see as an East-West conflict would be deterred from taking any aggressive action which might endanger the vital interests of the other.

It was not long, however, before smaller nuclear weapons of various designs were produced and deployed for use in what was assumed to be a tactical or theatre war. The belief was that were hostilities ever to break out in Western Europe, such weapons could be used in field warfare without triggering an all-out nuclear exchange leading to the final holocaust.

I have never found this idea credible. I have never been able to accept the reasons for the belief that any class of nuclear weapons can be categorised in terms of their tactical or strategic purposes.

Next month I enter my eightieth year. I am one of the few survivors of the First World War who rose to high command in the Second and I know how impossible it is to pursue military operations in accordance with fixed plans and agreements. In warfare the unexpected is the rule and no one can anticipate what an opponent's reaction will be to the unexpected.

As a sailor I saw enough death and destruction at sea but I also had the opportunity of seeing the absolute destruction of the war zone of the western front in the First World War, where those who fought in the trenches had an average expectation of life of only a few weeks.

Then in 1943 I became Supreme Allied Commander in South East Asia and saw death and destruction on an even greater scale. But that was all conventional warfare and, horrible as it was, we all felt we had a "fighting" chance of survival. In the event of a nuclear

war there will be no chances, there will be no survivors—all will be obliterated.

I am not asserting this without having deeply thought about the matter. When I was Chief of the British Defense Staff I made my views known. I have heard the arguments against this view but I have never found them convincing. So I repeat in all sincerity as a military man I can see no use for any nuclear weapons which would not end in escalation, with consequences that no one can conceive.

And nuclear devastation is not science fiction—it is a matter of fact. Thirty-four years ago there was the terrifying experience of the two atomic bombs that effaced the cities of Hiroshima and Nagasaki off the map. In describing the nightmare a Japanese journalist wrote as follows:

Suddenly a glaring whitish, pinkish light appeared in the sky accompanied by an unnatural tremor which was followed almost immediately by a wave of suffocating heat and a wind which swept away everything in its path. Within a few seconds the thousands of people in the streets in the centre of the town were scorched by a wave of searing heat. Many were killed instantly, others lay writhing on the ground screaming in agony from the intolerable pain of their burns. Everything standing upright in the way of the blast—walls, houses, factories and other buildings, was annihilated . . . Hiroshima had ceased to exist.

But that is not the end of the story. We remember the tens and thousands who were killed instantly or worse still those who suffered a slow painful death from the effect of the burns—we forget that many are still dying horribly from the delayed effects of radiation. To this knowledge must be added the fact that we now have missiles a thousand times as dreadful; I repeat, a thousand times as horrible.

One or two nuclear strikes on this great city of Strasbourg with what today would be regarded as relatively low yield weapons would utterly destroy all that we see around us and imediately kill probably half of its population. Imagine what the picture would be if larger nuclear strikes were to be levelled against not just Strasbourg but ten other cities in, say, a 200 mile radius. Or even worse, imagine what the picture would be if there was an unrestrained exchange of nuclear weapons—and this is the most appalling risk of all since, as I have already said, I cannot imagine a situation in which nuclear weapons would be used as battlefield weapons without the conflagration spreading.

Could we not take steps to make sure that these things never come about? A new world war can hardly fail to involve the all-out use of nuclear weapons. Such a war would not drag on for years. It could all be over in a matter of days.

And when it is all over what will the world be like? Our fine great buildings, our homes will exist no more. The thousands of years it took to develop our civilisa-

tion will have been in vain. Our works of art will be lost. Radio, television, newspapers will disappear. There will be no means of transport. There will be no hospitals. No help can be expected for the few mutilated survivors in any town to be sent from the neighbouring town—there will be no neighbouring towns left, no neighbours, there will be no help, there will be no hope.

How can we stand by and do nothing to prevent the destruction of our world? Einstein, whose centenary we celebrate this year, was asked to prophesy what weapons would be used in the Third World War. I am told he replied to the following effect:

"On the assumption that a Third World War must escalate to nuclear destruction, I can tell you what the Fourth World War will be fought with—bows and arrows".

The facts about the global nuclear ams race are well known and as I have already said SIPRI has played its part in disseminating authoritative material on world armaments and the need for international efforts to reduce them. But how do we set about achieving practical measures of nuclear arms control and disarmament?

To begin with we are most likely to preserve the peace if there is a military balance of strength between East and West. The real need is for both sides to replace the attempts to maintain a balance through ever-increasing and even more costly nuclear armaments by a balance based on mutual restraint. Better still, by reduction of nuclear armaments I believe it should be possible to achieve greater security at a lower level of military confrontation.

I regret enormously the delays which the Americans

and Russians have experienced in reaching a SALT II agreement for the limitation of even one major class of nuclear weapons with which it deals. I regret even more the fact that opposition to reaching any agreement which will bring about a restraint in the production and deployment of nuclear weapons is becoming so powerful in the United States. What can their motives be?

As a military man who has given half a century of active Service I say in all sincerity that the nuclear arms race has no military purpose. Wars cannot be fought with nuclear weapons. Their existence only adds to our perils because of the illusions which they have generated.

There are powerful voices around the world who still give credence to the old Roman precept—if you desire peace, prepare for war. This is absolute nuclear nonsense and I repeat—it is a disastrous misconception to believe that by increasing the total uncertainty one increases one's own certainty.

This year we have already seen the beginnings of a miracle. Through the courageous determination of Presidents Carter and Sadat and Prime Minister Begin we have seen the first real move towards what we all hope will be a lasting peace between Egypt and Israel. Their journey has only just begun and the path they have chosen will be long and fraught with disappointments and obstacles. But these bold leaders have realised the alternative and have faced up to their duty in a way which those of us who hunger for the peace of the world applaud.

Is it possible that this initiative will lead to the start of yet another even more vital miracle and someone somewhere will take that first step along the long stony road which will lead us to an effective form of nuclear arms limitation, including the banning of Tactical Nuclear Weapons?

After all it is true that science offers us almost unlimited opportunities but it is up to us, the people, to make the moral and philosophical choices and since the threat to humanity is the work of human beings, it is up to man to save himself from himself.

The world now stands on the brink of the final Abyss. Let us all resolve to take all possible practical steps to ensure that we do not, through our own folly, go over the edge.

THE ILLUSTRATED MAN
David Levine / 1980

A Proposal for International Disarmament

George F. Kennan

George F. Kennan made the following address in accepting the Albert Einstein Peace Prize on 19 May 1981 at the Marriott Hotel in Washington, D.C. Preliminary remarks have been omitted; the remaining text is complete.

Adequate words are lacking to express the full seriousness of our present situation. It is not just that we are for the moment on a collision course politically with the Soviet Union, and that the process of rational communication between the two governments seems to have broken down completely; it is also—and even more importantly—the fact that the ultimate sanction behind the conflicting policies of these two governments is a type and volume of weaponry which could not possibly be used without utter disaster for us all.

For over 30 years wise and far-seeing people have been warning us about the futility of any war fought with nuclear weapons and about the dangers involved in their cultivation. Some of the first of these voices to be raised were those of great scientists, including outstandingly that of Albert Einstein himself. But there has been no lack of others. Every president of this country, from Dwight Eisenhower to Jimmy Carter, has tried to remind us that there could be no such thing as victory in a war fought with such weapons. So have a great many other eminent persons.

When one looks back today over the history of these warnings, one has the impression that something has now been lost of the sense of urgency, the hopes, and the excitement that initially inspired them, so many years ago. One senses, even on the part of those who today most acutely perceive the problem and are inwardly most exercised about it, a certain discouragement, resignation, perhaps even despair, when it comes to the question of raising the subject again. The danger is so obvious. So much has already been said. What is to be gained by reiteration? What good would it now do?

Look at the record. Over all these years the competition in the development of nuclear weaponry has proceeded steadily, relentlessly, without the faintest regard for all these warning voices. We have gone on piling weapon upon weapon, missile upon missile, new levels of destructiveness upon old ones. We have done this helplessly, almost involuntarily: like the victims of some sort of hypnotism, like men in a dream, like lemmings heading for the sea, like the children of Hamlin marching blindly along behind their Pied Piper. And the result is that today we have achieved, we and the Russians together, in the creation of these devices and their means of delivery, levels of redundancy of such grotesque dimensions as to defy rational understanding.

I say redundancy. I know of no better way to describe it. But actually, the word is too mild. It implies that there could be levels of these weapons that would not be redundant. Personally, I doubt that there could. I question whether these devices are really weapons at all. A true weapon is at best something with which you endeavor to affect the behavior of another society by influencing the minds, the calculations, the intentions, of the men that control it; it is not something with which you destroy indiscriminately the lives, the substance, the hopes, the culture, the civilization, of another people.

What a confession of intellectual poverty it would be—what a bankruptcy of intelligent statesmanship— if we had to admit that such blind, senseless acts of destruction were the best use we could make of what we have come to view as the leading elements of our military strength!

To my mind, the nuclear bomb is the most useless weapon ever invented. It can be employed to no rational purpose. It is not even an effective defense against itself. It is only something with which, in a moment of petulance or panic, you commit such fearful acts of destruction as no sane person would ever wish to have upon his conscience.

There are those who will agree, with a sigh, to much of what I have just said, but will point to the need for something called deterrence. This is, of course, a concept which attributes to others—to others who, like ourselves, were born of women, walk on two legs, and love their children, to human beings, in short—the

Dorothy Day, Peacemaker, by David Levine

most fiendish and inhuman of tendencies.

But all right: accepting for the sake of argument the profound iniquity of these adversaries, no one could deny, I think, that the present Soviet and American arsenals, presenting over a million times the destructive power of the Hiroshima bomb, are simply fantastically redundant to the purpose in question. If the same relative proportions were to be preserved, something well less than 20 per cent of those stocks would surely suffice for the most sanguine concepts of deterrence, whether as between the two nuclear superpowers or with relation to any of those other governments that have been so ill-advised as to enter upon the nuclear path. Whatever their suspicions of each other, there can be no excuse on the part of these two governments for holding, poised against each other and poised in a sense against the whole northern hemisphere, quantities of these weapons so vastly in excess of any rational and demonstrable requirements.

How have we got ourselves into this dangerous mess?

Let us not confuse the question by blaming it all on our Soviet adversaries. They have, of course, their share of the blame, and not least in their cavalier dismissal of the Baruch Plan so many years ago. They too have made their mistakes; and I should be the last to deny it.

But we must remember that it has been we Americans who, at almost every step of the road, have taken

I STILL FEEL INSECURE

OAN

the lead in the development of this sort of weaponry. It was we who first produced and tested such a device; we who were the first to raise its destructiveness to a new level with the hydrogen bomb; we who introduced the multiple warhead; we who have declined every proposal for the renunciation of the principle of "first use"; and we alone, so help us God, who have used the weapon in anger against others, and against tens of thousands of helpless non-combatants at that.

I know that reasons were offered for some of these things. I know that others might have taken this sort of a lead, had we not done so. But let us not, in the face of this record, so lose ourselves in self-righteousness and hypocrisy as to forget our own measure of complicity in creating the situation we face today.

What is it then, if not our own will, and if not the supposed wickedness of our opponents, that has brought us to this pass?

The answer, I think, is clear. It is primarily the inner momentum, the independent momentum, of the weapons race itself—the compulsions that arise and take charge of great powers when they enter upon a competition with each other in the building up of major armaments of any sort.

This is nothing new. I am a diplomatic historian. I see this same phenomenon playing its fateful part in the relations among the great European powers as much as a century ago. I see this competitive buildup of armaments conceived initially as a means to an end but soon becoming the end itself. I see it taking possession of men's imagination and behavior, becoming a force in its own right, detaching itself from the political differences that initially inspired it, and then leading both parties, invariably and inexorably, to the war they no longer know how to avoid.

This is a species of fixation, brewed out of many components. There are fears, resentments, national pride, personal pride. There are misreadings of the adversary's intentions—sometimes even the refusal to consider them at all. There is the tendency of national communities to idealize themselves and to dehumanize the opponent. There is the blinkered, narrow vision of the professional military planner, and his tendency to make war inevitable by assuming its inevitability.

Tossed together, these components form a powerful brew. They guide the fears and the ambitions of men. They seize the policies of governments and whip them around like trees before the tempest.

Is it possible to break out of this charmed and vicious circle? It is sobering to recognize that no one, at least to my knowledge, has yet done so. But no one, for that matter, has ever been faced with such great catastrophe, such inalterable catastrophe, at the end of the line. Others, in earlier decades, could befuddle themselves with dreams of something called "victory." We, perhaps fortunately, are denied this seductive prospect. We have to break out of the circle. We have no other choice.

How are we to do it?

I must confess that I see no possibility of doing this by means of discussions along the lines of the negotiations that have been in progress, off and on, over this past decade, under the acronym of SALT. I regret, to be sure, that the most recent SALT agreement has not been ratified. I regret it, because if the benefits to be expected from that agreement were slight, its disadvantages were even slighter; and it had a symbolic value which should not have been so lightly sacrificed.

But I have, I repeat, no illusion that negotiations on the SALT pattern—negotiations, that is, in which each side is obsessed with the chimera of relative advantage and strives only to retain a maximum of the weaponry for itself while putting its oponent to the maximum disadvantage—I have no illusion that such negotiations could ever be adequate to get us out of this hole. They are not a way of escape from the weapons race; they are an integral part of it.

Whoever does not understand that when it comes to nuclear weapons the whole concept of relative advantage is illusory—whoever does not understand that when you are talking about absurd and preposterous quantities of overkill the relative sizes of arsenals have no serious meaning—whoever does not understand that the danger lies not in the possibility that someone else might have more missiles and warheads than we do but in the very existence of these unconscionable quantities of highly poisonous explosives, and their

existence, above all, in hands as weak and shaky and undependable as those of ourselves or our adversaries or any other mere human beings: whoever does not undersand these things is never going to guide us out of this increasingly dark and menacing forest of bewilderments into which we have all wandered.

I can see no way out of this dilemma other than by a bold and sweeping departure—a departure that would cut surgically through the exaggerated anxieties, the self-engendered nightmares, and the sophisticated mathematics of destruction, in which we have all been entangled over these recent years, and would permit us to move, with courage and decision, to the heart of the problem.

President Reagan recently said, and I think very wisely, that he would "negotiate as long as necessary to reduce the numbers of nuclear weapons to a point where neither side threatens the survival of the other."

Now that is, of course, precisely the thought to which these present observations of mine are addressed. But I wonder whether the negotiations would really have to be at such great length. *What I would like to see the President do, after due consultation with the Congress, would be to propose to the Soviet government an immediate across-the-boards reduction by 50 per cent of the nuclear arsenals now being maintained by the two superpowers—a reduction affecting*

in equal measure all forms of the weapon, strategic, medium-range, and tactical, as well as all means of their delivery—all this to be implemented at once and without further wrangling among the experts, and to be subject to such national means of verification as now lie at the disposal of the two powers.

Whether the balance of reduction would be precisely even—whether it could be construed to favor statistically one side or the other—would not be the question. Once we start thinking that way, we would be back on the same old fateful track that has brought us where we are today. Whatever the precise results of such a reduction, there would still be plenty of overkill left—so much so that if this first operation were successful, I would then like to see a second one put in hand to rid us of at least two thirds of what would be left.

Now I have, of course, no idea of the scientific aspects of such an operation; but I can imagine that serious problems might be presented by the task of removing, and disposing safely of, the radioactive contents of the many thousands of warheads that would have to be dismantled. Should this be the case, I would like to see the President couple his appeal for a 50 per cent reduction with the proposal that there be established a joint Soviet-American scientific committee, under the chairmanship of a distinguished neutral figure, to study jointly and in all humility the problem not only of the safe disposal of these wastes but also the question of how they could be utilized in such a way as to make a positive contribution to human life, either in the two countries themselves or—perhaps preferably—elsewhere. In such a joint scientific venture we might both atone for some of our past follies and lay the foundation for a more constructive relationship.

It will be said: this proposal, whatever its merits, deals with only a part of the problem. This is perfectly true. Behind it there would still lurk the serious political differences that now divide us from the Soviet government. Behind it would still lie the problems recently treated, and still to be treated, in the SALT forum. Behind it would still lie the great question of the acceptability of war itself, any war, even a conventional one, as a means of solving problems among great industrial powers in this age of high technology.

What has been suggested here would not prejudice the continued treatment of these questions just as they might be treated today, in whatever forums and under whatever safeguards the two powers find necessary. The conflicts and arguments over these questions could all still proceed to the heart's content of all those who view them with such passionate commitment. The stakes would simply be smaller; and that would be a great relief to all of us.

What I have suggested is, of course, only a beginning. But a beginning has to be made somewhere; and if it has to be made, is it not best that it should be made where the dangers are the greatest, and their necessity the least? If a step of this nature could be successfully taken, people might find the heart to tackle with greater confidence and determination the many problems that would still remain.

It will also be argued that there would be risks involved. Possibly so. I do not see them. I do not deny the possibility. But if there are, so what? Is it possible to conceive of any dangers greater than those that lie at the end of the collision course on which we are now embarked? And if not, why choose the greater—why choose, in fact, the greatest—of all risks, in the hopes of avoiding the lesser ones?

We are confronted here, my friends, with two courses. At the end of the one lies hope—faint hope, if you will—uncertain hope, hope surrounded with dangers, if you insist. At the end of the other lies, so far as I am able to see, no hope at all.

Can there be—in the light of our duty not just to ourselves (for we are all going to die sooner or later) but of our duty to our own kind, our duty to the continuity of the generations, our duty to the great experiment of civilized life on this rare and rich and marvelous planet—can there be, in the light of these claims on our loyalty, any question as to which course we should adopt?

In the final week of his life, Albert Einstein signed the last of the collective appeals against the development of nuclear weapons that he was ever to sign. He was dead before it apeared. It was an appeal drafted, I gather, by Bertrand Russell. I had my differences with Russell at the time as I do now in retrospect; but I

would like to quote one sentence from the final paragraph of that statement, not only because it was the last one Einstein ever signed, but because it sums up, I think, all that I have to say on the subject. It reads as follows:

> We appeal, as human beings to human beings: Remember your humanity, and forget the rest.

No Last Plague

Howard H. Hiatt

This is adapted from a speech delivered at a symposium in New York City, September 27, 1980. Howard Hiatt, M.D., is Dean of the Harvard School of Public Health and Professor of Medicine at Harvard Medical School.

The destruction wrought by an atomic weapon on Hiroshima provides, along with the similar experience in Nagasaki, direct evidence of the consequences of nuclear warfare, but there are many theoretical appraisals upon which we may also draw. For example, in response to a request from the Senate Committee on Foreign Relations, the Office of Technology Assessment of the Congress of the United States, with the assistance of the Congressional Research Service, the Department of Defense, the Arms Control and

Disarmament Agency, and the Central Intelligence Agency last year [1980] published a study that described in detail the effects of nuclear attacks on Detroit and on Leningrad.

The effects of a nuclear explosion in or over New York may be found in several places, including an article by Kevin Lewis in *Scientific American* last year. The description that follows is taken from materials prepared by the U.S. Arms Control and Disarmament Agency.

The scenario is conservative. While the one-million ton bomb involved in the attack is more than 50 times more powerful than that dropped on Hiroshima, so, too, is it far less destructive than the largest contemporary weapons. And this hypothetical attack involves the detonation of only a single bomb, whereas contemporary military planning and technological capabilities make it far more likely that several will be used in each attack.

New York City's trial by nuclear attack begins with the detonation of a one-million ton air burst bomb 6,500

feet above the Empire State Building. The area of total destruction, the circle within which even the most heavily reinforced concrete structures do not survive, has a radius of 1.5 miles. That circle extends from the Brooklyn Bridge to Central Park Lake and from Long Island City to Hoboken. Included within it are the Empire State Building, Lincoln Center, the Stock Exchange. And within this circle, almost all of the population is killed.

At a distance of three miles from the center of the blast, past Jersey City and Elmhurst, past the Brooklyn Museum in the south and 145th Street in the north, concrete buildings are destroyed. The heat from the explosion and the spontaneous ignition of clothing cause third-degree flash burns over much of the body, killing most people in this area.

More than four miles from the center, brick and wood frame buildings are destroyed and fires caused by the intense heat are fanned by 160-mile per hour winds.

In a circle extending to Hastings on Hudson, Livingston, New Jersey, and beyond Far Rockaway to the sea, brick and wood frame buildings sustain heavy damage. The heat exceeds 12 calories per square centimeter, and all individuals with exposed skin suffer severe third-degree burns. At the outer limit of this circle, brick and wood frame structures sustain moderate damage.

Miles beyond this last ring, people suffer second-degree burns on all exposed skin, and additional burns from flammable clothing and environmental materials. Retinal burns resulting from looking at the fireball may cause blindness. As high winds spread the fires caused by the initial blast and thermal radiation, the number of casualties grows.

If we assume a population for the metropolitan area of 16 million, more than 1,600,000 are killed. Even more—2,800,000—are injured. Many of these survivors are badly burned, blinded, and otherwise seriously wounded. Many are disoriented. These are the

short-term effects; the problem of radiation sickness, including intractable nausea, vomiting, bleeding, hair loss, severe infection, and often death, will grow in the days and weeks ahead. Fallout from the bomb will spread well beyond the area of impact.

The population is devastated; many survivors are in need of immediate medical care, food, shelter, clothing and water. The communities in which they have lived have, in many cases, virtually ceased to exist as physical entities as well. Government is barely existent. The transportation system, including many roads, has been destroyed. Remaining food, water, and medical supplies are dangerously inadequate.

And what of the medical response to such a disaster? In Hiroshima, 65 of the city's 150 doctors were killed in the bombing and most of the survivors were wounded. Some 10,000 wounded made their. way to Hiroshima's 600-bed Red Cross Hospital. There, only

six doctors and 10 nurses were able to help them. John Hersey described the struggle of one of those physicians:

> Sasaki . . . realized . . . that the casualties were pouring in from outdoors. There were so many that he began to pass up the lightly wounded; he decided that all he could hope to do was to stop people from bleeding to death. Before long, patients lay and crouched on the floors of the wards and the laboratories and all the other rooms . . . and in the driveway and courtyard, and for blocks each way in the streets outside. Wounded people supported maimed people; disfigured families leaned together. Many people were vomiting . . . The people in the suffocating crowd inside the hospital wept and cried, for Dr. Sasaki to hear, "Sensi! Doctor!" and the less seriously wounded came and pulled at his sleeve and begged him to go to the aid of the worse wounded. Tugged here and there in his stocking feet, bewildered by the numbers, staggered by so much raw flesh, Dr. Sasaki lost all sense of profession and stopped working as a skillful surgeon and a sympathetic man; he became an automaton, mechanically wiping, daubing, winding, wiping, daubing, winding.

For New York we can take as our base a figure of 29,000 physicians in the metropolitan area. Extrapolating from the casualties suffered by the general population, we may project that 3,000 doctors will be killed immediately and some 5,100 will be seriously injured. Thus, 21,000 surviving physicians will be responsible for the care of 2,800,000 patients with grave wounds. It will be essential that these wounds be attended to as quickly as possible, yet for each of these patients to be visited once—for fifteen minutes—will require every surviving physician to work a thirty-four hour shift.

In fact, it is likely that many fewer physicians will survive, for they are concentrated, during working hours, in an area close to the center of the blast. But whether the post-attack physician-to-patient ratio is 1:300 or 1:1000, where will treatment take place?

The bomb will massively reduce the number of hospital beds, within the City alone, and the amount of medical equipment and supplies are similarly inadequate. Can the seriously injured be treated at New York Hospital-Cornell Medical Center? It no longer exists. St. Vincent's Hospital? It, too, has been destroyed. In ruins, as well, are Bellevue Hospital, Beth Israel Medical Center, Mount Sinai Medical Center, and several others. The geographic distribution of surviving medical facilities will be another problem, some requiring physicians to enter more highly radioactive areas, and thus expose themselves to greater personal danger, in order to treat the injured. The shortage of nurses will be severe.

With a decimated professional community, physical

facilities largely in ruins, and a complete disruption of communications, the task of treating the wounded will be hopeless.

If you have any doubts, you will understand my use of the term hopeless after I describe a twenty-year-old man who was recently a patient in the Burn Unit of one of Boston's teaching hospitals. He had been in an automobile accident in which the gasoline tank exploded, and had incurred very extensive third-degree burns. During his hospitalization, he received 281 units of fresh-frozen plasma, 147 units of fresh-frozen red blood cells, 37 units of platelets, and 36 units of albumin. He underwent six operative procedures, during which wounds involving 85 percent of his body surface were closed with homograft, cadaver allograft, and artificial skin. Throughout his hospitalization, he required mechanical ventilation and monitoring with central venous lines, arterial lines and an intermittent pul-

monary artery line. Despite these heroic measures, which stretched the resources of one of the country's most comprehensive institutions, the man died on his 33rd hospital day. His injuries were likened by the person who supervised his care to those described for many of the victims of the Hiroshima bomb.

Keeping that one patient alive for 33 days required the extraordinary resources of one of the world's major medical centers. No amount of preparation could provide the human and physical resources required for the care of even a few such patients hospitalized simultaneously in any city of the nation. Yet one must assume that hundreds of thousands of patients would be in that condition in a post-attack New York. At least tens of thousands of such casualties would result in *every* large metropolitan center hit by a nuclear weapon.

New York is perhaps the most favored American city with respect to resources for burn victims: it has 48 beds devoted to the care of acutely burned patients. Yet at least one-half of these beds would be destroyed in the first seconds after the blast.

This is but one reason that it is futile to suggest a meaningful medical response to the overwhelming health problems that would follow a nuclear attack. Further, only the most limited medical measures can be visualized to deal with the burden of cancer and genetic defects that would afflict survivors and future generations. Temporary evacuation has been suggested as an approach, but radioactivity would make the blast area uninhabitable for months. Most of the area's water supply, sanitation resources and transportation and industrial capacity would be destroyed.

At present more than 50,000 nuclear warheads are deployed and ready. Most dwarf in destructive power the bomb used against Hiroshima. Sufficient nuclear bombs exist outside the United States to subject every major American city repeatedly to the destruction that was described for New York. Six nations are now acknowledged possessors of nuclear weapons, but other countries almost surely share that "privilege." Every addition to this list increases the degree of instability.

What purpose, one may ask, is there in describing these unthinkable conditions? But the conditions are not unthinkable; rather they are infrequently thought about. Among the painful results of the silence are the continuing proliferation of nuclear weapons and the failure to reject out-of-hand nuclear war as a "viable option" in the management of world problems.

Physicians for Social Responsibility and the Council for a Livable World have joined to sponsor meetings to break the silence on this issue. There is, of course, no reason to consider the consequences of nuclear war in strictly medical terms. But if we do so, we must pay heed to the inescapable lesson of contemporary medicine: where treatment of a given disease is ineffective *or* where costs are insupportable, attention must be given to prevention. Both conditions apply to the effects of nuclear war—treatment programs would be virtually useless and the costs would be staggering. Can any stronger arguments be marshalled for a preventive strategy?

A physician attempts to make a persuasive case for prevention without frightening the patient by describing in clinical detail the most unpleasant aspects of the disease in question. If the patient fails to pay heed, however, the doctor is justified in calling attention to the consequences, however stark they may be. Our "patients" at present include the political leaders of the principal nations of the world. Many appear not to understand the medical realities of nuclear confrontation. Therefore, we have come together to paint this picture in its true dimensions. If the horror of that picture is offensive—and how can it be otherwise?—ascribe the horror not to hyperbole or irresponsibility on the part of the speakers, but reather to a realistic story that has no precedent in devastation and will almost surely be followed by none.

The dividends of a successful campaign for prevention could extend far beyond the immediate one of survival. The United States and the Soviet Union might, for example, agree to commit to health programs a fraction of the resources saved by freezing, at present levels, their stockpiles of nuclear weapons. Compare the $30 to $60 billion cost estimate for the proposed MX missile system or similarly expensive developments in the Russian arsenal with the $2 billion needed to wipe out malaria, which kills one million children per year, in Africa alone. Or compare the cost of these weapons with the $300 million spent, according to the World Health Organization, for the successful WHO campaign that eliminated smallpox from the face of the earth.

Confrontation, *Winter 1981*

The BOMb

The Ideas by Which We Are Ruled

Within the decade the three dominant figures in the Air Force have given considered voice to their views on foreign policy and the proper American response. They deserve to be better read.

From General Thomas S. Power, USAF (Ret.)

"The Soviet leadership is irrevocably committed to the achievement of the ultimate Communist objective, which is annihilation of the capitalist system and establishment of Communist dictatorship over all nations of the world."

"Soviet rulers are not like the leaders of other nations with whom one can reason and conclude agreements to be approved and honored by the people whom they represent."

"But the military aspects of the Communist threat represent just one phase of the most insidious and gigantic plot in history. There are the economic, technological, political, ideological and other phases, all designed for one objective only, and that is the accomplishment of the ultimate Communist goal of total world domination."

"With 700 million people, one-quarter of the world's population, it [Communist China] is under the absolute control of fanatic and ruthless dictators who are determined to conquer all of southeast Asia . . . once they have succeeded in building up a sufficient stockpile of nuclear weapons and delivery vehicles they will doubtless embark on a major and sustained campaign of aggression against their neighbors."

From General Nathan F. Twining, USAF (Ret.)

"I can summarize my views on national security planning into two sentences. The leaders of an organized conspiracy have sworn to destroy America and the Free World by one means or another, and there is no real evidence available at this time to indicate that their objective has been changed. Therefore we had better be prepared to fight to maintain our liberty."

"Red China under its present leadership seems to me at this writing to be practically a hopeless case. Naked force seems to be the only logic which the leadership of that unfortunate nation can comprehend."

"From America's conduct of the Korean War, the Sino-Soviet Bloc had learned three important things: one, the U.S. was not going to use the atomic bomb, even tactically; two, it had no stomach for tangling with the Chinese Communists; and three, this nation never even considered carrying the war back to the U.S.S.R.—the real instigator of the aggression. The homeland of the Sino-Soviet Bloc [sic] was therefore secure."

". . . another course of action which could have been considered. I call this course 'containment plus,' because it includes all the elements of containment and adds *initiative*. This course of action would *not necessarily* [italics added] have required a calculated and deliberate first nuclear blow against Communist powers. . . . The United States *could* have said:

> The United States does not intend to initiate military conflict, but it will have to begin it if the U.S.S.R. and Communist China persist in their attempts to enslave more of the free world. The United States will be ready to fight. The Communist apparatus is trying to destroy this nation with every trick at its command, therefore, the United States will also use every economic, technical, political, psychological, and subversive method which can be contrived. This nation must refuse to be bound to the dogmatic principles of statesmanship while its enemy lives by the law of the jungle. The stakes to humanity [sic] are too high."

From General Curtis E. LeMay, USAF (Ret.)

"To begin with it is necessary to understand that Vietnam is part of a much larger and much longer war—a war between communism and the Free World. . . . Although the war has many facets, it has but one objective: Communist control of the entire world."

"I should think that with the evidence of Korea and Vietnam we should begin to see the errors in the limited war doctrine we now practice."

". . . We must see to it that Communist aggression results in Communist disaster. This we cannot obtain at the negotiating table."

". . . America languors with an illness of euphoria brought on by our leaders who have proclaimed an international détente in the struggle against communism. This détente is unwarranted."

". . . I sincerely believe any arms race with the Soviet union would act to our benefit. I believe that we can out-invent, out-research, out-develop, out-engineer and out-produce the U.S.S.R. in any area from sling shots to space weapons, and in so doing become more and more prosperous while the Soviets become progressively poorer. This is the faith I have in the free enterprise economy. . . ."

John Kenneth Galbraith, How to Control the Military, *N.Y., Signet, 1969.* © *Doubleday & Co.*

Fear and trembling.

In April 1982 a group of European visitors urging disarmament in Moscow's Red Square were knocked down by K.G.B. agents and taken away for questioning. The Soviet action reflects their uneasiness that the stress on support for European peace movements could have important consequences within the Soviet Union. *Sovietskaya Rossiya*, a newspaper, denounced signs of support for disarmament among the Russian people as "toothless pacifism." Reports indicate that growing numbers of the Russian young gather in Moscow and other Soviet cities to sing peace hymns, many taken from the American antiwar movement of the 1960s. Marshal Nikolai V. Ogarkov, chief of staff of the Soviet armed forces, a hardliner and a hawk, wrote a pamphlet "Always Ready to Defend the Fatherland," in which he complained of such "easy-going attitudes and carelessness . . . a dangerous phenomenon, fraught with grave consequences."

The lesson? Nikolai, meet Thomas, Nathan and Curtis.

No Angels, No Devils

John M. Swomley, Jr.

John M. Swomley Jr. is Professor of Social Ethics at St. Paul School of Theology in Kansas City and author of many books, among them The Military Establishment *and* American Empire. *He was formerly executive secretary of the Fellowship of Reconciliation.*

The United States, the Soviet Union and their respective allies are on a collision course unless something significant changes in their relation to each other. Neither side could win a worldwide war, and the common people of all nations would die by the scores of millions. In the light of this possibility of horror, previous misunderstandings of the conduct of foreign policy need to be re-examined.

Formerly it was assumed that one nation's foreign policy is necessarily antagonistic to another's—because international politics, ruled by a laissez-faire philosophy, presupposes that successful operators who have accumulated power will determine the outcome of geography, economics and history by their exercise of power, which includes military cartels known as alliances.

Today the overriding purpose of foreign policy ought to be the avoidance of war, especially as any war could be the trigger of a nuclear conflagration. Foreign policy, in effect, is too important to be left in the hands of governments and the power elites that run them. People must become aroused so that they participate in decision-making.

The problem for people concerned about peace is how to move from the laissez-faire philosophy of international politics or from power blocs organized militarily against each other to a system of mutual cooperation. One approach is to suggest to ordinary Americans a new attitude toward the Soviet Union which does not gloss over the differences that exist in our philosophies of government.

That new attitude should begin with a recognition that the Soviets are not devils and we are not angels. There are aspects of their system which are evil as there are aspects of ours. An oversimplification which has in it a great deal of truth would trace their evil to totalitarianism and ours to monopoly capitalism, sometimes referred to as multi-national conglomerates or cartels. Both sides are heavily militarized, under the grip of a military-industrialized complex and an internal elite of economic, political and military interests.

That new attitude should also begin with a recognition that we must appeal to peoples rather than to government elites for change, an appeal which must be couched in actions expressing a new attitude. Without trying to be comprehensive, I suggest the following answers to the question: "What should be our attitude toward the Soviet Union?"

1. We should treat the Soviet Union as we want it to treat us. In terms of trade we should export food, medicines, machinery and other products that will enhance life for all the Soviet people. However, we should not make or trade items that can be used for the torture of persons, or for surveillance and other police-state measures that contribute to totalitarianism or for the waging of war. There is no point to selling another nation weapons, or factories and processes for the making of weapons and subsequently argue that we need a draft of young men and women in order to deal with that nation's use of those weapons.

2. We should stop the steady verbal criticism of other nations as if we have provided a superior standard of morality by which all other nations shoud be judged. Self-criticism is always more constructive than criticism of others. If we were to demonstrate a superior

way of life it would be far more effective in changing the Soviet Union than any criticism delivered in the press or before the United Nations.

George Kennan, in his *American Diplomacy*, pins his hope on a society which by contrast with Russia's is so ideal that it will be the incentive for the Russian people to change their own society. He implies that this should be America's role. He writes of "his faith that if the necessary alternatives are kept before the Russian people, in the form of the existence elsewhere on this planet of a civilization which is decent, hopeful and purposeful, the day must come—soon or late, and whether by gradual process or otherwise, when that terrible system of power . . . will be distinguishable no longer as a living reality . . ."

3. When the Soviet Union intervened in Afghanistan it did not create a new pattern of international immorality. The U.S. intervened in the Dominican Republic to keep the Bosch forces from controlling the government. The U.S. intervened in Iran, Chile, Guatemala, Vietnam and in various other countries. The surest way to establish a new pattern of international morality is to change our own policy by publicly renouncing any future intervention in other nations, and also to seek in the United Nations formal acceptance of a policy of non-intervention by states in the affairs of other states, whether invited to intervene or not.

4. We Americans ought not to hold the Soviet people hostage for the conduct of their government. This can be illustrated at two levels. The withholding of food, medicine or other products essential to the life or health of the people is not a good way of influencing government policy. In a totalitarian society the people are not directly responsible for the actions of government. Even in a more democratic society people are not consulted before government announces its policies.

Confrontation, *Winter, 1981*

Steven Brodner

The Absent Danger

Not since the hysteria over Sputnik two decades ago have we Americans felt so anxious about our place in the world. Part of our anxiety is firmly grounded in material life. Millions are out of work with little prospect of returning soon, inflation seems permanently into double digits, few can afford a new house or even a car. But these specific problems merge into a greater unease. Just yesterday, it seemed, we were living in the American Century, when the dollar was "good as gold," American industrial products were the international standard, and GI Joe patrolled the world (backed by our nuclear monopoly). No longer. Cassandras of both political parties exploit this emotional link between economic distress and a general feeling of

powerlessness. They say the greatest threat to our way of life comes from abroad. Our defenses are weak, they say, our influence is diminished, our example is scoffed at, our very future is imperiled. They wish to redirect our attention to the Kremlin and its master plan to take over the world.

Yet the new sense of powerlessness was inflicted most forcefully on Americans not by anything the Russians did, but by Moslem nationalists who seized our embassy in Iran. That symbolized everything that had gone wrong. Worst of all, it was a slap in the face. The hostage issue triggered an intense emotional reaction among Americans. Unlike the Vietnam War, which induced puzzlement, futility, and often guilt, we could feel at last that we were the aggrieved party. We had been maligned and mistreated—and, so far as we could tell, through no fault of our own. Patriotism became fashionable once again. We waved the flag, which was not a bad thing to do, now that we were not fighting any colonial wars to be embarrassed about. We shook our fists, which made us feel good, though it was not much help to the hostages. And we floundered for some way to assert ourselves. But we could not figure out how to do it. We could not put pressure on the Iranians because they did not even have a government. Or at least not one responsive to bribes or threats. And there was virtually no way we could use force and still get the hostages out alive. (This is why the hostages' families can be thankful that the "rescue" mission was bungled.)

We were consumed by a terrible frustration for which there was no outlet. Then along came Afghanistan and the rampaging Russians. What a relief! Here at last was an adversary worthy of our indignation: one who, like us, measured power in terms of brigades, flotillas, and megatons. We could flex our muscles once again. Last December and January, (1979-80), adrenaline flowed in Washington like Perrier. Men girded for war and made solemn vows of fortitude. They evoked visions of Munich and recited irrefutable "lessons" of the past.

The only problem was trying to explain exactly what was the threat in Afghanistan. The United States hardly could be said to have a vital stake in a country with which it has had virtually no economic or political contact, and which, for all practical purposes, fell under Soviet control two years earlier. Nor could we be said to be upholding the sacred principle of non-intervention. After all, we had intervened a few times ourselves to help our "friends" stay in power. True, the Kremlin's insistence that it was merely responding to a call for help from a beleaguered ally was a pretty flimsy excuse. But it was just as flimsy when we used it in the Dominican Republic in 1965.

We were disturbed about Afghanistan not because it suddenly assumed strategic significance, but for the more emotional reason that we were tired of being "pushed around." Without the humiliation American pride suffered in Iran, Afghanistan would have seemed little more than a settling of accounts among Communists. We would have dismissed it with a shrug and a sermon, just as Lyndon Johnson dismissed the Soviet occupation of Czechoslovakia in 1968 and John Foster Dulles dismissed the suppression of the Hungarian revolt in 1956.

But the American public was agitated by the events in Tehran, and the Carter administration was in trouble. President Carter needed an issue with which to redeem himself. A tough stance would bolster the public's morale, and maybe the administration's ratings as well. Afghanistan suddenly became crucial. It was time to stand up to the Russians and show that we would not be "pushed around" anymore. Lost somewhere in the shuffle was the fact that it was not the Russians, but the Iranians, who were pushing us around. But never mind. The Kremlin was being pushy. It was sending

ships into "our" Indian Ocean. It was mucking around in black Africa. It was building missiles as big as ours. And, worst of all, it now seemed to be inching toward the Persian Gulf, the watery site of all our current oil anxieties. A minor annoyance elevated to the level of a major crisis.

Suddenly Reds under the bed are fashionable again. Richard Nixon, resurrected once more (this time, it would seem, as the "old Nixon"), tells us in his recent book, *The Real War* (Warner Books), World War III already has started and the Reds are gunning for us. This is a bit odd coming from the man whose whole foreign policy was built on detente, and who signed an arms control agreement with Moscow and opened the door to Peking. It is even odder to hear the same sort of stuff from Henry Kissinger, who worked out a succession of cozy deals with the Russians amounting virtually to a US-Soviet condominium over the world. But now, in his new guise as a Republican office-seeker, Kissinger finds it expedient to repudiate the policies he pursued so energetically in office.

Similar noises emerge from an assemblage of academics, litterateurs, businessmen, and retired military officers known as the Committee on the Present Danger. The phrase, "the present danger"—vague, but ominous—entered the political vocabulary as a password for a new bipartisan hawkish consensus. Norman Podhoretz, editor of *Commentary*, uses this password as the title for his recent little volume, *The Present Danger* (Simon & Schuster), an extended version of a *Commentary* article earlier this year. In now-familiar present-danger rhetoric, Podhoretz tells us that our civilization may be in its last quarter-hour. The threat, to his mind, is not atomic destruction or economic collapse, but rather Soviet imperialism. The Russians are "dedicated to the destruction" of our society, and the balance of power is "tilting" toward them. Our "Finlandization," whatever that is, lies just around the corner, and because we have indulged in a "culture of appeasement," we may soon find that "surrender or war are the only remaining choices." The book is a main selection of the Conservative Book Club.

The current unhappy state of affairs, according to Podhoretz, results from the fact that all the presidents

from Ike the Good have foolishly sought "detente" with the Russians when they should have held faithfully to the brand of "containment" pursued by Harry Truman and Dean Acheson in the early days of the cold war. By containment he means the classic formulation of George Kennan in 1947: The US should confront the Soviets with the "adroit and vigilant application of counterforce at a series of constantly shifting geographical and political points." In other words, the US should draw a military line against any "communist" advance.

The only trouble with this doctrine, as Kennan himself soon realized, was that it made no distinction between Soviet power and indigenous nationalist movements in which local "Communists" were involved. And further, as Walter Lippmann pointed out at the time, it would make the United States hostage to every dictator wanting American help to prop up his regime. It would mean, Lippmann wrote, "recruiting, subsidizing and supporting a heterogeneous array of satellites, clients, dependents and puppets." It meant, in short, the Vietnam War, the logical application of the containment strategy. Kennan later repudiated his own doctrine, and has become one of the most ardent critics of the attitudes Podhoretz exemplifies.

Podhoretz's argument is a familiar one—we have been hearing it, in one form or another, ever since 1945—and so is his prescription. We should reverse the "retreat" of American power initiated by (of all people) Nixon. We should not be squeamish about supporting our tried and true friends in places like the Philippines and South Korea, though they may play a little rough sometimes. We should get rid of the pernicious "no more Vietnams" syndrome. We should build more missiles and bombers, overcome our "articulated horror over the prospect of nuclear war," "unleash" the CIA, and resist the insidious "self-Finlandization" (one of the few awkward phrases in an elegantly written essay) that, so he assures us, has already infected our European allies.

To buttress his points Podhoretz occasionally cites certain historical "facts." For example, he tells us that after World War II the Russians "had been permitted" by the US to occupy most of Eastern Europe. They had not been "permitted" to do anything. They were in Eastern Europe because they had pushed back the German army, and because it had been US and British policy to make them carry the brunt of the war against the Nazis. The Americans and British later tried to get them out of Eastern Europe by economic and political pressure, but failed. Podhoretz also states that in 1947 Greece and Turkey were "threatened by the same fate." They were not. The Russians sought joint control with Turkey over the Dardanelles. They cited the fact that Turkey had been an ally of Nazi Germany, that they were seeking less than the British enjoyed at Suez and the Americans in Panama, and that FDR had given tacit approval to their claims. The Turks, with American support, refused. That was the end of it. There was never a threat of invasion. As for Greece,

the Russians—honoring their 1944 pact with Churchill—gave the British a free hand in mopping up the Communist and leftist forces. The guerrillas got support not from the Russians but from the Yugoslavs, who were pursuing their own national objectives—in this case a slice of Macedonia. Had Podhoretz consulted Milovan Djilas, whom he quotes approvingly on the need not to be frightened by nuclear war, he would have noted that Stalin washed his hands of the Greek Communists and made no threats against Greece.

One more example. In discussing the application of the containment doctrine in Korea, Podhoretz declares that, "In refusing to do more in Korea than repel the North Korean invasion . . . the United States served notice on the world that it had no intention of going beyond containment to rollback or liberation." To the contrary. As early as August 1950, the Truman administration hinted that its ultimate objective was to unify Korea by force. That month Warren Austin, US delegate to the UN, told the Security Council that all Koreans "must attain complete individual and political freedom. . . . Shall only a part of the country be assured of this freedom? . . . I think not." On October 7, three weeks after the Inchon landing, American troops crossed the 38th parallel and drove toward the Yalu with instructions to proceed until they met Chinese or Russian resistance. Short-circuiting the Security Council, where the Russians had a veto, the US secured an endorsement of the action from the General Assembly. Later, after it all went wrong, Truman and Acheson claimed that MacArthur had taken matters into his own hands. But it was they, with the concurrence of the Joint Chiefs, who had tried to roll back communism. And it was not the Russians, but the Chinese, who stopped them.

Pordhoretz's "facts" are really metaphors designed to show that only American stupidity, or perhaps even betrayal, allowed communism to spread its tentacles. The real-life fact that communism has hardly spread anywhere, and that the term itself—as a description of a nation's economic or foreign policy—has become largely meaningless, does not diminish the urgent breathlessness of his argument, for the argument is one that rests on faith, and on fear.

This is why Afghanistan has been such a blessing, for the Soviet presence in that forsaken land nourishes American anxieties. And chief among those anxieties is oil. Thus we have Podhoretz arguing that the real reason the Soviets are in Afghanistan is to creep down toward the Gulf. And why do they want to get there? Why, to shut off the West's oil supply. It is a curious scenario that lacks political, as well as logistical, plausibility; but this in no way diminishes the dogmatism with which it is presented.

Yet ultimately it is not the invasion of Afghanistan, or even the threat that the Russians *somehow* will be able to seize, operate, and protect oil fields spread across a hostile area bigger than Europe, that has led Podhoretz to such grim forebodings. For he is not primarily concerned with Russian power. Rather it is communism as an ideology that disturbs him. The Soviet Union, he asserts, is not a nation like any other. Rather it is, like Nazi Germany, a revolutionary state determined to impose an international order congenial to its interests and ideology. One could, to be sure, say this of all powerful states. But for Podhoretz the primary question is a moral one. "Communism," he declares, quoting liberally from apostates like Djilas and Solzhenitsyn, "whether dominated by Moscow or not, has been a curse." Now this may well be true. But it is not an observation that offers much direction to American policy. It doesn't tell us what to do about Afghanistan, let alone the MX missile, Persian Gulf oil, and an economy reeling under the burden of geopolitical decisions made three decades ago and not seriously reexamined since.

Podhoretz is not so much a Churchill warning us to awake, or even a Cassandra predicting terrible woes, as he is a Jeremiah with a litany of grievances. There is something shrill, and disturbingly intolerant, about his moral crusade against the various evils he lumps together under the category of "communism." He finds it hard to accept that others, in perfect good faith, might disagree with him. Thus he declares that critics of US military interventionism are poisoned by "self-hatred," that restraint in foreign policy is a "euphemism for unilateral disarmament;" that those dubious about the virtues of the CIA and an imperial presidency are "isolationists," and that liberals are consumed by an "anti-Americanism that makes them reflexively blame the United States for everything evil that happens in the world." There is also something distasteful about a morality that hails the salutory effects of McCarthyism because it was able to "mobilize support for an anti-Communist foreign policy by making the danger of Communism seem domestic and immediate."

Perhaps what inspires former liberals who worry aloud about "the present danger" has less to do with morality than with indignation. Neoconservatives like Podhoretz are tired of being "pushed around"—not only, to judge by the articles in his magazine, by Iranians and Russians, but by affirmative action minorities, equal rights women, and shameless gays. He is outraged that the Arabs dare charge so much for their oil. We should have invaded them in 1973, when it all started, he asserts.

Underneath so many of these complaints lies a deep concern over status. That concern, at least for many ex-liberals, began in the mid-1960s, when black militants stopped being grateful for white liberal largesse, when expensively educated white children stopped showing respect for their parents and teachers, when the sacred bastion of the academy was invaded. That is when scholars started to flee Berkeley and Columbia, and when *Commentary* made a sharp turn to the right.

Today we face serious problems with the Soviet Union. Not because it is ruled by fanatical Communists panting to grab our oil, but because lines of communi-

cations and mutual interest have virtually broken down. The recent resurrection of the Red peril is not due to any sudden increase in Soviet power and influence. For all its missile building, the Soviet Union remains a society with an inefficient and now stagnant economy, with little influence outside areas policed by the Red Army, with restive satellites seeking their own deals with the West, and with the world's most populous and powerful nations arrayed in alliance against it: the United States, Western Europe, China, and Japan. The view from the Kremlin must be very grim indeed.

Then why Reds under the bed once more? Because the certainties of our own world have collapsed. Because we no longer can count on our prosperity, on our ability to order events, on assuming that the future will be better than the past. Today the United States is going through a kind of nervous fit, showing some of the symptoms of an imperial power on the decline. The situation is still under control. It is not yet a nervous breakdown. The American people, for all their anxiety, are still relatively calm. But they are under assault—by demagogues, by ideologues, by politicans and intellectuals intent on self-assertion.

The pronouncements of those who have made "the present danger" a vogue phrase are not just symptoms of the current unrest. They are fuel that could ignite a panic. That may be the intention.

Ronald Steel, The New Republic, *August 16, 1980*

Curti, National Review

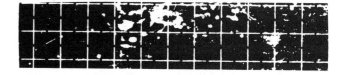

Inflating the Soviet Military Threat

Threat inflation is still the name of the game. James Fallows, in his perceptive book *National Defense*, cites a classic example of this technique. On the front page of the Jan. 9, 1981, *Washington Post* appeared this headline: "Soviets Launch Huge New Attack Submarine." The article first described how the Soviets had shocked American intelligence people by launching a new cruise-missile-firing submarine.

The story went on to tell how the giant submarine was nearly twice the size of the largest operational U.S. attack submarine. From beginning to end, the article stressed the idea that bigger was inevitably better—a concept far from accurate. A submarine's effectiveness depends not on size, but on its ability to operate quietly.

The fright campaign goes on with one of our leading scaremongers, Lt. Gen. Daniel O. Graham, former head of the Defense Intelligence Agency, contending that a nuclear war would result in 10 million Russian deaths, as opposed to 100 million Americans. A more reliable source, however, states that 400-500 megatons of nuclear explosives could kill more than 100 million Russians. What would be the result if we unloaded the thousands of megatons in the 10,000 nuclear bombs and warheads now in our arsenal?

The most fantastic of the fears peddled by our arms advocates was one conjured up by George K. Keegan, former U.S. Air Force major general. The Soviets, he said, are on the verge of developing a particle-beam weapon capable of destroying incoming U.S. nuclear warheads. The Pentagon, however, says there is little support in U.S. technical and intelligence circles for his assertion. Particle-beam weaponry is considered many years away from becoming a reality.

These and other scare tactics, exemplified by the Foxbat Syndrome, have been the primary means of promoting war fever and military expansion since the early 1950s. More recently, the Soviet invasion of Afghanistan has generated a new "security crisis" and with it the biggest arms buildup in our history.

"It is part of the general pattern of misguided policy that our country is now geared to an arms economy which was bred in an artificially induced psychosis of war hysteria and nurtured upon an incessant propaganda of fear." These are not the words of an anti-military crank, but of Gen. Douglas MacArthur, delivered May 15, 1951.

General, where are you when we need you?

George Ott has written for the U.S. Naval Institute Proceedings, Armed Forces Journal, Military Review *and* National Defense.

The Problem as Seen from the Right

"America's lack of effective civil defenses would create a major disadvantage in any future confrontations with the USSR that raised the specter of nuclear war. The Soviets, with as few as ten million or a few tens of millions of their people at risk in a strategic nuclear war could risk escalating a crisis to an extremely threatening level while realistically expecting the U.S., with 190 million of its people at risk, to back down.* The principle involved is that the side likely to lose the most by escalating a crisis will make the greatest concessions to avoid escalation—or even to avoid confronting an opponent when such confrontation might escalate. . . ." (*The number of Soviet fatalities projected depends on the conditions assumed for the exchange, but what is important to realize is that most of these conditions are subject to control by the Soviet Union.) T.K. Jones in "Strategic Options for the Early Eighties: What Can be Done?" William R. van Cleve and W. Scott Thompson.

An opposing point of view is as follows:

1). Calculations of the effectiveness of Soviet civil defense can never be relied upon by Soviet decision-makers because—in the light of the thousands of warheads available to the U.S. even after a Soviet first strike—they require that many uncertainties be resolved favorably: e.g., the Soviet population would have to be out of the Soviet cities when the war came; it would have to be assumed that the U.S. had not decisively compensated for that movement by changes in targeting; Soviet industry would have to be protected effectively so that survival means were

PAS

available to the surviving Soviet population; environmental and ecological uncertainties would have to have turned out reasonably well; it would probably have to be summer not winter.

2). Even conceding that these uncertainties could be controlled or relied upon, the disaster that would be represented by nuclear war is so great that the Soviet leadership is likely to be quite as deterred as the American leadership and its degree of boldness in subnuclear war maneuvers determined by lesser considerations. Losing a very large fraction of one's nation in a few days is not relevant to the calculations of politicians who are maneuvering their ships of state to avoid even much more minor collisions. In short, these calculations appear to be an opiate of strategists, not politicians.

3). Further, were a confrontation between the superpowers to be influenced because the Soviet Union threatened, much less tried, a strategic evacuation, the result would be a Western weapons buildup, or shift in weapons tactics, which ensured that no such tactics would ever work again. The resultant shift in Western attitudes would, by itself, seem to deter such maneuvers.

4). As a consequence, this approach, taking relative civil defense capabilities as strategically meaningful, requires that one believe that the world is moving toward a single cataclysmic crisis that will determine everything—and determine it as if in a war game.

The Great Fear Returns

Bob Seeley

In 1961 I spent the summer with the American Friends Service Committee in California. With three others, I traveled and spoke on peace before groups ranging from Friends' Meetings to the Optimist's Club.

It was not a good time for peace. The country had just exchanged "massive retaliation" for the Messianic America of John F. Kennedy's inaugural address. In my high school, the primary topic of discussion during the 1960 election had been whether Kennedy could "stand up" to Khrushchev. A Berlin crisis was in progress that summer. Yet to come were the Bay of Pigs, the Cuban Missile Crisis, and, of course, Vietnam.

The Great Fear was king, and all else bowed to it. If the economy was being depleted by massive arms expenditures, so be it; they were a necessary defense. If the draft infringed on citizens' rights, that, too, was necessary. And if the competition for superiority in nightmare weaponry put the world in mortal danger, that was the rational response to an unreasoning, malevolent force that sought to undermine our way of life.

Vietnam brought the country face-to-face with its own responsibilities. By 1969 it was not necessary to argue—as I had in 1961—that "defense" could easily become aggression. Our culpability was writ large in body counts, in support for a crumbling dictatorship, and in our own casualties, dead and alive. We had learned that we were not always the peaceful giant fighting reluctantly at our friends' uttermost need. The Great Fear was dead or forgotten; we had urgent concerns of our own.

Now that fear is returning. Quietly, almost without our realizing it, the Soviet Union has regained its leading position in America's mythology of terror. Worse: the myth-makers, by persistently rejecting disarmament, have made it politically unthinkable. Now they are trying to make arms control equally difficult. We could never hope for peace, they argue; now we cannot even hope to keep the world's peril at its current level. Agreement is foolhardy because the Soviets are building up their military forces while the U.S. position deteriorates.

We have, of course, had Red Scares before. At budget time, the Soviet military regularly grows, necessitating ever higher defense spending. But the current myth-making is more apocalyptic, and hence more dangerous, than any in recent years. Once accepted, it leaves no way out through negotiation or U.S. initiative. The prospect is rather for a growing military establishment and security, such as it is, through more and more sophisticated weaponry.

The argument is familiar, but it bears repeating. The Soviet Union has been expanding its weapons technology, its Navy, and its military ground forces. At the same time, it has begun an intensive program of civil defense. It is deploying more and more tanks, more and more troops, in the Warsaw Pact countries, just across the border from NATO forces. Hence, in the words of the Committee on the Present Danger, "The principal threat to our nation, to world peace, and the cause of human freedom is the Soviet drive for dominance based upon an unparalleled military buildup." Hitler's ghost is invoked; planners now talk of a Soviet *blitzkrieg* in Europe. And there is ominous talk of Soviet "first-strike capability."

Much of this argument is questionable, particularly its unspoken assumption that the Soviets *must* be arming for a first strike if they are arming at all. But the reality is less important than the myth.

For the Great Fear, whatever its basis in fact, is not merely a series of trial balloons in the press. It is a position held by influential people—among them Walt Rostow, Saul Bellow, and Adm. Elmo Zumwalt (Ret.)—and argued not only in the popular press but in specialist journals catering to the intelligence and diplomatic community.

Writing in *Policy Review* for Fall, 1977, Colin S. Gray of the Hudson Institute argues that "Western publics should understand that arms control has never offered a satisfactory alternative path to the national security, as compared with unilateral military effort." An article in the *International Defense Review* describes Soviet civil defense as one of the major threats to world peace. Paul Nitze, chairman of policy studies for the Committee on the Present Danger, argues in yet another article that not negotiation but more arms are needed. Articles too numerous to count bemoan the state of NATO. And on and on.

Gray is trying to save arms control from the "liberal arms-control establishment." Nitze is trying to stop it altogether. Yet both use the same assumptions. Both accept the Great Fear.

Such analysis has consequences beyond abandonment of arms control or disarmament as policy goals. It means, for one thing, that the President must negotiate not only with the Soviet Union, but with the U.S. myth-makers. In fact, as Daniel Yergin pointed out in a recent issue of *Harper's* (June, 1977), he must do so *before* he negotiates with the Kremlin. There is much besides arms control that could decrease tensions between the two countries, but in an atmosphere of terror it is difficult to make concessions or to reach agreements of any sort.

Individual soldiers and civilians of military age, too, are affected. Our perceptions of our adversaries, however inaccurate, determine how we place weapons, how we recruit our troops and where they are stationed, and what we believe the military's mission to be. If we believe that our adversary is expanding, unreasoning, and malevolent, we will act accordingly.

We will, first of all, revive conscription. The myth-makers are worried because we abandoned it at all. We must, they suggest, maintain the flexibility that the draft provided us in the event of emergency. And the emergency is coming. The Warsaw Pact countries are already more heavily armed than the NATO states.

Soviet forces could cut through Europe quickly (one estimate was 48 hours) with little resistance, leading to an "intensive land war" for which the U.S. is ill-prepared without the draft.

This argument surfaced most clearly in the recent draft debate. Draft advocates based their cries of alarm on a feared Soviet invasion of Western Europe; so, for that matter, did the Ford Administration in arguing that standby registration was not necessary.

For those who will fight the war should it come, the Great Fear means the neutron bomb, assignments in Europe, long sea cruises pursued by Soviet submarines which are pursued by American submarines (all just for practice), and the ever-present worry that this might be The Day. It means that The Day could come by accident, for *both* sides have their share in the Great Fear.

It also means stringent limits on action to improve military rights or working conditions. Senate Bill 274, which purports to outlaw military unions but also outlaws much heretofore legitimate activity, is no accident. Neither are the anti-counseling provisions of Senate Bill 1437, successor to the notorious Senate Bill 1. In an emergency atmosphere, there will be emergency legislation to "preserve military effectiveness." If that legislation is badly drawn, it will still pass because protecting national security has become paramount. It may not even be read or debated.

None of this is new. What is new is the hysteria of groups like the Committee on the Present Danger. We are not merely confronted with a powerful adversary, they say; we are on the brink of defeat.

A proposition does not become false because those who espouse it are predictable or improperly moti-

vated—as many myth-makers with ties to the arms establishment surely are. The crucial question is whether the reality supports the myth. If it does, there is a real danger of war by a combination of arms race and miscalculation; and those who are concerned about peace confront two implacable opponents who will not be brought together because they refuse to be. But if reality does not support the myth, efforts to end militarism and war must begin by countering the fear.

The Great Fear is in fact hollow. Yergin suggests that, while the Soviet Union has apparently increased its military expenditures, to conclude that there has been a dramatic Soviet military buildup is misleading. The Central Intelligence Agency, which had previously estimated Soviet military costs as 6-8% of USSR gross national product, suddenly last year produced an estimate of 11-13%. But "the revised figures are upward revisions of estimates of what it costs the Soviets to pay for their military force and equipment; they have nothing to do with any real change in the number or kinds of weapons."

Analyses of Soviet civil defense, and prognostications based upon them, are even more suspect. According to Soviet calculations quoted in a recent article in *National Review* (January 20, 1978), USSR losses in a nuclear war would be only 5%.

But to take these figures at face value ignores the first law of Soviet life, known to anyone who has lived or visited there: Nothing Works As It Is Claimed to Work, and Everyone Knows That It Doesn't Work. Hedrick Smith, in *The Russians,* gives example upon example of Soviet inefficiency, coverup, and common knowledge of both inefficiency and coverup. Surely even the Soviet authorities who made the civil defense calculations made certain they came out as they did. They thereby impressed both the higher-ups and the West, and no doubt earned promotions.

In any case, Yergin argues, "the [Soviet] civil defense program is far too small-scale for a potential 'offensive.' One might just as readily conclude that the Russians are afraid of a war. . . . World War II is very much part of contemporary Soviet culture, and was a very painful period in Soviet history. . . . Twenty million [Soviet] citizens died, and virtually every family was touched. Only 2 percent of that number of Americans was killed. Were experiences reversed, most American leaders would feel compelled to pay obeisance to civil defense."

The "massive rearmament" of the Warsaw Pact nations, also, is less awesome than it appears for three reasons: It is not as massive as fear would make it (though it does exist); many Soviet troops are in Eastern Europe because of Soviet problems with Eastern Europe; and Soviet equipment may not be as reliable as the myth-makers claim (one high-ranking military defector claimed that one-third of the Warsaw Pact's armored vehicles failed to start in practice maneuvers).

In a world of huge armies, overkill, and the ever-present chance that the human race will be extermi-

nated within days, it seems odd to speak of the U.S. or the U.S.S.R. as "weak." Yet that is what the myth-makers would have the public believe. That such views attain the hearing that they do shows more clearly than any other fact our susceptibility to the Great Fear.

Therein lies a real danger. For American policy toward the Soviet Union is the subject of a major debate. Not all of this debate is public, and much of it is based on hysterical myth. The outcome of the debate may determine the fate of humankind. It will almost certainly control what will happen to the draft, to soldiers and sailors who will have to fight should war come, and to many significant free speech rights. We who are concerned about peace and conscience must be involved.

CCCO Notes

Rabbi Hoffman:
Pacifist and Jew

Rob Polner

All young men of draft age in 1940 were faced with the narrow choice of complying with induction orders, or going to jail or a work camp. Jewish men were rarely granted conscientious objector status, yet they had nowhere to turn among fellow Jews if they didn't want to go, didn't want to kill.

That is, until Rabbi Isidor B. Hoffman, the Jewish chaplain at Columbia from 1934 to 1967, the pre-eminent American Jewish pacifist, the Jewish Dorothy

Day, came along. Obsessed by peace the way most men of his day were obsessed by war, in 1941 Hoffman helped found the Jewish Peace Fellowship to aid Jews who refused military service. Previously, Jews were forced to go to the Quakers and other Christian peace churches, or rely on political groups for assistance.

In that war and in subsequent wars, Hoffman, who died Jan. 27, changed the lives of thousands of men. Everett Mendelson, now a Harvard professor, was referred to Hoffman shortly after the outbreak of the Korean War. He was drafted, but unsure if he wanted to serve. After talking to Hoffman for 45 minutes, he decided he indeed had pacifist inclinations and he applied for and received conscientious objector status. Max Kampelman, chief U.S. delegate to the recent Madrid Conference on the Helsinki Accords, was a

Rabbi Hoffman

conscientious objector during World War II and was counselled regularly by Hoffman.

Last Wednesday more than 50 people paid tribute to Hoffman in a memorial service in Earl Hall conducted by Rabbi Charles Sheer. It was a quiet tribute to an extraordinary life.

"It was Isidor Hoffman who played an often dominant role through unflagging speaking, writing, contacting, to win to our cause, either as committed pacifists, or non-pacifist defenders and sympathizers, some of the great personalities of our times, including Albert Einstein," said Jane Evans of the Union of American Hebrew Congregations, who founded the Fellowship with Hoffman.

"And it was Isidor, as I can personally attest, who appeared before many rabbinic, professional and lay agencies to explain and plead the cause of nonviolence and Jewish pacifists," she continued.

Hoffman devoted his life to establishing a Jewish presence in the country's peace movement. A tall broad-shouldered man who spoke with an air of conviction but never dogmatically, he was a devout religionist in an age of science, a pacifist in the bloodiest century in history. And he won the respect of a wide range of people, Jews and non-Jews alike, who could not always agree with his deeply held beliefs about the universality of Jewish ideals and the sanctity of life.

The Rabbi's greatest interest was peace, but it is not possible to understand this obsession without recognizing that his motivations and wellsprings were what he perceived to be Judaism's strong identification with pacifism. Though Judaism is not a pacifist religion, Hoffman believed—along with other influential Jews of his day—that it had a strong strain of nonviolence running through it. He drew on the biblical prophet Isaiah, for instance, who said that peace was God's highest blessing. To this end he believed, with Einstein, that the pioneers of a warless world were the young men who refused military service.

Hoffman's actions were based on religious learning; his views, in one sense, transcended politics. Still, "one of his greatest disappointments," said an admirer after the service, "was that so many Jews turned right—not so much as a political betrayal but as a rejection of the needy and the acceptance, however vicariously, of war."

In creating the Jewish Peace Fellowship, Hoffman joined about 100 others in assisting Jewish war resisters. By and large, only men of Quaker, Mennonite or other "historic peace" churches were granted C.O. status by draft boards. He travelled widely to prisons and work camps, where he brought objectors packages from families and literature on the war. He comforted parents, counselled young men about Judaism and the draft law, and saw to it that no one whose conscience prevented him from participating in wars was abandoned or forgotten.

"For me and for quite a number of my fellow conscientious objectors," Hoffman told this reporter a year ago, "we had a sense of role in service to our country and humanity. It wasn't that we were superciliously or self-righteously condemning our fellow Americans who did engage in military service—many of them had good motives we felt.

"But it is the people who stayed out of that contagion, who kept their eye on the causes of war—how did we get into this, what brought on a great nation to act like beasts as the Nazis did, how can we so reorder society that there won't be another such occasion—who, as pacifists, were effective beyond their number in studying and understanding the longtime struggle for the elimination of war," he said.

Today the Jewish Peace Fellowship has 4,000 members and an ample budget. It actively opposes registration and the draft and has a network of 75 trained draft counselors across the country. The Fellowship maintains contacts with peace groups in Israel and recently submitted a friend-of-the-court brief in Indiana on behalf of a Jehovah's witness who was denied unemployment insurance after he refused to work on munitions in a civilian factory.

Hoffman was the first Jew to join the National Interreligious Service Board for Conscientious Objectors, an umbrella agency for religious organizations; and other Jewish groups now belong. He worked closely with Socialist Party leader Norman Thomas as a member of the board of directors of SANE, a peace and disarmament group. Hoffman also served on both the conservative Rabbinical Assembly and the reform Central Conference of American Rabbis.

Hoffman often expressed disappointment about the turn of events in the Middle East, especially since he worked with philosopher Martin Buber and others 50 years ago in an attempt to establish a bi-national state in Palestine. In recent years he advocated reconciliation between Israelis and Arabs, and was troubled by both the lack of Arab pacifists and near-pacifists who would speak out for peace and by those in the Middle East who sought to turn their countries into military bases for the Great Powers.

It was evident at the memorial service that Hoffman was regarded highly even by those, like Sydney Morgenbesser, Columbia professor of philosophy, who didn't always agree with his views. "His concerns were sincere, his visions sincere, his views worthy of respect," Morgenbesser said.

Just before he died of a heart attack—he was 82—Hoffman organized a dozen residents of the retirement village in Connecticut where he lived into a peace group, which among other things protested the building of a Trident nuclear submarine in nearby Groton. A frequent speaker in local high schools, he was an active pacifist until the very end.

Lying on a hospital bed in Connecticut after his attack, he told his wife, Ida, "I have a great zest for life, but if I have to go I'm ready." For those who knew him and for the thousands of people he helped, Isidor Hoffman's spirit of non-violence and love of life will always survive.

Broadway (Columbia University Spectator), March 19, 1981.

Afghanistan—Why We Should Care

Robert Canfield, Associate Professor of Anthropology, Washington University in St. Louis

In Badakhshan, a remote province of Afghanistan, a pregnant woman strapped explosives to her body, threw herself under a Soviet tank, and blew it up.

In Kabul, the capital city, unarmed men stood before machine-gun emplacements, daring the gunners to shoot them; when they were shot down other men took their places and were also killed; they did this, according to the *Christian Science Monitor,* "until the soldiers were so ashamed they ran away."

Also in Kabul, women and children threw blankets soaked in kerosene over tanks and tried to set them on fire with Molotov cocktails.

In Paktia, an eastern province, villagers attacked a group of Soviet-led Afghan soldiers with swords, knives, antiquated rifles, handguns, even shovels.

In the western city of Herat, rioting crowds decapitated 35 Soviet "advisers" and paraded the heads on poles in the streets.

In other places, children plastered mud on the gunsights and peepholes of Soviet tanks so that snipers would pick off the tank crew as they emerged to clean off the mud.

These reports appeared in 1980 in such diverse sources as the *Afghanistan Times,* the *Omaha World-Herald,* the *National Review,* and the *New York Times.* They tell of the acts of violence and courage by which the people of Afghanistan resist the Soviet occupation.

To most Americans, Afghanistan is one of the most remote countries on earth. The Soviet invasion there appears no more than a distant, isolated tragedy. The Europeans, generally more interested in international events, feel likewise. A prominent European political analyst quoted in *U.S. News and World Report* said, "Many in Europe want to close their eyes to the change that has occurred. . . ."

If indeed change has occurred as a result of the Soviet invasion, understanding that change requires more than the obvious reasons for the Soviet invasion. The moves of a chess master must be understood as part of a plan; in the case of Soviet intentions, it is as necessary to study the moves that are not made as the ones that are. Truth is not served by the authorities who tell us that the Soviet invasion is only an isolated event, a local act, merely an attempt by the Soviets to control a local irritation on their southern flank.

The truth is that the invasion has already affected political relations all over the world and will continue to do so. The Soviets have both a long-range plan that involves Afghanistan and an immediate, short-range goal in the specific situation that precipitated the inva-

sion. The Afghan people may be far away, but their struggle does relate closely to U.S. affairs and the outcome of their struggle will affect America's future.

First, certain geophysical conditions have obliged the Soviet Union to have a vital interest in Afghanistan for more than a century. One of these conditions is that Russia, despite many material advantages—rich agricultural lands and diverse and abundant mineral resources—has the major problem of no year-round port on the open sea, except on the Pacific. The northern ports are frozen in winter and the Black Sea ports are controlled by the Turks at the Dardanelles and Bosporus Straits. This condition contributed to the "great game" in the 19th Century between the British, who controlled India and had close ties with Persia, and the Russians, who considered it a kind of "manifest destiny" that they should expand into neighboring territories and obtain direct access to the sea, either the Mediterranean or the Indian Ocean. This problem is not now defunct, as some people suppose: early in the Iranian crisis, Turkish officials stopped all traffic through the straits for a few days, thus immobilizing Soviet ships in the Black Sea.

The other geophysical feature influencing political affairs in Central Asia is that Afghanistan sits astride the historic corridors of trade and conquest between the great population centers of Eurasia. Through this region have passed the caravans that linked India, China, Europe, and the Middle East. Also through this region have passed the great conquerors of Asia: Alexander, Mahmood of Ghazni, Genghis Khan, Tamerlane, Babur, Nadir Shah, and many others. Formerly, the importance of this region lay in its position on the way to India to the southeast and to Persia and Mesopotamia to the southwest—the flow of conquest normally moving from north to south. At the current time its importance lies in its control of the corridors between the Soviet Union to the north and Baluchistan and Pakistan to the south, which have shores on the Indian Ocean, and its control of certain corridors into Iran.

That makes Afghanistan, along with Baluchistan, a piece of real estate precious to the Soviet Union. The *U.S. Naval College Review* noted several months before the invasion: "Soviet access through Pakhtoonistan and Baluchistan to the Indian Ocean, a distance of only 300 miles, would enable the Soviet navy to operate for extended periods at a great distance from Russian shores, to service Soviet ships that increasingly patrol the area, and permit a Soviet naval presence in areas close to important oil tanker routes to Western Europe, the United States and Japan."

The importance of an Indian Ocean seaport to the Soviet Union should be evident in this: in the last 10 years it has constructed the largest and most modern navy in the world.

Context two involves the locations of vital resources. The most prominent resource in or near the Central Asian region is, of course, oil. Most of that lies on the Persian Gulf. The United States imports about half the oil it uses, Europe 85 percent, and Japan 100 percent.

Most of that oil—about two-thirds of the non-communist industrial world's oil supply—comes from the Persian Gulf.

Another major source of oil in this Central Asian region lies in the opposite direction: within the Soviet Union. The Soviet Union is the world's largest oil producer—12.1 million barrels a day—and it is the second largest oil exporter—about 3.3 million barrels a day. Most of its exported oil goes, of course, to satellite countries, but about a third of it is sold to western Europe and Japan. So the Soviet Union, unlike the other major powers, has more than enough oil for its own needs. And this is true despite its poor petroleum technology; depths that Western technology can drill in six months take Soviet technology five years.

However, because of rising domestic consumption, the Soviet Union may have to import oil within five or six years. How long it will be before Soviet petroleum needs outstrip production is unclear, and how the Soviets will deal with the problem is likewise unclear. They could improve technology, limit export, or acquire oil from the Middle East, most likely from the Persian Gulf region.

Besides the oil of the Persian Gulf there is another

set of valuable resources that could be reached easily by the Soviet Union through Afghanistan and Baluchistan. This is in southern Africa, where there are some of the richest mineral deposits in the world. Over 90 percent of the world's supply of chromium, vital to the aircraft industry, is found in two countries, South Africa and Zimbabwe. The Soviet Union also has vast chrome deposits, so denying African sources to the West puts the USSR in an even more advantageous position.

Besides chromium, Africa also has large deposits of other industrially important minerals: copper, uranium,

platinum, manganese; not to mention the commercially valuable deposits of diamonds, gold and silver.

The third context is political—the policies of the great powers. The political policies of the major powers have always been an important factor in Central Asian affairs. For the British in the 19th Century and for the United States since World War II, the policy has basically been the same: to contain the Russians on their southern flank. American policy, further, included the idea of developing a "northern tier"—Turkey, Iran, Afghanistan, and Pakistan—as the barrier against Soviet expansion to the south. Iran in recent years became a main bulwark of that tier. In 1953, fearing that the duly elected Premier Musaddiq would not respond well to Western pressures, the CIA overturned him and restored to power the Shah, whom Musaddiq had ousted. The United States sold the Shah a massive package of foreign assistance, most of it military aid, and it was largely paid for by Iranian oil. By 1975 Iran had the fourth most powerful military machine in the world—after the United States, the USSR, and Israel.

In the U.S. plan, Afghanistan was to be a buffer zone, not a military bastion against the Soviet Union as Iran was. Thus, when Afghan Prime Minister Daood requested military aid from Vice President Nixon in 1954, Nixon turned him down. The United States would offer some forms of domestic aid, he said, but no military assistance.

Daood eventually took his military needs to the Soviet Union, and Afghanistan thus became the first nation to receive aid from both the United States and the Soviet Union. The desire to win Afghan friendship was the aim of both sides, and the Afghans were the beneficiaries. This suited United States policy, since the Shah still guarded the real prize, Iran and the Persian Gulf. As long as the Shah was strong, Afghanistan's importance lay only in its remaining friendly and neutral. This was presumably acceptable, if not ideal, to the Soviet Union as well.

As far as the Soviets were concerned, the real worry was China. Mao had long since pulled out of Soviet control. The border between China and the USSR, the longest in the world, had been the site of many skirmishes. And after 1972, relations between China and the United States dramatically warmed up. A coalition of the United States and China along with the European nations and Japan promised to be a formidable bloc indeed.

These conditions set limits on viable political activity for the Soviet Union in Central Asia. The conditions placed a high value on any development in the nations of the "northern tier" that would favor the Soviet Union. A weakening of the barricade would provide an opening for the Soviet Union to make moves that could outflank this China-western coalition and strengthen the Soviet position in relation to the Persian Gulf and Eastern Africa.

Two developments in Central Asia made such a move possible and those were the specific circumstances that precipitated the invasion. One was the collapse of the Shah. When the Shah fell, the "northern tier" policy fell with him. If the Shah had stayed in power, he would have had the ability to undermine any serious Soviet activity in Afghanistan, Pakistan, or Baluchistan. Prince Daood, who took over Afghanistan in the coup of 1973, had been sensitive to that. Eventually losing confidence in the Soviet Union, he eased closer to the Shah. When he began to remove the Marxists in his own cadre, they overturned him in April 1978.

That was the second critical development. It was a break for the Soviet Union that the Shah began to have troubles of his own after the Afghanistan coup. These developments in Iran and Afghanistan tipped the balance of power along the "northern tier" and made it possible for the Soviet Union to make more decisive moves in Central Asia.

The leader of the coup that overturned Daood in April 1978 was Nur Muhammad Taraki; the group that he led was known as the Khalq ("masses") party. The name is misleading because not one of the key figures in this party identified with the traditional Islamic culture of the masses. All of them had been trained abroad, all spoke and wrote at least one western language well. It was as western, as urban, and as middle class a group as you could find in Afghanistan. They were, however, ideological Marxists of an extreme sort, having split away from another, more moderate Marxist party, the Parcham ("banner") party.

Even though the new regime was well received at first, the attitude of the masses soon became quite negative. By the summer of 1978 repressive measures were required in order to get the people to cooperate. Popular resentment gathered quickly. This took shape, at first, as complaints against Hafizullah Amin, Taraki's second in command. But it soon also took form as localized rebellions. By the end of the year there was trouble in every rural area of the country. Popular resentment was also evident in the growing number of desertions from the Afghan army—which of course Amin used to enforce his policies.

By March 1979, less than a year after Taraki's coup, separate rebellions were exploding all over the country. Without coordination, without even trusting each other, rebel groups were attacking convoys and military bases, blowing up bridges, and assassinating government officials. Members of the Khalq party were captured, and, if not killed, deprived of their mustaches and, sometimes, of their upper lips—the mustache having become an informal mark of party membership.

In spring 1979 Soviet advisers took command of the Afghan air force and began to supervise the army more closely. They tried to intimidate the Afghan people. In March, retaliating for an uprising in Herat, helicopter gunships attacked people as they were coming home from Friday prayers. These "flying tanks" can fire 6,000 rounds a minute; they can level a forest or village in a few minutes. On that day in March, several thousand people died in the attack. In the northern part of the country Afghan security forces, advised by Soviet officers, drowned 1,500 Hazara young men.

But the more the Soviets became involved, the more fiercely and sacrificially the Afghan people resisted. Herat, decimated as it was, rose up again in a general strike and public rioting. In the north, 1 million Tajiks were in open revolt. The rebels claimed full control of 12 provinces. At least one of these areas, the Kunar valley, set up its own adjudicative and administrative structure to serve the needs of its population.

Soviet officials, plainly mystified by the intensity and breadth of the resistance, sent in three study groups to look at the situation. The first came in spring 1979. Another group arrived in the early summer. Finally, in mid-August a delegation of 118 people, including 12 Soviet generals, was sent to blanket the whole country.

They stayed for two months, trying to find out why the Khalq regime was collapsing. While this study was in the field, one of the most obvious countermeasures was determined: Hafizullah Amin would have to be removed. The decision was apparently made while Taraki was at the conference of non-aligned nations in Cuba. Taraki stopped in Moscow on the way back and was informed of the plan. Amin was too, however, because Taraki's bodyguard was a personal friend of

Amin's. On Sept. 13, 1979, Amin was invited to the Palace (now called the People's House). A shootout took place and Taraki was killed, apparently by military personnel loyal to Amin. Amin assumed control of the government.

Amin acquired a bundle of problems. The grassfire had become an inferno. On the day after Taraki was killed, a leading person in Kandahar was wounded in an assassination attempt; on the way to the hospital in a taxi he was killed by another rebel group. About the same time the Kabul chief of police was killed while traveling in Logar.

Soon afterward rebels stormed the Soviet embassy, killing six members of the embassy staff, and also, reportedly, the head of the military police in Kabul. Amin apparently controlled only Kabul. Roads were unsafe, and desertions from the army had hit an all-time high. The economy was in trouble. New conscription orders and a doubling of military salaries did not stanch the hemorrhage afflicting the military. The troops that remained showed no heart to fight. Even the "People's Defense Committees," civilian militias set up by the Khalq regime, were disappearing and their weapons were falling into rebel hands. For that reason, Amin withdrew support from them. He attempted to secure his position by surrounding himself with trusted associates—most of whom, in traditional Afghan custom, were relatives. One of those was soon assassinated.

This was the condition of Amin's government in November 1979. Soviet officials had been spending a few weeks reviewing their research on the rebellion, trying to decide what to do about it. The following must have been weighed in their deliberations:

• The Soviets knew that the rebels had nothing more than ordinary small arms. Despite their accusations of CIA or Pakistani or Chinese complicity, the Soviets knew very well that there was little modern weaponry on the other side to oppose them. Never since World War II had the Soviet Union invaded a country where it expected to be

met by fully armed opposition.

- The Soviets also knew that if they withdrew their already sizable support from the Afghanistan government, the regime would fall into militant Islamic hands. What that would mean was already becoming evident in Iran.
- The Iranian revolution was of course by now boiling. The American hostages were taken at the very time the Soviets were pondering their options in Afghanistan. Conceivably, the Soviets expected the United States soon to attack Iran. A Soviet move into Afghanistan in December 1979 or January 1980 might have been calculated to correspond with an American action in Iran, and might have blunted world reaction against the Soviets.

They may also have considered the risk involved in invading Afghanistan, but probably not very seriously. Soviet leaders probably did not think there was much danger of a military setback. By the end of 1980, of course, it was clear that the Afghans have done better than expected. A loss could undermine Soviet control of Central Asia, where the Russians are not popular anyway. A decisive loss could weaken Soviet control of their own country, just as the defeat of Russia by the Japanese in 1905 eventually led to the collapse of the Czar. The Russian people have not forgotten the toll of World War II.

In any case, the decision was made to invade and to remove Amin. The immediate tasks were political and military. The political side of the invasion was to arrange for the legitimation of the invasion. That did not work out. A Soviet deputy minister for foreign affairs was sent to Kabul to persuade Amin to do two things: to request the Soviets formally to send troops into Afghanistan, and to step aside so that Babrak Karmal, of the more moderate Parchami wing of the Marxist group, could take over. Amin apparently refused to do either.

There was more fighting in the "People's House" and Amin and several other persons, including the Soviet deputy minister, were killed. This deprived the Soviets of the legitimacy they wanted. They could only claim, as they did, that the man they had killed had been the one who invited them in. Also, the bitter resistance of the Afghan troops in Kabul in the first few days showed how welcome the Soviet troops were. Moreover, Babrak Karmal was not in place to take over the government immediately. The *Manchester Guardian* reported that after the invasion began, his voice was broadcast, as if on Kabul Radio, announcing his ascension to power. Actually, the broadcast came from Radio Tashkent in the USSR; Kabul Radio carried on its usual programming all day long.

The military side of the invasion went well. On Christmas Day 1979, air transport planes began to land at Kabul airport. More than 150 flights in two days brought in as many as 10,000 troops. Convoys crossed the border in the north in two places. For a number of days troops poured in. Eventually nine or 10 divisions were ensconced in the country and another four or five were poised at the border—altogether, about 100,000 men.

Besides the military and political dimensions of the invasion, there was an administrative one. In January 1980, after the military phase was well under way, the Soviets flew in 5,000 bureaucrats to run the country. These were not advisers. They were native speakers of Tajik-Dari who knew how to read and write the Dari (Persian) language, capable of wading into, and making order out of, the bureaucratic mess left by disheartened and recalcitrant Afghan bureaucrats. One Afghan official who escaped the country said he was ordered "not to show my face in the office unless it is to collect my pay."

Now it is possible to summarize the Soviets' reasons for invading: They were obviously concerned about putting out the grassfire resistance against the Khalq regime. This was a precipitating cause, but not the only one; the long-range goals were those set by the geopolitical context. They invaded in order to establish a better position from which to do the following: to establish a base on the Indian Ocean; to gain control over oil on the Persian Gulf; to strengthen their relationship with, and influence over, the nations of southern Africa; and to outflank the China-American coalition.

The Soviet invasion of Afghanistan has probably been more costly than Soviet officials foresaw. There is a chance they now see some risks in the operation they had not noticed before—like the risk of having the world's strongest war machine embarrassed by a motley assemblage of tribesmen, merchants, civil servants, women and children.

But even if the Soviets have not done as well as expected, their plan is by no means foiled. The Soviets have a firm grip on Afghanistan, and they have the military might to continue to hold it. Once the 1980 Moscow Olympics were over, the Soviets were free to send in additional troops without so much world notice. Even before that, in April 1980, N. H. Kaul reported in *The Press Trust* of India that the Russians had already moved ballistic missiles into the country, some of them possibly carrying nuclear warheads. They have 300 agents working among the Baluch, to soften the resistance which they should reasonably expect there. It may take time, but as long as they have the resources, time can be on their side. They need not complete the game at once to win it, and they have reason to believe at this point that they will win it.

The Soviets are committed to holding Afghanistan. They may have been drawn in too soon by the brushfire and under undesirable circumstances, and they may have botched their invasion politically; but having been drawn in, they are going to stay—even if the price is high, as it may be.

That is why the resistance of the Afghanistan peoples is so important. The Afghans are now the immediate, if not the ultimate, deterrent against a Soviet push to the Indian Ocean and/or the Persian Gulf.

This article is reprinted from the Washington University magazine.

Citizens! hold fast—discipline Your Fear—it is for the Good ✚ of the People
on this the Law is clear............................this Way quickly—he's hiding here
within—the cowering conscript Prays............while we've a War to win

Francis A. Fitzgerald

106

Alternatives To War

Progress with Chemistry

Chemical disarmament has been a major topic for discussion at the United Nations for the past 10 years or so, but as yet, no international agreement has been reached. Indeed, since the conclusion some years ago of a separate convention on the prohibition of the development, production and stockpiling of biological weapons and on their destruction, there has been virtually no progress towards the prohibition of the production and stockpiling of chemical weapons. At the same time, recent progress in military chemical technology has resulted in the imminent possibility of a new generation of chemical weapons—the binary nerve-gas weapons—appearing in the chemical arsenals. Such a development may have grave consequences for the prospects of reaching agreement on chemical disarmament.

The need for a convention prohibiting the possession of chemical weapons makes it necessary to study problems connected with the destruction and conversion of these weapons. In particular, we need to discuss the problems connected with the destruction and conversion of present stockpiles of chemical warfare (CW) agents and munitions; the destruction and conversion of CW research and development facilities; the verification of such destruction and conversion, and confidence-building measures; and the environmental and occupational health hazards involved in maintaining and handling stockpiles of CW agents and munitions.

SIPRI

What Do We Really Need for National Security?

While more money may add to military strength, it doesn't necessarily add to our national security. What do we really need?

- **Fiscal Responsibility in the Pentagon:** We don't want to compete with the Russians by building up ineffective or simply excessive military forces. Many new U.S. weapons are overpriced, and the mix of weapons is tilted too much toward complex, expensive systems. The Pentagon also has failed to make hard choices between new programs, preferring to reduce maintenance and stretch out production rather than cut something out entirely. Just because we spend more doesn't mean we're stronger.
- **Military Restraint:** Simply adding to military strength doesn't assure our security either. As Vietnam demonstrated, we invite disaster when we overestimate the usefulness of military force. We need to be smart as well as strong, and these days being smart means showing military restraint.
- **Arms Control:** Effective arms control will ensure our security better than an unrestrained nuclear weapons race. Reagan does not seem eager to pursue arms control; but he'll blow the top off the budget without it.
- **A Strong Economy:** Ensuring the health of our economy and diversifying our energy sources is at least as important to national security as military strength. As one economist put it, our failure to achieve energy independence is the "moral equivalent of defeat."

Military quick-fixes are no answer to the complex political and economic problems facing the world today. Throwing more and more money at the Pentagon is no substitute for a more effective foreign policy.

Coalition for a New Foreign and Military Policy

Some Other Approaches to Comprehensive Treaties

Besides freezes or SALT-plus-reductions, there are other formulations. Prime Minister Pierre Elliott Trudeau proposed a method of "suffocation" of the nuclear arms race by negotiating four measures: a comprehensive test ban; an agreement to stop the flight-testing of all new strategic delivery vehicles; a prohibition on production of fissionable material for weapons purposes; and an agreement to limit and then reduce military spending on strategic systems. (It is admitted that the latter would require a Soviet openness in reporting, comparing and verifying such expenditures, which is, of course, wholly non-existent now on the Soviet side.)

For those who are technically minded, there is the proposal of Professor Sidney Drell that the sum total of warheads plus launchers be limited to 10,000 at most (e.g., a ten-headed missile could be turned into ten single-warheaded missiles and still stay below the limit; thus, this is an upper limit with much flexibility below). (See *International Security*, Winter, 1980.)

Still another approach is that of Ivan Selin, who argues (op. cit.) that Soviet-American relations are likely to continue to be bad, that SALT agreements can occur only when they happen to be improving, but that, even so, unless these agreements are significant *militarily*, ratification on both sides will not occur. He believes future agreement should focus on maintaining the survivability of land-based ICBMs on each side; maintaining the viability of the U.S. bomber force to penetrate Soviet air defenses; and trading off the vulnerability of Western medium-range missiles in Europe against diminutions in the threat to Europe from comparable missiles in the Soviet Union.

Federation of American Scientists, 1981.

Zero in Moscow

Ground Zero Week came to the Soviet Union on April 19 [1982]. It lasted less than two minutes.

What was the subversive message that caused the K.G.B. plainclothesmen to pounce instantly on seven demonstrators and the banner they unfurled in Moscow's Red Square? The banner read "Bread, Life, and Disarmament." And what was the dangerous appeal contained in the leaflets the K.G.B. seized before they could be distributed? The leaflets called on the Soviet government to shift spending from arms to food aid.

The incident underlines the difficulties facing the European and American anti-nuclear campaigns. The Soviet Union has greeted those campaigns with encouragement, but it will not allow even the most innocuous of peace messages to reach its population through channels not subject to government control. So the pressures exerted on East and West are distinctly asymmetrical.

This does not mean, as some defenders of established Western arms policies have suggested, that the anti-nuclear campaigns are doing more harm than good. It does mean that those elements of the peace movement who are truly convinced that *bilateral* disarmament is the only likely disarmament will have to make their position dramatically clear. One way to do so is to take advantage of the fact that not all representative symbols of the Soviet government lie within K.G.B. territory. Every demonstration of discontent with American and NATO policy—and may there be many!—must be matched by equally vigorous and visible demonstrations outside Soviet embassies, consulates, travel bureaus, etc. The message may not get through to the Soviet people but at least it will reach the Soviet government: that the prospects for backing away from nuclear suicide are dim unless both sides are resolved to back away together.

Commonweal, May 7, 1982

Mea Culpa

Formerly I was a very dedicated nuclear warrior. I was all for developing nuclear weapons like neutron bombs to help our allies stay free. But I've come to the realization that it's not going to work.

Samuel Cohen, the father of the neutron bomb, defending it as a humane weapon but recognizing that its use would trigger nuclear war "and we'll be wiped out as a free nation." March 27, 1982

Ditty

Anonymous U.S. soldier, WW II (written on a latrine wall in Great Britain)

Quiz

"Why doesn't the U.S., which is still proud of its own revolution, befriend an occasional revolution in the twentieth century?"

Bill Monroe to Secretary of State Haig on "Meet the Press," April 4, 1982

A Scenario: The Aftermath (1 Year Later)

It is hard to continue to feel a major tragedy for a full year. After a while numbness sets in and blocks that part of the mind. We now pay attention to the daily functions of our lives and try not to dwell too much on the past.

The people miss being part of a nation—yet they are still afraid of their "neighbors" in the nearby towns which are not part of our Association, an "alliance" of all the towns in this county and two from the next one.

This arrangement enables us to get by and we trade with some of our "neighbors" who belong to other Associations. So far only local governments have survived the attack (except for Alaska, N. Dakota, Oregon and New Hampshire, which are still organized on a state basis). There are supposed to be about 1,500 fragments of what only last year was the United States of America. There are rumors that the nation will come together again but I think it will take a long time. There are still regions of the country which people simply avoid. The Eastern megalopolis, for example, is a nightmare which is usually observed by airplane.

From a Hudson Institute scenario of a nuclear war in which 5,000 megatons reached the U.S. (The Nuclear Crisis of 1979, William M. Brown)

Living, Mothering, Resisting

Molly Rush

One day, two weeks after my arrest for taking part in a protest against nuclear weapons, I had a vision of what a long jail term would mean to my family and friends. I wrote a reflection on it in my notebook.

At the preliminary hearing, my husband and six children had been on hand to support me. They had come to visit me in jail the previous day. They want me home again. I want to return, to make roast chicken or spaghetti sauce, their favorites. I want to watch Bob, 14, and Greg, 12, grow up, as I have the older ones.

This is what I wrote:

> Today I felt my death to all that. In the vision I have died and my ghost lives on, watching. I saw the boys grow tall, begin to shave, making occasional visits or sending notes, remembering me with fondness and, perhaps, resentment.
>
> I've cracked their world open. As time goes on and the ragged edges heal, I'll be left out of their everyday reality, tombed behind glass. If I were really dead, they might feel my presence, as I do my mother's. Instead, they'll visit and I'll wonder at the changes in them, no longer daily and imperceptible, but visible and startling. Talk won't be free and easy, but self-conscious.
>
> Perhaps I'll become a sort of myth: "Remember when she did this?" or "We went there with Mom." But my daily, living reality has perished— at least for months, perhaps years.
>
> I've just begun to realize because it was my own decision to interfere with the production of nuclear weapons that could kill them, they may experience the same guilt/anger reaction a close relative may have toward a suicide.
>
> In any case, as the first grief passes, friends and family will find that the intensity of pain and loss will subside.
>
> I'm reminded of my mother's bout with cancer.

On the day of her operation we, eight brothers and sisters, huddled together during the more than 12 hours of waiting. For days we kept vigil outside the intensive care unit. Later, we visited frequently; she was constantly in our thoughts. But as time passed, after her homecoming, I'd find myself thinking with a start that a whole day might pass without a thought of her penetrating my busy life.

Eventually, over the five-year illness, she became scheduled into my life; every week or two I'd take the day off to accompany her to the oncology clinic. Certainly, at other times, I would think, pray, cry or visit. But days might go by without her pain and suffering penetrating my consciousness. Visits actually cheered me up because my imaginings of her condition were worse than the reality. She'd smile and her eyes would dance; clearly she enjoyed the small pleasures that life gave her. I'd feel relief and less guilt as she'd assert, "I'm fine."

So now I picture my absence as involving a lessening of grief, as life goes on without me, as my presence is gradually forgotten, as new patterns of living emerge without my being a part. The pain will numb, then go away. I pray I can stand being a living corpse.

It's nearly four weeks since I wrote that in my notebook. Finally, I will try to integrate what I felt that day with what brought me here, to a maximum security prison, held in lieu of $125,000 bail, facing eight charges ranging from burglary and criminal conspiracy to criminal mischief, charges that may mean years in prison, walled off from the world I love, a world of family and friends, my satisfying, frustrating work for peace and justice, of walks in the country, laughter over a beer, listening to good music, joking with my kids, all the things that bring joy to my life.

Yet I feel a quiet peace, even a sense of joy as I sit in my cell reading my mail or pondering scripture in solitude, but in unity with hundreds who share our vision of a world in which we can offer peace as a gift to our children.

"Our destiny is to live out what we think, because unless we live what we know, we don't even know it." (Thomas Merton, *Thoughts in Solitude*)

Merton has been one of my guides, especially over the past seven years. It was his vision of linking con-

templation with a world of action that has inspired the work of the Thomas Merton Center in Pittsburgh.

Larry Kessler founded it in 1972, as a response by Catholics to the Viet Nam War. Ecumenical and independently funded from the start, we took the motto from Paul VI, "If you want peace, work for justice." In 1973, my youngest of six children, Greg, was entering kindergarten.

In the previous 10 years I'd been very active with the Catholic Interracial Council (CIC) of Pittsburgh. It began in 1963, at the height of the civil rights movement, when CIC members leafleted my parish, St. Bernard, located in an affluent suburb, Mt. Lebanon, that borders our own more modest borough of Dormont. I was a member of the Christian Mothers group in the parish and had gone to hear Father John LaBauve, a black priest, speak at one of our monthly meetings.

Until then the story of the civil rights struggle had come to me only on television. I remember being deeply inspired by the moral strength shown during the lunchcounter sit-ins as demonstrators sat in dignity while louts poured ketchup on their heads. I was ashamed that, busy as I was with four young children, I was doing nothing to help in the struggle. So I sent in my $5 dues and became a member of CIC.

Acting for Change

I soon found myself leafleting churches, too, and learning as I went along. Soon I was marching in protests and helping with a study of Catholic grade school texts. I'd been stunned to read in a text used by my fourth grader, Gary, that "the Jews are the world's

saddest people because they turned away from Christ." This, nearly 20 years after Hitler's gas ovens! Despite church teachings against racism, children were being taught with textbooks studded with stereotypes. Our report, when published, hit *The New York Times*. With all the pressure from many sources, school textbooks around the country were revised. Black stories and faces began to appear in their pages. I saw that change was possible. I also learned that it was usually just a few determined people who brought about change.

So it was in 1973, when Larry was leaving for Boston, having made our storefront peace and justice center a reality. He asked me to take over. There would be three nuns working full time, but he thought it important that a layperson be director. "But I can only work part time." That was okay (there being no alternatives). In July 1973, then, with no college education and no experience beyond my 10 years with CIC, I plunged in, again learning as I went along. It was the year of the Sahel drought; the problem of world hunger went to the top of our agenda alongside the moral atrocity of Viet Nam.

I began studying the causes of hunger. They went far beyond droughts, to the injustice of a worldwide system that was built and secured with military might. We put together a slideshow that explained some of this, and it was widely used.

Meanwhile, I was learning that a few multinational corporations were making it impossible for poor people to grow their own food, as they bought up tracts for export crops. At the same time they were increasing

"YOU'RE IN FOR MURDER? FUNNY, I'M IN FOR REFUSING TO!"

monopoly control of more and more of the US food industry, and kept food prices up. And these politically powerful companies were influencing the US Government to support military dictators around the world who, with an elite few in every country, would exploit their own people for their own benefit.

As time went on, the center became involved in a wide variety of projects, from a food cooperative, a soup kitchen and a food bank, to recovering food that might otherwise be wasted from supermarkets, restaurants, etc., and distributing it to people in need of it. We have organized, lobbied and demonstrated for desegregation and welfare rights, against nursing home abuses and the B-1 bomber.

In recent years I have devoted a great deal of time in studying the terrifying injustice of the nuclear arms race, which, as the Vatican has stated, is a "machine gone mad" and a "theft from the poor."

Last year, $600 million was spent worldwide on armaments, including first-strike nuclear weapons that imperil everyone and make no one secure. Worldwide nuclear stockpiles are the equivalent of 1,300,000 Hiroshimas. But that isn't enough.

The cold war revival of the 80's is far more dangerous than the 50's version. Then, deterrence was the official policy. Leaders seemed to understand that nuclear war would bring unimaginable destruction to our planet. Today, the emphasis is on fighting and winning a "limited" nuclear war, although how long such a war could remain limited is a matter of conjecture. The development of first-strike weapons that can target and destroy enemy missile silos places nuclear war on a hairtrigger. The spread of nuclear bombs to more and more nations multiplies the risks.

For these reasons, most experts agree that nuclear war will occur in the coming decades. We are slouching, not toward Bethlehem, but toward Armageddon.

Who is doing anything to prevent such a disaster? The build-up of weapons is speeding up; the time to stop the madness is frighteningly short. Yet we sleepwalk toward the abyss of nuclear destruction, pretending it doesn't exist in the "real world" but only in the increasingly unreal fantasies of the arms specialists, those who plan and, in the face of our silence, will carry out the deaths of our children, of life on our planet.

> The desert [Merton wrote] is the home of despair. And despair, now, is everywhere. . . . Despair is an abyss without bottom. Do not think to close it by consenting to it and trying to forget you have consented.

This, then, is our desert: to live facing despair, but not to consent.

I was finding that people felt helpless against a menace that they at least subconsciously knew threatened their future.

I learned that around the country there were a few staunch souls who had dedicated their lives and risked their freedom to confront the nuclear beast. Philip and Daniel Berrigan were among these. Famous for draft board raids in the 1960's, they had, with faith, persisted against the Bomb long after the media had lost interest.

Philip and his wife, Liz McAlister, had founded Jonah House in Baltimore and with a few friends had maintained a persistent, dogged presence at the Pentagon. With symbolic acts, pouring blood and ashes, they had tried to speak the truth of what was the dirty secret of the shiny technology being developed—they would be used to kill.

Like Old Testament prophets who called for the destruction of our nuclear idols and a return to faithfulness, Phil and Liz acted on their words, again and again going to jail for their acts of civil disobedience to the government in obedience to God.

When I first met Phil in Pittsburgh, I felt fascinated and challenged by the man. But I resisted, feeling he was too judgmental. My stance has always been to encourage any sign of hope, of activity on behalf of justice. He seemed to be saying these were all worthless, that we were called to risk even our lives if we were to be faithful to God's judgment. I was pragmatic, not certain his methods were bringing any more results than mine. I continued to Read *Year One*, Jonah House's newsletter, with increasing interest. But what could I do? I had a family. I couldn't be traipsing down to the Pentagon, getting arrested. What about my children?

As time went on the question became, indeed, what *about* my children? Would they live to grow up or would these weapons with their pushbutton death management go off first?

As I began to speak more and more on the subject, I watched people's reactions. People would lean forward in frightened fascination as I described the threats posed by the arms race. Then they would fold their arms, hugging themselves in a gesture of self-protection. Finally, as though a curtain had come down, I would see that they were shutting it out, the implications were too frightening. What, after all, could *they* do?

I began to be more ready to hear the Berrigan message. When I was invited to be a resource person in Cleveland at a retreat with Dan Berrigan, I agreed to come. That retreat changed my life. We spent the weekend reflecting on the Epistle of James. I prepared a dialogue between Merton and the Apostle James for my section, the first chapter. For two days we reflected together on the Gospel in light of today's world.

James 1:22-25 reads:

> Only be sure that you act on the message and do not merely listen; for that would be to mislead yourselves. A person who listens to the message but never acts upon it is like one who looks in a mirror at the face nature gave, glances and goes away, and at once forgets the image. But the one who looks closely into the perfect law, the law that makes us free, and who lives in its company,

does not forget what is heard, but acts upon it; and that is the one who by acting will find happiness.

No word about results. Those were in God's hands. At last, I was ready to take a step, to act on my beliefs.

In the next year, I was arrested several times, at the arms bazaar in Washington, then at Rockwell International. For years I had leafleted and protested at the headquarters in Pittsburgh of this major military contractor. I had watched friends in Christian Peacemakers be arrested and hauled off for symbolic protests. I never quite had the nerve to join them. Yet the arrest in Washington had taught me what a freeing experience it was: "We count those happy who stood firm." (James 5:11)

As I let go of my trust in myself and began to trust more in God, fears that earlier immobilized me faded away. I was more and more living and acting at one with my conscience.

One of the things that began to happen was very disturbing. I call it the sanctification process. Some people began to respond to me in a sort of hero-worship manner. "*You* take risks. *I* could never do that." Yet I knew my strength was not simply my own. God supplies what you need. It began to seem an evasion of responsibility, to attribute special gifts to someone who essentially was the same old Molly, full of the same weaknesses as they. I wanted to say, "Let go. Let go of your fears, of your need for security. Trust just a little, take a first step, and God will give you the grace to take the second."

Signs of the Times

So, when the idea of the witness at GE was presented to me, I knew I had to consider it seriously. In the past year the signs have been piling up until anyone with half an eye can see which direction we are taking. The SALT II treaty was scuttled after the Soviet invasion of Afghanistan. The Soviet act, instead of being seen as a sign of weakness, their version of the Viet Nam quagmire, has been used as the pretext for a massive new build-up of arms, one which began *before* they sent in troops.

All the lessons of Viet Nam were quickly forgotten, including the fact that we lost despite our huge array of armaments and our use of sophisticated technology. History was rewritten to suggest that even *more* was needed than the massive bombing, 500,000 troops and $150 billion to put down revolution in one small country. Instead of seeing that we lost because the people supported the other side and opposed massive intervention by an outside power, we are allowing preparations for a repeat performance somewhere else. Rapid deployment forces are being readied, this time so that we can destroy our oil supply in order to save it.

Rather than question the sanity of such madness, public opinion has reverted to support for being No. 1.

Frustration over seemingly insoluble economic and social problems in this country has been displaced by support for massive military spending. We can expect to see $1 trillion or more spent on dangerous new weapons systems and provocative intervention forces. These will not guarantee our security. They will guarantee, however, that economic and social problems will worsen, adding to the spiral of tension.

As for the new weapons, we are buying Trident submarines, MX missiles, cruise missiles and, finally, the Mark 12A missile.

The Mark 12A reentry vehicle represents a central threat in that it is planned as a first-strike weapon. In addition to its use on 300 Minuteman III ICBMs, it is being considered for MX, the mobile missile, and for second-generation Trident missiles. Its accuracy and explosive power (335 kilotons, compared to the 11-12 kilotons of the Hiroshima bomb) indicates that it would be used against hardened Soviet missile silos before their ICBMs could be launched.

This is in accordance with the Carter 1980 Presidential Directive No. 59, released for the 35th anniversary of the Hiroshima bombing. It is part of ongoing Pentagon plans since announcement in 1974 by James Schlesinger of a US counterforce policy. For the first time, it is official US policy, formally approved, to prepare for a preemptive first-strike attack against the Soviet Union. No longer is our nuclear weaponry designed solely to deter war; we are equipping ourselves to fight and win a "limited" nuclear war.

Between 1969 and 1978, our nuclear warheads stockpile quadrupled, to 8,000 warheads. With the introduction of these new weapons, our uncertainty increases. With the temptation to use them, our security decreases.

What about the Soviet Union? In each of these new technological developments, the US has led the way. The SALT II treaty, even if signed, will not slow or halt the new weapons system from being deployed. Faced with this new "hair-trigger" nuclear policy and with lack of public understanding of the threat posed, I saw it was clearly time to step up resistance to this new, and infinitely more deadly, cold war of the 1980's.

Further warning signals have been sent to us, in the form of three false nuclear alerts caused by computer foul-ups within the past year that could easily have led to nuclear war by error. Our early warning system allows 15-20 minutes before our weapons are launched. We were six minutes into an alert in November 1979. *Nine minutes from nuclear war*, and the papers carried a paragraph or two. The media have cooperated with Cold War II, playing down protests and publishing without comment scare stories of the invincible Soviet threat. The Soviets' inability to deal with a determined uprising by Polish workers was headlined, but seldom was the point made that all the Soviet weapons were useless against a people determined to resist.

Why should any nation continue to pile up useless weapons that can cut short the passage of life on our beautiful earth?

Family and Future

I love my children very much, from red-headed, quiet Gary, 25, and Danny, 18, with his curly brown hair and beautiful smile, to my younger boys, Bob, 14, sensitive and loving, and Greg, 12, pert, bright and independent. Linda, 23, full of heart and common sense, is married and lives nearby; Janine, 22, athletic, "born again," with a great sense of humor is a senior, studying special education.

I look at them and think about their lives being quenched out by insane government policies that very few pay attention to or understand. Linda wants to have a baby. Can I welcome a grandchild with open arms, then wait for his or her future to be stolen away? My brothers and sisters have tried to understand. But they, like most people, refuse to take in the reality of the threat to their own kids. So they see only the very painful separation we've had to face.

After his last visit to jail, my Bobby had his first asthma attack in a couple of years. I cry that I'm not with him, or Greg.

My husband was opposed, then bewildered, now is doing all he can to support me. It's been a hard struggle for all of us to face up to the reality of my being in jail.

I could have closed my eyes and hoped for the best. But that hope would have been a blind hope based on refusal to see and refusal to act responsibly. Dom Helder Camara writes of the "Abrahamic minorities who, like Abraham, hope when all hope is gone."

So, I exist on a faith that God will see my children

through, not only my jailing, but the darkness of a world of the blind, one that promises them the darkness of death. It is not in nuclear weapons that I place my trust. It is not in that world of blindness and fear and hatred where I place my trust.

"Praise the Lord, all nations,
extol him all you peoples;
for his love protecting us is strong,
The Lord's constancy is everlasting,
O praise the Lord."—(Psalm 117)

"And what is faith? Faith gives substance to our hopes, and makes us certain of realities we do not see."—(Heb. 11:1)

Christianity and Crisis, *December 8, 1980*

Summaries of Five General Sources of War

1. Economic—Quarrels over

   (1) Territory
   (2) Colonies
   (3) Trade
   (4) Roadways
   (5) Waterways
   (6) Boundaries
   (7) Islands
   (8) Ports
   (9) Cities
   (10) Mines
   (11) Industries
   (12) Taxation
   (13) Disbursements
   (14) Monopolies, etc.

2. Dynastic—Disputes over
   (1) Heredity
   (2) Divine Right
   (3) Genealogy
   (4) Right of succession
   (5) Primogeniture
   (6) The qualified electorates

3. Nationalistic causes
   (1) Patriotism
   (2) Racial pride
   (3) National pride
   (4) Envy
   (5) Jealousy
   (6) Traditions
   (7) Spirit of the crowd

4. Religious causes
   (1) Conscientious devotion
   (2) Varying forms of worship
   (3) Fanaticism
   (4) Intolerance
   (5) Persecution
   (6) Rise of science
   (7) Liberalism
   (8) Willingness for martyrdom, etc.

5. Sentimental
   (1) Vision
   (2) Hope
   (3) Sense of right
   (4) Longing for emancipation
   (5) Sympathy
   (6) Temptation to intervention

Words most familiar to the Spelling Book of War

1. Ambition
2. Arrogance
3. Audacity
4. Fanaticism
5. Independence
6. Zeal
7. Persecution
8. Aggression
9. Cruelty
10. Clannishness
11. Adventure
12. Revenge
13. Presumption
14. Vindictiveness
15. Servility
16. Contempt
17. Progressiveness
18. Prejudice
19. Dread
20. Suspicion
21. Ruthlessness
22. Deception
23. Intrigue
24. Greed
25. Consciousness of power

44. Personal magnetism
45. Perfidy
46. Threats
47. Evasions
48. Conspiracies
49. Coalitions
50. Personal rivalry
51. Breaking treaties
52. Plunder
53. Tariff
54. Blockade
55. Popular delirium
56. Love of adventure
57. Disputes
58. Blunders of diplomats
59. Different types of civilization
60. Lust for wealth
61. Spirit of liberty
62. Inhumanity
63. Bigotry
64. Slavery
65. Sectionalism
66. Atrocities
67. Discovery of wealth
68. Agitation for justice
69. Obstinacy
70. Precipitation
71. Assassination
72. Martial spirit
73. Untrustworthiness
74. Insane rulers
75. Racial prejudice
76. Lack of assimilation
77. Intervention
78. Preparedness
79. Proximity
80. Standing armies
81. Secret diplomacy
82. Deliberate provocation
83. Haughtiness
84. Hypocrisy
85. Disappointment
86. Easy-going pacifists
87. Violation of neutrality
88. Ignorance
89. Credulity
90. Betrayal
91. Usurpation
92. Hatred
93. Tyranny
94. Starvation
95. Arson
96. Rape
97. Cruelty
98. Rapacity
99. Murder
100. Slaughter

26. Jealousy
27. Envy
28. Quarrels between subjects
29. Patriotism
30. Reaction in government
31. Repression of progressiveness
32. Exploitation
33. Heavy taxation
34. Democracy
35. Excesses
36. Long past extravagance
37. Confiscation
38. Destitution
39. Despair
40. Genius
41. Longing for glory
42. Love of conquest
43. Visions of empire

Tell A. Turner, Causes of War and The New Revolution *(Boston: Marshall Jones, 1927)*

Life After Nuclear War
The Economic and Social
Impacts of Nuclear Attacks
on the United States

Arthur M. Katz 1982 452 pages $27.50

The nuclear disarmament movement: "Protestant angst" or rational outcry? Bureaucratic gladiators try to convince us it's the former, while a growing rebellion—involving prominent scientists, physicians, educators, and clergymen as well as people from all walks of life—continues to seethe. This concerted effort to alert the public to the immediate and long-range consequences of both limited and full-scale nuclear attacks is substantiated by the data and analysis contained in *Life After Nuclear War*, a new Ballinger publication.

Life After Nuclear War presents a grim scenario of what life will be like for survivors of a nuclear exchange. It fuels the argument that even a limited nuclear war will have no winners. Originally undertaken as a study for the Joint Congressional Committee on Defense Production, *Life After Nuclear War* is an expanded and updated version of that 1979 report, written by Dr. Arthur Katz, a former consultant to the Committee.

Those who believe that a limited nuclear war is acceptable—even winnable—have based their claims on quantitative estimates: how many buildings left intact? how many people will survive? Katz's study goes farther, asking: what will life be like? His is the first thorough consideration of the economic, social, psychological, physical, and political traumas faced by survivors. Questions such as these are answered:

Could medical personnel, assuming enough survive, cope with a decimated drug industry?

What psychological traumas will the sight of untreated dying produce?

Will a transportation system remain intact to deliver food and other vital, but highly centralized, resources?

Will political control, necessary to rebuild society, exist?

Ballinger Publishing Company, P.O. Box 281, 54 Church St., Cambridge, MA. 02138.

But what they killed each other for
I could not well make out.
—*Southey*

Religious Organizations

Roman Catholics, Jews, Baptists, Presbyterians, Evangelicals, Lutherans, Brethren, United Church of Christ, Unitarians, Disciples, Methodists, Episcopalians, Muslims, Orthodox, Buddhists and leaders of virtually every other religious body have taken stands opposing the arms race and nuclear war. To get in touch with others working on this issue contact the local or national office of your denomination, or:

- NATIONAL COUNCIL OF CHURCHES, 110 Maryland Av. NE., Washington, DC 20002, (202) 544-2350.
- UNION OF AMERICAN HEBREW CONGREGATIONS, 2027 Massachusetts Avenue, N.W., Washington DC 20036, (202) 387-2800.
- U.S. CATHOLIC CONFERENCE, 1312 Massachusetts Avenue N.W., Washington DC 20005, (202) 659-6600.
- INTERFAITH CENTER TO REVERSE THE ARMS RACE is a regional/national information resource serving the religious community: 132 N. Euclid Avenue, Pasadena, CA 91101, (213) 449-9430 or 681-4292.
- WORLD PEACEMAKERS is compiling an updated list of such religious statements, and can inform individuals of activities within their denomination. 2852 Ontario Rd., N.W., Washington DC 20009, (202) 265-7582.
- QUAKER PEACE ACTION CARAVAN (Q-PAC) is a project of Quaker Peace and Service, a department of the Religious Society of Friends in Great Britain and Ireland. A Mobile Training and Resource Center, Q-PAC travels to Quaker groups, youth groups or interested service organizations offering their skills and materials in this creative work for peace. They stay for a few days in each location during which time they promote the ideas of disarmament and world peace through films, theatre, puppet shows and general discussions, and through distributing literature. For further information write to: Q-PAC, Friends House, Euston Road, London NW1 2BJ.

CLERGY AND LAITY CONCERNED (CALC), 198 Broadway, New York, N.Y. 10038. For over a decade CALC has been uniting the efforts of civic leaders and religious groups—Protestant, Catholic, Jewish, Buddhist and others—with those of tens of thousands of other citizens who share a justified anxiety over government's misuse of its many powers. In the past CALC has taken up many controversial issues such as U.S. involvement in Vietnam and a nationwide campaign to halt construction of the B-1 bomber. Today it is engaged in spearheading a nationwide movement to:

. . . halt the development, testing and production of nuclear weapons;

. . . stop the construction of new nuclear plants and phase out all operating reactors;

. . . develop safe, renewable energy sources and, in the process create jobs to aid the troubled economy.

Although Clergy and Laity Concerned is now focusing its efforts on achieving a nuclear moratorium, that work is only one facet of its overall program. The volunteers and staff of Clergy and Laity Concerned are engaged in ongoing education/action programs to help bring about desperately needed changes that will help the millions in the world who are victims of injustice or inhuman treatment or who are suffering from hunger. To carry out its work, Clergy and Laity Concerned asks for a $20.00 membership fee.

THE OTHER SIDE: Justice Rooted in Discipleship, P.O. Box 12236, Philadelphia, PA 19144, U.S.A. A monthly magazine; $16.75 in the U.S., $18.75 for out-of-U.S. subscribers. This magazine presents the pressing issues of today's world in a straightforward and personal style. Each issue revolves around a particular theme—world peace, disarmament, the Middle East—with articles and interviews by people who have had direct experience and/or knowledge of the area under discussion. There is an emphasis upon the need for a true manifestation of the Christian spirit in the world today which means, most simply, the focusing upon the commonality which is found among all peoples everywhere—the brotherhood of man. Each issue also contains letters and suggestions by the readership.

THE SOCIETY FOR INTERNATIONAL DEVELOPMENT (SID) "is the largest non-governmental organisation of its kind in the area of international development." Its aims are "to encourage the creation—at national, regional and international levels—of a sense of community among individuals and organizations committed to development; to promote international dialogue on major development issues; to advance the art and science of social and economic development through educational means, including research, publication and discussion, and to provide support and services for national development constituencies committed to these objectives."

For information contact: SID International Headquarters, Palazzo Civitta del Lavoro, 00144 Rome, Italy; SID World Conference Headquarters, 1834 Jefferson Place, N.W., Washington, DC 20036, U.S.A.; SID U.K. Chapter, 6 Homington Court, Albany Park Road, Kingston on Thames KT2 5SP, U.K.

Following are the most recent additions to our ongoing list of groups and organisations that are working for peace and disarmament:

The Atlantic College Peace Studies Project
St. Donat's Castle
Llantwit Major
South Glamorgan CF6, 9WF, U.K.

Campaign Against Militarism
6 Endsleigh Street
London WC1H ODX, U.K.

Central Committee for Conscientious Objectors
2208 South Street
Philadelphia, PA 19146, U.S.A.

Center for Peace Studies
St. Martin's College
Lancaster LA1 3JD, U.K.

Centre Martin Luther King
Avenue de Bethusy 56
1012 Lausanne, Switzerland

Children's Campaign for Nuclear Disarmament
Box 550, RD#1
Plainfield, VT 05667, U.S.A.

CHOICE
1005 Pearl Street
Boulder, CO 80302, U.S.A.

Community for Creative Non-Violence
1345 Euclid Street N.W.
Washington, DC 20009, U.S.A.

Community of the Peace People
224 Lisburn Road
Belfast BT9 6GE
Northern Ireland

Conscience & Military Tax Campaign—U.S.
44 Bellhaven Road
Bellport, NY 11713, U.S.A.

Conscientious Objection to Military Tax (COMIT)
1789-14, Toke-Cho
Chiba City
299-31 Japan

Covenant Peacemaking Program
Fellowship of Reconciliation
Box 271
Nyack, NY 10960, U.S.A.

Creative Mind
26 Linnet Lane
Liverpool, L17 3BQ, U.K.

Dag Hammarskjold Information Center on the Study of Violence and
    Peace
110 Eton Place
Eton College Road
London NW3 2DS, U.K.

Educators for Social Responsibility
c/o Roberta Snow
25 Kennard Road
Brookline, MA 02146, U.S.A.

Federalist Caucus
P.O. Box 19482
Portland, OR 97219, U.S.A.

The Institute for Education in Peace and Justice
3700 West Pine
St. Louis, MO 63108, U.S.A.

International Association of Educators for World Peace
Box 705
Clarksville, MD 21029, U.S.A.

International Peace Research Association Faculty of Law
University of Tokyo
Bunkyoku
Tokyo 113, Japan

International Student Peace Network
Box 282
Kingston, NJ 08528, U.S.A.

Jobs With Peace National Network
2990 22nd Street
San Francisco, CA 94110, U.S.A.

Members of Congress for Peace Through Law
501 House Annex 2
Washington, DC 20515, U.S.A.

Mennonite Central Committee
Peace Section (International)
21 South 12th Street
Akron, PA 17501, U.S.A.

Movement International de la Reconciliation
35 rue van Elewijck
1050 Brussels, Belgium

MX Information Center
232½ University Street
Salt Lake City, UT 84102, U.S.A.

National Mobilization for Survival
48 St. Marks Place
New York, NY 10003, U.S.A.

The New Manhattan Project
15 Rutherford Place
New York, NY 10003, U.S.A.

Non-Violent Direct Action Group
Vale Cinema Road
Chavakachcheri, Sri Lanka

The Nonviolent Tactics Development Project
454 Willamette
Eugene, OR 97401, U.S.A.

Nuclear Weapons Freeze Campaign
4144 Lindell Blvd., 2nd Floor
St. Louis, MO 63108, U.S.A.

Operation Dismantle
Box 3887, Station "C"
Ottawa K1Y, 4M5, Canada

Parliamentarians for World Order
336 East 45th Street
New York, NY 10017, U.S.A.

Peace Advertising Campaign
P.O. Box 24
Oxford OX1 3J2, U.K.

Peace Education Project
Lansbury House Trust Fund
6 Endsleigh Street
London WC1H 0DX, U.K.

The Peace Project
Aloha #244
1290-D Maunakea Street
Honolulu, HI 96817, U.S.A.

Project Ploughshare
Conrad Grebel College
Ontario N2L 3G6, Canada

SANE
514 "C" Street, N.E.
Washington, DC 20002, U.S.A.

Society for Prayer for World Peace
5-26-27 Nakakokubun
Ichikawa, Chiba 272, Japan

Syracuse Peace Council
924 Burnet Avenue
Syracuse, NY 13202, U.S.A.

The Voice of Humanity
8548 Temple Road
Philadelphia, PA 19150, U.S.A.

World Goodwill Newsletter, Transition.

MINI-DIRECTORY OF PEACE STUDIES PROGRAMS

ANTIOCH INTERNATIONAL, Individualized M.A. in Peace Studies, Yellow Springs OH 45387. 513-767-1031
Purpose: Combines theory and action, research and colloquia, independent study, practical skills, overseas experience.
Educational Level: Master of Arts in Peace Studies
Director: Dean Ewell Reagin

ASSOCIATED MENNONITE BIBLICAL SEMINARIES, 3003 Benham Ave., Elkhart IN 46417
Purpose: Provide program of reflection and action in area of church's ministry of reconciliation, facilitate peace witness of members in local congregations and larger communities.
Educational Level: Master of Arts (Peace Studies).
Director: LeRoy Friesen

BETHEL COLLEGE, Peace Studies, N. Newton, Kansas 67117 316-283-2500
Themes: Conflict resolution, war/peace theory, international or transnational studies, and religious and moral dimensions.
Educational Level: Undergraduate with a bachelor degree available as a double major or area of concentration.
Director: Robert S. Kreider

BOSTON COLLEGE, Program for Study of Peace and War, Chestnut Hill MA 02167 617-969-0100
Themes: Conflict resolution, War/Peace theory, and human rights.
Educational Level: Undergraduate level with Associate Degree.
Directors: James Halpin, David Toscano

Center for Conflict Resolution, UNIVERSITY OF WISCONSIN, 731 State St., Madison, WI 53703
Themes: Conflict resolution, social change.
Educational Level: Undergraduate level with possible bachelors degree (in American Institutions with a concentration in Conflict Studies).

Center for Peace Studies, UNIVERSITY OF AKRON, Akron, OH 44325
Themes: Conflict resolution, war/peace theory and international or transnational studies.
Educational Level: Undergraduate level, no degree available.
Director: Warren F. Kuehl

Center for Peaceful Change, KENT STATE UNIVERSITY, Kent, OH 44240
Theme: Conflict resolution, war/peace theory.
Educational Level: Undergraduate level with bachelor degree in peace studies.
Director: Dennis Carey

Center for Teaching International Relations, Graduate School of International Studies, UNIVERSITY OF DENVER, Denver, CO 80218
Educational Program: Recognized as an established academic program but non-degree granting. Research.
Director: Michael G. Fry, Dean

CHAPMAN COLLEGE, Peace Studies Program, Orange CA 92666 714-997-6621
Themes: Conflict resolution, techniques of reconciliation, disarmament, non-violence, history of peace movements.
Educational Level: Undergraduate, minor with required internship.
Chairperson: Barbara E. G. Mulch

COLGATE UNIVERSITY, Program in Peace Studies, Hamilton NY 13346 315-824-1000
Themes: Problems of war and peace, social and economic justice, non-violence and conflict resolution in theory and practice.
Educational Level: Bachelors degree in peace studies
Director: Carolyn Stephenson

Conflict and Peace Studies, UNIVERSITY OF COLORADO, Boulder, CO 80309
Themes: Problems of conflict and peace; social sciences view
Educational Level: Undergraduate level with either a major or area concentration within a social science department.
Director: Elaine Yarbrough

Peace and Conflict Studies, CONRAD GREBEL COLLEGE, University of Waterloo, Waterloo, Ontario, Canada N2L 3G6
Themes: Analysis of sources of conflict at interpersonal and group levels and means for controlling and resolving these conflicts to establish peace, nonviolent social change, international peacekeeping.
Educational Levels: Undergraduate degree; research and public education program "Project Ploughshares" a church and community sponsored project.
Director: Conrad Brunk

CORNELL UNIVERSITY, Peace Studies Program, 180 Uris Hall, Ithaca NY 14580
Educational Level: Graduate Program only.
Director: George Quester

CONRAD GREBEL COLLEGE, Peace and Conflict Studies, University of Waterloo, Waterloo, Ontario, Canada, N2L 3G6 519-885-0220
Themes: Analysis of sources of conflict at interpersonal and group levels and means for controlling and resolving these conflicts to establish peace, nonviolent social change, international peacekeeping.
Educational Level: Undergraduate degree: research and public education program, "Project Ploughshares": a church and community sponsored project.
Director: Conrad Brunk

EARLHAM COLLEGE, Peace and Conflict Studies, Richmond IN 47374 317-962-6561, ext. 305
Themes: Systematic study of conflict in human societies, ideals of peace, nonviolence, freedom and justice, economic reasons for conflict.
Educational Level: Certificate or major in peace studies.
Directors: George Lopez, Howard Richards

EARLHAM SCHOOL OF RELIGION, Box 36, Earlham College, Richmond IN 47374
Purpose: Acquaint students with historic peace testimony of the Friends and its application in world.
Educational Level: Master of Arts (research oriented), M. Min. enables development of some skills for occupation in peace field.
Director: Alan Kolp

GARRETT-EVANGELICAL PEACE AND JUSTICE CENTER, 2121 Sheridan Rd., Evanston IL 60201 312-866-3962
Purposes: Provides ministerial students with biblical, theological, and ethical basis for understanding and supporting peace, justice, liberation, and world affairs. Students become involved in research, participate in courses, field education or internships, peace organizations, and outreach activities for peace sponsored by the Center.
Educational Level: M. Div., M.T.S., Ph.D. (with Northwestern University)
Director: Walter Cason

GEORGETOWN UNIVERSITY, Center for Peace Studies, 2 O'Gara, Washington, DC 20057, 202-625-4240
Purpose: Works to integrate faith, action, and research into the process of peace, with particular emphasis on nuclear tehcnology problem.
Educational Level: Undergraduate peace studies major under interdisciplinary program.
Director: Richard T. McSorley, S.J.

GODDARD COLLEGE, Plainfield, VT 05667
Purpose: Involves multitude of questions about the origins of war and the possibilities for peace and what individuals can do about these matters.
Educational Level: B.A., in Adult Degree Program, low residency
Core Faculty Member: Richard Hathaway

GOSHEN COLLEGE, Co-major in Peace, Goshen IN 46526 219-533-3161
Themes: Economics, conflict resolution, war/peace theory.
Educational Level: Co-major bachelor degree.
Director: J. R. Burkholder

GUSTAVUS ADOLPHUS COLLEGE, St. Peter MN 56082 507-931-4300
Purpose: An informal program of lectures, campus activities and faculty efforts to infuse the entire curriculum and campus life with themes of peace, justice, and global identity. An explicit commitment *not* to have formal courses or major in peace studies, but to increase the commitment of the entire school to peace and justice creatively.
Contact Person: Normal Walbek.

JUNIATA COLLEGE, Peace and Conflict Studies, Huntington PA 16652 814-643-4310, Ext. 360
Purpose: Applied liberal arts: all disciplines contribute to understanding of problem of war. Accessible to every student through the program of emphasis, which encourages interdepartmental study.
Educational Level: Bachelor degree
Director: M. Andrew Murray

KENT STATE UNIVERSITY, Center for Peaceful Change, Kent OH 44242 216-672-3143
Themes: Conflict resolution, war/peace theory.
Educational Level: Undergraduate with bachelor degree in peace studies.
Director: Dennis Carey

MANCHESTER COLLEGE, Peace Studies Institute, North Manchester IN 46962 219-982-2141
Themes: Understanding of war and peace, social change and conflict reduction, systemic justice, historical perspective and technical aspects of cultural analysis.
Educational Level: Undergraduate major, B.A. or B.S. degree.
Director: Ken Brown.

MANHATTAN COLLEGE, Peace Studies Institute, Bronx, NY 10471
Themes: Economics, conflict resolution, war/peace theory, international and/or transnational studies, arms control, literature, philosophy, religious studies, biology and sociology.
Educational Level: Bachelor of Arts degree, graduate program.
Director: Joseph J. Fahey

SAINT JOSEPH'S UNIVERSITY, Faith/Justice Institute, 5600 City Ave., Philadelphia PA 19131 215-879-7906.
Principal Goal: To "serve faith and promote justice" in an educational context by exploring the ethical implications of the major human problems of our times—local, regional, national, and international.
Educational Level: Certificate
Director: Fr. Al Jenemann S.J.

SOUTHERN ILLINOIS UNIVERSITY AT EDWARDS-VILLE, Peace Studies Program, Edwardsville IL 62026
Purpose: An interdisciplinary minor for students who wish to gain a comprehensive understanding of one of the major issues of contemporary society, the problem of eliminating war in favor of less violent means of resolving disputes.
Educational Level: Undergraduate minor.
Chairperson: Ronald J. Glossop, School of Humanities.

SYRACUSE UNIVERSITY, Program in Nonviolent Conflict and Change, 249 Physics Bldg., Syracuse NY 13210, 315-423-3870
Focus: Transdisciplinary study of nonviolent means of managing conflicts and bringing about or resisting change.
Educational Levels: Major concentration (B.A. degree) for undergraduate students in College of Arts and Sciences; interdisciplinary research and training concentration on graduate level in conjunction with Social Science Ph.D. program in Maxwell School of Citizenship and Public Affairs.
Director: Neil Katz

UNIVERSITY OF AKRON, Center for Peace Studies, Akron OH 44325 216-375-7008
Themes: Conflict resolution, war/peace theory and international/transnational studies.
Director: Warren F. Kuehl

UNIVERSITY OF BRADFORD, School of Peace Studies, Bradford, West Yorkshire BD7 1DP, England 0274-33466, Ext. 565
Purpose: Systemized study of conditions for development of harmonious and constructive relationships and creative nonviolent methods of change; to understand circumstances in which conflict, tension, and violence prevail. Disciplinary concentrations: Politics,

History, and Sociology.
Educational Level: Undergraduate (B.A.) graduate (M.A., Ph.D.)
Contact Person: N.J. Young (Reader in Peace Studies)

UNIVERSITY OF DENVER, Center for Teaching International Relations, Graduate School of International Studies, Denver CO 80208 303-753-3106
Purpose: Dedicated to assisting classroom teachers become more proficient in the teaching of global, social science and educational skill topics.
Educational Program: Recognized as an established academic program but nondegree granting. Research.
Director: B. Abrahamsson, Acting Dean.

UNIVERSITY OF HAIFA, Peace Studies, Haifa, 31 999 Israel 04-240111, 04-240050
Themes: Peace thinking and conflict regulation, the Arab-Israeli conflict, peace research, game simulation, disarmament and arms control.
Educational Level: one or two semesters, undergraduate*, M.A. major
Director: Joseph D. Ben-Dak
*in English and Hebrew

UNIVERSITY OF NOTRE DAME, Program in Nonviolence, Notre Dame IN 46556
Themes: Emphasizes nonviolence.
Educational Level: no degree in peace studies available
Director: John H. Yoder

UNIVERSITY OF MISSOURI/COLUMBIA, 22 Middlebush Hall, Columbia MO 65211
Purpose: Provides the student with an opportunity to explore and contribute to a significant problem area not thoroughly covered by any one department. It encourages an interdisciplinary approach to the topic of peace and allows the student to intergrate personal academic concerns into a coherent pattern of studies related to the conditions of peace.
Educational Level: B.A. (Area of Concentration.)
Chairperson: Dr. Marvin Rogers

UNIVERSITY OF PENNSYLVANIA, Peace Science Society, 3718 Locust Street, Philadelphia PA 19174
Themes: Economics, conflict resolution and war/peace theory.
Educational Levels: Masters and Doctoral degrees available.

UNIVERSITY OF WISCONSIN, Center for Conflict Reoslution, 731 State Street, Madison WI 53703
Themes: Conflict resolution, social change.
Educational Level: Undergraduate level with possible bachelor's degree (in American Institutions with a concentration in Conflict Studies.)

WAYNE STATE UNIVERSITY, Center for Peace and Conflict Studies, 5229 Cass Ave., Detroit MI 48202 313-577-3453
Purpose: Searches for ways to lessen global conflict. Directs its attention to an analysis of the sources of domestic conflict and the modalities of conflict resolution and management.
Educational Level: Undergraduate Program—Co-Major in Peace & Conflict Studies, cross-listed with Political Science and History.
Director: Lillian Genser

WILMINGTON COLLEGE, Peace Studies program, Pyle Center, Box 1183, Wilmington OH 45177 513-382-6661 Ext. 219. Also houses the Hiroshima/Nagasaki Memorial Collection, 513-382-5338
Purpose: To prepare students for careers in agencies and organizations dedicated to peacemaking activities and to enable those entering other careers to become effective as lay leaders and to fulfill their responsibilities as citizens.
Educational Level: Undergraduate level with a major or minor
Director: Earl W. Redding; newsletter editor Helen Redding

(Thanks to: Center for Peaceful Change, Kent State University, and the Wilmington College Peace Resource Center.

The Greens

. . . are a West German party of environmentalists who will accept nothing less than a Europe free of nuclear arms. Increasingly influential as a political party and a symbol of reluctance to be incinerated, the Greens sharply condemn the truculent policies of the United States *as well as* Soviet policies.

First Things First

The Priorities Working Group (PWG) is an open task force of the Coalition for a New Foreign and Military Policy, working on priorities, conversion and federal budget transfer amendments. The PWG brings together both Coalition and non-Coalition members, and includes representatives of a broad range of religious, peace, community, public interest, service and trade union organizations.

Formed in July 1977, the PWG combines grassroots constituent education and organizing efforts, with coordinated activity on Capitol Hill.

The organizations associated with the PWG come from a wide range of interests and orientations. Many produce useful resources and educational material on specific programs and issues related to priorities including health, energy, food and nutrition, conversion, housing, community development, farm and rural

issues, jobs, and military spending. If you are interested in more information on these issues, or would like to receive regular bulletins from the PWG, contact the Coalition for a New Foreign and Military Policy, 120 Maryland Avenue, NE, Washington, D.C. 20002, or call (202) 546-8400.

Working for Disarmament and Peace

REFERENDUM is a global referendum for world peace. The campaign was begun in March 1979 and since that time has gathered the signatures of over 25 million people from 54 countries. The Referendum is printed in ten languages and has been circulated to the press and private people in 180 countries. It has been based on the belief that the vast majority of the world's people are already in agreement concerning world peace. "If we the people could just show each other that we bear no hate in our hearts, we could build a ring of friendship round the world that nobody could stop." For further information write: REFERENDUM, Box 78, 1441 Drøbak, Norway.

Transition.

INTERNATIONAL ORGANIZATIONS AND PERIODICALS

CENTER FOR DISARMAMENT (NGO Liaison), Rm 3577, United Nations, NY 10017 USA'

CHRISTIAN MOVEMENT FOR PEACE, 46 rue de Vaugirard, 75006 Paris, France *Sec* Laurence Eberhard

CHRISTIAN PEACE CONFERENCE, Jungmannova 9, 111 21 Praha 1, Czechoslovakia (24 88 66). *Gen-Sec* Dr. Karoly Toth. *Christian Peace Conference,* qtly, $4 pa. *Ed* Dr Jirl Svoboda

DISARMAMENT CAMPAIGNS c/o NVA, Kerkstr. 150,2000 Antwerp (031 350272) *Ed* Mark Heirman $14 pa.

EIRENE (P, TW) D545 Neuwied 1, Engerser Str. 74B West Germany (02631 22011), *Sec* Jean-Luc Tissot

ESPERANTO MOVEMENT FOR WORLD PEACE (P) *Sec* Dr Renato Corsetti, via Strabone 1,I-00176 Roma, Italy. *PACO*

EUROPEAN NUCLEAR DISARMAMENT CAMPAIGN 6 Endsleigh, London WC1H 0DX Gt Britain (01-380 0532) *Sec* Meg Beresford. *END Bulletin* bimthly, £5 pa *Ed* Tony Simpson

INST. FOR WORLD ORDER 777 United Nations Plaza, New York, NY 10017 (212 490 0010) *Pres* R.C. Johansen, *Alternatives* qtly, $15 pa.

INTERNATIONAL ATOMIC ENERGY AGENCY (IAEA), Kaerntnerring 11, A-1010 Wien, Austria (524511). *Dir-Gen* Dr. Sigvard Eklund

INTERNATIONAL COLLECTIVE RESISTANCE 35 Van Elewyckstraat, 1050 Bruxelles, Belgium. *Sec* Jean Fabre

INTERNATIONAL CONFEDERATION FOR DISARMAMENT AND PEACE and CONFLICT EDUCATION LIBRARY TRUST 6 Endsleigh St, London WC1H 0DX, Gt Britain (01-387 5754). *Peace Press,* mtly. £2 ($5) pa. *Vietnam International,* mtly £2 ($5) pa

INTERNATIONAL FELLOWSHIP OF RECONCILIATION (FoR, IPB) Hofvan Sonoy, 1811LD Alkmaar, Netherlands (01031 72 123014). *Co-ord* James H. Forest. *IFoR Report,* 6pa $12, *Ed* Marty Deming

INTERNATIONAL PEACE ACADEMY, 777 United Nations Plaza, New York, NY 10017, USA (212 986 3540)

INTERNATIONAL PEACE BUREAU, rue de Zurich 41, CH-1201 Genéva, Switzerland (0041 22316429), and GENEVA INT. PEACE RESEARCH INST.

INTERNATIONAL PEACE RESEARCH ASSOC, POB 70, 33100 Tampere 10, Finland (931 23571).

NATIONAL MOBILIZATION FOR SURVIVAL 853 Broadway, Room 2109 New York, NY 10003, USA (212 533 0008)

NONVIOLENT ALTERNATIVES INT. SERVICE NETWORK, Kerkstr. 150, B-2000 Antwerpen, Belgium (031 350272). *Sec* Coen de Vocht. *Peace Action News,* $5.

PAX CHRISTI INTERNATIONAL, Kerkstr 150,2000 Antwerpen (03135 0218). *Sec* Etienne DeJonghe

PONTIFICAL COMMISSION JUSTITIA ET PAX (PC) Piazza San Calisto 16, Vatican City, Italy

SERVICIO PAZ Y JUSTICIA (orientacion nonviolenta) FoR). Casa de la Paz, Mexico 479, 1097 Buenos Aires, Argentine (34 8206). *Dir* Adolfo Perez Esquivel. *Paz y Justicia,* mtly $20pa

THE RIGHT TO REFUSE TO KILL (HR, WRI), 12 Hamcau de Bois Préau, F-92500 Rueil-Malmaison, France (00331 7493816). *Ed* Gerd Greun. $6 pa.

WAR RESISTERS' INTERNATIONAL (WRI, I), 55 Dawes St., London SE17 1EL, Gt. Britain (01-703 7189). *Sec* John Hyatt. *WRI Newsletter,* £3 pa

WISE/WORLD INFORMATION SERVICE ON ENERGY, Blassiusstr. 90, 1091 CW Amsterdam, Netherlands (31 20 924204). *Wise,* bi-mtly. £3.75

WOMEN'S INTERNATIONAL LEAGUE FOR PEACE AND FREEDOM (I.WIL), 1 rue de Varembe, 1211 Genéva 20, Switzerland (33 61 75). *See* Edith Ballantyne. *Pax et Libertas.* qtly.

WORLD ASSOC OF WORLD FEDERALISTS, AND WORLD FEDERALIST YOUTH (F), Leliegracht 21, GR1016, Amsterdam C. Netherlands (020 227502). *Sec* Jos Lemmers

WORLD CONFERENCE ON RELIGION AND PEACE, 777 United Nations Plaza, New York, NY 10017, USA (212 687-2163). *Sec-Gen* Dr. Homer A. Jack. *Religion for Peace,* qtly £2 pa. apply for national addresses in Australia, Austria, Bangladesh, Belgium, Canada, France, Germany (FR), Gt. Britain, India, Italy, Japan, Netherlands, Sri Lanka, Singapore, USA

WORLD DISARMAMENT CAMPAIGN (WRI 1PB, I), 41 rue de Zurich, CH1201 Genéva, Switzerland (0041 22 316429). *Sec* Gerd Greune

WORLD FED. OF SCIENTIFIC WORKERS 40 Goodge St., London W1P 1FH, Gt Britain (01-580 8688). *Sec* Prof J.M. Legay. *Scientific Workers,* qtly £3 pa. *Ed* K. Dutton

WORLD PEACE THROUGH LAW CENTER, 400 Hills Bldgs, Washington DC 20006, USA (202 247-77992). *Sec* Ms M. Henneberry. *World Jurist, Law and Computer Technology* bi-mtly $10 pa.

WORLD PEACE THROUGH LAW CENTER, 400 Hills Bldgs, Washington DC 20006, USA (202 247-77992). *Sec* Ms M. Henneberry. *World Jurist, Law and Computer Technology* bi-mtly $10 pa.

Working for Disarmament and Peace

Armament and Disarmament Information Unit
The Science Policy Research Unit
University of Sussex
Falmer
Brighton BN1 9RF, England

Campaign for Nuclear Disarmament
29 Great James Street
London WC1N 3EY, England

International Fellowship of Reconciliation
Hof van Sonoy 15-17
1811 LD Alkmaar, The Netherlands

National Peace Council
29 Great James Street
London WC 1N, England

Pax Christi International
150 Kerkstraat
2000 Antwerp
Belgium

Bertrand Russell Peace Foundation
Bertrand Russell House
Gamble Street
Nottingham NG7 4ET, England

Stockholm International Peace Research Institute
Sveavagen 166
S-113 46 Stockholm
Sweden

United Nations Association
3 Whitehall Court
London SW1, England

War Resisters International
55 Dawes Street
London, SE 17 England

WMSE Publications
c/o CAAT
5 Caledonian Road
London N1 9DX, England

World Disarmament Campaign
21 Little Russell Street
London WC1 4HF, England

World Goodwill
866 United Nations Plaza
Suite 566-7
New York, New York
U.S.A. 10164

World Goodwill
3 Whitehall Court
Suite 54
London, England SW1A 2EF

Bonne Volonte Mondiale
1 Rue de Varembé (3e)
Case Postale 31
1211 Geneva 20
Switzerland

Transition

Basic Ideas for a Strategy for Stopping the Arms Race

1. The purpose of this campaign is to build public support for stopping the arms race.
2. The method will be to persuade as many others as possible of our own concern that the arms race is the number one threat to humankind which is likely to lead to a catastrophic war. Even without a war the $400 billion the world now spends on arms destroys all possibility of decent development, social justice, and democracy—here in the United States as well as abroad.
3. The slogan of the movement will be "Stop!" The idea of "Stop" is important in two ways. First, it signifies the need to take action now to stop the arms race. It implies a political program of halting further weapons acquisition and transferring funds to meeting basic needs. Second, it signifies a need for every person to stop and reflect on the issue of security, what it means to base security on the amassing of killing power, whether there are alternative sources of security, and how could these alternative sources of security become the foundations of an alternative national security policy.
4. The campaign seeks to enlist two groups of persons. The first are the many thousands of Americans who are privately convinced of the insanity of the arms race but who know no way to express their concerns or are diffident about it because they think that they are alone. There are many millions of Americans who believe that the time for discussing disarmament is over and that we have only a few short years to implement a program to lead the world decisively away from the brink of nuclear catastrophe. The second group includes millions more who are sincerely troubled about the issues of security and arms but are afraid to move off the path of military escalation. They believe that leaders who recommend ever bigger military bud-

gets know best, that they have access to secret information and that the issues are too complicated for ordinary people. But many of these would be open to serious reflection about security, particularly what teaching the Bible has to offer modern man about the basis of security. They would be open to receiving and discussing information on a regular basis on the arms race and alternatives.

5. The WORLD PEACEMAKERS facilitate this effort through a loose, informal organization. A person may join with us by committing herself or himself to writing personal letters to persons she or he is in contact with—personal friends, fellow members of groups, etc.—urging these persons to do one or more of the following:

a) call President Reagan (202-456-1414) urging him to take the initiatives detailed in "A TIME TO STOP."

b) write letters to Congresspersons, President, Secretary of State, Secretary of Defense, etc., urging the President to take the initiatives detailed in "A TIME TO STOP";

c) host a dinner or lunch with community leaders or other influential persons to persuade them to do the same;

d) contact local talk show on radio and TV to get spokespersons for WORLD PEACEMAKERS to make presentation;

e) support other local or established peace organizations with money or volunteer services;

f) form local conversion committees to discuss alternative uses of local military industry;

g) establish ongoing seminars, retreats, courses, conferences on security. Develop lists of speakers who would go to local communities for these activities;

h) conduct training sessions in various parts of the country so that church and synagogue people will become expert in the issues;

i) facilitate distribution of pamphlets, tracts, and backup studies to the growing network;

j) raise substantial funds to support peace organizations and institutes preparing the materials;

k) recruit and support candidates for local and national office who will take strong positions on ending the arms race;

l) finance and produce TV programs on security and the arms race;

m) finance and write newspaper ads on the various campaigns.

WORLD PEACEMAKERS
2852 Ontario Rd. NW
Washington, D.C. 20009

Jared Miller

Jobs with Peace

Does the U.S. government spend too many of our tax dollars on the military? Can the country afford both guns and butter? These questions form the basis of the Jobs with Peace (JWP) campaign, a grassroots, nationwide effort to rebuild the economy by shifting funds from the military to the civilian sectors.

Basic to all JWP initiatives is the link between military and social spending. As war-making currently takes up 58% of every tax dollar, precious little money is left for human needs programs. Yet this increasingly small proportion of the budget is the sole beneficiary of the "belt-tightening" so favored by administration budgeteers.

Military spending has other harmful effects as well. Inflation is caused, since no consumer goods or services are produced, by military spending. Furthermore, while you cannot consume military goods, workers in the defense industries still demand these goods and services. A stable stock of goods must make do for all workers, driving prices up.

Partially due to Reagan's social cuts and military increases, the JWP campaign is flourishing. Next November, referenda are planned in Boston, Seattle, Pittsburgh, Milwaukee and in parts of northern California. In the South, the Southern Organizing Committee for Economic and Social Justice (SOC) vows "to put the issue of military spending as opposed to human needs in the forefront in Southern Communities" through a series of JWP-like initiatives. The Reagan administration's guns over butter policy will be receiving more and more challenges in the upcoming years.

Science for the People

A World Peace Guard

A Proposal for an Unarmed Agency for Peace-keeping

A. THE BASIC IDEA

A World Peace Guard (WPG) would be an agency for peacekeeping, transnational in composition with a Ready Reserve, able to carry out missions for a regional organization, the United Nations, or other political authority. It would carry out functions which have already been exemplified in United Nations actions, in Cyprus for example, except for armed actions; and in some examples of nonviolent action initiated by coalitions of private and governmental groups. Tasks in management and control of overt or threatened conflict would be undertaken under a discipline of nonviolent action.

Its major and almost exclusive direct fiunction would be in the field of security. It may serve a liaison function regarding peacemaking tasks or facilitating community service projects. These would usually be carried out by other agencies: local, regional, national, international.

Examples of functions for a WPG might be the following:

++ Patrol a demarcation line

++ Receive arms or supervise disarmament of both sides

++ Observe and report in unsettled situations

++ Investigate and report on specific complaints of violations

++ Interpose when necessary

++ Aid in mediation and conciliation

++ Recruit specialists & other volunteers as parties require

++ Participate in special maneuvers, ceremonies, patrols, teams

++ Police an area where agents of law & order have fled

++ Use good offices to facilitate resolution of conflicts.

Larry Fabian, in his valuable study, *Soldiers Without Enemies*, concluded:

"There seems to be wide agreement that peacekeeping institutions and skills are distinguishable by these two integral qualities: political impartiality and noncoerciveness."

He adds that impartial intent may not preclude partisan effects, and noncoercive methods may be tinged with coercion at times. He nevertheless insists that these two qualities "embody norms that peacekeepers are guided by; they are the underlying sources of peacekeepers' strength and influence."

More Information from: Charles C. Walker, Box 92, Cheyney, Pa. 19319.

Careers in Peacemaking

We want to talk to you about something very basic, something as basic as PEACE. We want to discuss with you how your life—time—talent—and interests are related to the search for PEACE.

Have you thought about how the work you choose to do may contribute to or hamper PEACE?

PEACE is more than just the absence of war. Injustice, prejudice, poverty, greed and pollution also hurt people. To us PEACE MEANS A CREATIVE PROCESS OF WORK AND STRUGGLE TOWARD A JUST AND SATISFYING WORLD FOR ALL PEOPLE.

A career for PEACE is one that helps and does not harm you, others, or your environment. It is a job you are proud of. This does not mean it must carry a large salary or fame. It does mean you enjoy doing it and want to share that joy with your family and others.

Right now you are probably searching for your personal direction and identity.

It is not uncommon at the age of 18 to feel anxious about what to do when you leave high school or go on to college. There are many people who really care about you who will try to help or give advice. Often this may confuse you more.

HOW ABOUT YOUR NEEDS?

You need a job to make money

You want to make your own decisions

You want a job that will teach you, challenge you, and make you feel useful, good about yourself, and will make others proud of you.

You look around and see few opportunities—but you also see something else. You see that there are many people doing exciting things. They are involved in jobs which are fun, useful and creative—the kinds of areas you feel drawn to. You ask yourself, How did they do it?

WHY NOT ASK THEM?

Some will say, "Hard work", others, "Luck". Well, both of these are true, but what they are not telling you is that they spent a great deal of time agonizing the same as you.

When they tell their story, their path seems haphazard. They feel they "lucked out" or "stumbled into" their great job. But we ask them to talk about what they were doing before that happened. They all did various things to prepare themselves, often without realizing how it would come out.

"Oh, I had lots of jobs; just to make money."

"I worked part time at a drive-in and took classes at night. It was hard!"

"I helped out in a garage on Saturdays just to learn about cars. But I had a crummy job pumping gas at night for money."

"While I was in high school I helped out at a day-care center. I liked the kids and learned a lot about them."

Not very exciting or romantic? Well it depends on your attitude. The interesting thing about these folks is that they tried many options, built experience, and eventually arrived at a satisfying job. The first person owns a plant store, the second is a drug and family counselor, the third an auto mechanic and the fourth a child-care worker. So you see, you will probably try on many hats before you choose. Some will fit better than others.

HOW TO GET STARTED

Begin by checking-out things about yourself. What do you know how to do already, your hobbies, talents and skills? What kind of settings do you like to be in— indoor or outdoor? Do you enjoy working with people, talking with them, or do you work better alone?

HOW ABOUT YOUR VALUES?

Values are those deeply rooted concerns which contribute so much to your image of yourself and your world. Such concerns as ecology, animals, music, friends, religion, art or children. The list would be personal and would represent the depth of your interest and desire to work for those values.

A few examples: If you care about animals: You might begin by seeking out places where you can help out and learn more about the life and care of various animals. Perhaps a pet shop, the zoo, a breeder or a veteranarian. Talk to the people who work there and find out what they do and how they learned to do it.

If you like children: Look for day-care centers, pre-schools, tutoring programs, juvenile projects, recreation centers. Volunteer your time, maybe just cleaning up,

maybe reading to the children or teaching them something you know. Many times you can work yourself into a job just by being in a place at the right time and having demonstrated your interest and capability.

PROFESSIONS

If you are interested in professions such as law, teaching, social work, medicine or music, for example, seek out the unions and organizations these folks belong to. Talk to professionals in your community to discuss new and more creative directions these careers are taking. Professional organizations usually include a minority, women's, or "radical" caucus—get in touch with the one that fits your interest.

Don't forget your guidance counselor and teachers. They can and will help if you let them know what you need. They have resources and contacts you can use. This is their job and they enjoy helping.

Finally, it's your life, your world and your future— take responsibility for them. There are people who want to help. Growth will come as you evolve into the person you want to be. If you choose a job for the wrong reasons, you are likely to be unhappy later, and may have to start all over again. Choosing a constructive, loving, helping career will be continually rewarding and will help to build a peaceful world.

BUT REMEMBER . . .

You may find out you are really not as interested in a certain career direction as you originally thought. That is OK. You will have found out before investing much of your life in it, and will have gained valuable experience.

Experience is important. Employers always ask about experience. Much of the time they want to find out if you have demonstrated to anyone that you are trustworthy and will put forth the effort needed to learn a job. Try to gain experience while still in school or in your spare time. Both job experience and volunteer experience are important to a potential employer.

There are many organizations right in your community where you can volunteer: The YMCA and YWCA, Red Cross, hospitals, Urban Service Agencies, Child Care and Food Co-ops, hot lines, counseling agencies, schools and churches.

Organizations such as ours are also in many cities. By contacting local church, synagogue or peace activists you can find out who and where they are. These groups are working for a peaceful world and social change in many different types of programs such as Peace Education, community relations, justice, and vocations for social change. Find the Ecology Action center in your community. They can tell you what is being done and how you might become part of the action.

(*Fran Donelan, AFSC, 317 E. 25th Street, Baltimore, MD 21218*)

Peace Sabbath Suggested Actions

1. Start a worship/study/action group in your congregation or community. Order materials from any of the co-sponsoring organizations of Peace Sabbath (addresses below).

2. Investigate militarism in your community, *e.g.,* weapons facilities, corporate headquarters of military contractors, universities with Pentagon contracts, draft boards being constituted. Contact NARMIC, 1501 Cherry St., Philadelphia, Pa. 19102.

3. Plan a demonstration at such a facility, pointing out the benefits of converting it to socially useful work. Contact FOR/AFSC Nuclear Weapons Facilities Project.

4. Provide draft counseling and offer support for young men facing registration or the draft. Contact CARD, 245 Second St., NE, Washington, D.C. 20002 or Draft Action, no. 534 Washington Bldg., 1435 G. St., NW, Washington, D.C. 20005.

5. Join the campaign calling for "an immediate, mutual freeze on all further testing, production, and deployment of nuclear weapons and of missiles and new aircraft designed primarily to deliver nuclear weapons." Contact CALC or FOR.

6. Celebrate a peace picnic, inviting the congregation and the community. Eat and play together, then plan to work together for peace.

7. Put peace on the ballot in your area, with propositions calling for a nuclear moratorium, for jobs with peace or for a shift of funds from the military budget to human needs. Contact Traprock Peace Center, Woolman Hill, Keets Road, Deerfield, Ma. 01342 and RTF/MFS.

8. Organize an ongoing clergy discussion group on disarmament. Order The Disarmament Reader from Riverside Church Disarmament Program.

9. Participate in a Mothers' Day demonstration at the Pentagon. Contact Womens Party for Survival, 7 Gilman St., Everett, MA 02149.

Liturgical Ideas for Peace Sabbath

1. Design special banners for display in your place of worship on Peace Sabbath.

2. Seek out and include hymns in your service that highlight Peace Sabbath concerns.

3. Since Peace Sabbath directly follows the Jewish and Christian celebrations of Passover and Easter, consider the ways that these important religious seasons can feed into the themes of Peace Sabbath, or the ways that Peace Sabbath can add to the meaning of these annual religious observances.

4. Explore the themes of Peace Sabbath in your church/synagogue school classes on that day.

5. Invite people in your congregation, at an appropriate point in the service, to come forward as a visible sign of their commitment or recommitment to the cause of peace and justice.

6. Think of the ways that the participation of children in the Peace Sabbath service might enhance the meaning of the day. You might include a special time to hear the prayers of young people with regard to their hopes and dreams about the world that they will inherit from this generation. A childrens' procession for life could also be a part of the service.

7. Try to arrange joint services with a neighboring church or synagogue.

8. Hold your services outside, so that your celebration of Peace Sabbath is given greater visibility in the community. Think about having a procession around the block after the service is over.

9. Consider taking a special offering to help fund continuing peace education efforts in the church/synagogue and in the surrounding community.

10. At some point in the Peace Sabbath service read your denomination's most recent statements about the arms race and militarism. If possible, pass out copies.

Preparing for Peace Sabbath

1. Announce your Peace Sabbath services in local newspapers.

2. Make a Peace Sabbath display for the lobby of your building. Have letter-writing materials on hand. (Think of other places in the community where this display could be used!)

3. Invite representatives from community groups which face budget cuts to participate in your services to attest to the human cost of the arms race.

Words of Peace from the Torah, the Psalms and the Prophets

For out of Zion shall go forth
the law, and the word of the
Lord from Jerusalem.
He shall judge between the
nations, and shall decide for
many peoples;
and they shall beat their
swords into plowshares,
and their spears into
pruning hooks;
nations shall not lift up sword
against nation,
neither shall they learn war
any more.

—Isaiah 2:4

Keep your tongue from evil,
and your lips from speaking
deceit.
Depart from evil, and do good;
seek peace and pursue it.

—Psalm 34:12-14

The way of peace they know
not and there is no justice
in their paths;
They have made their roads
crooked, no one who goes
in them knows peace.

—Isaiah 59:8

I call heaven and earth to
witness against you this day,
that I have set before you life
and death, blessing and curse;
therefore choose life, that you
and your descendants may
live . . .

—Deuteronomy 30:19

Then justice will dwell in the
wilderness, and
righteousness abide in the
fruitful field.
And the effect of
righteousness will be peace,
and the result of
righteousness quietness and
trust forever.
My people will abide in
peaceful habitation, in
secure dwellings, and in
quiet resting places.

—Isaiah 32:16-18

And I will make for you a covenant on that day with the beasts
of the field, the birds of the air,
and the creeping things of the
ground; and I will abolish the
bow, the sword, and war from
the land; and I will make you lie
down in safety.

—Hosea 2:18

You have plowed iniquity,
you have reaped injustice,
you have eaten the fruit of
lies
Because you have trusted in
your chariots and in the
multitude of your warriors,
therefore the tumult of war
shall arise among your
people and all your
fortresses shall be
destroyed.

—Hosea 10:13-14

Words of Peace from the Gospels and the Epistles

Jesus came and stood among the disciples and said to them, "Peace be with you." When he had said this, he showed them his hands and his side. Then the disciples were glad when they saw the Lord. Jesus said to them again, "Peace be with you. As the Father has sent me, even so I send you."

—John 20:19-21

Then Jesus said to him, "Put your sword back into its place; for all who take the sword will perish by the sword."

—Matthew 26:52

For the kingdom of God does not mean food and drink but righteousness and peace and joy in the Holy Spirit; one who thus serves Christ is acceptable to God and approved by others. Let us then pursue what makes for peace and mutual up-building.

—Romans 14:17-19

The devil took Jesus to a very high mountain, and showed him all the kingdoms of the world and the glory of them; and he said to him, "All these things I will give you, if you will fall down and worship me." Then Jesus said to him, "Begone, Satan! for it is written 'You shall worship the Lord your God and him only shall you serve.'"

—Matthew 4:8-11

Blessed are the peacemakers, for they shall be called children of God.

—Matthew 5:9

For where jealousy and selfish ambition exist, there will be disorder and every vile practice. But the wisdom from above is first pure, then peaceable, gentle, open to reason, full of mercy and good fruits, without uncertainty or insincerity. And the harvest of righteousness is sown in peace by those who make peace.

—James 3:14-18

He has shown strength with his arm,
he has scattered the proud in the imagination of their hearts,
he has put down the mighty from their thrones,
and exalted those of low degree;
he has filled the hungry with good things,
and the rich he has sent away empty...

—Luke 1:51-53

And when Jesus drew near and saw the city he wept over it, saying, "Would that even today you knew the things that make for peace! But now they are hid from your eyes."

—Luke 19:41-44

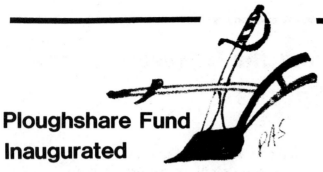

Ploughshare Fund Inaugurated

At a recent press conference in Alkmaar, Holland, Adolfo Perez Esquival, the 1980 Nobel Peace Prize recipient, inaugurated the "Ploughshare Fund." The fund, operated by Church and Peace, an international and ecumenical coordinating board for peace church groups, is making financial assistance available to individuals and churches working on the conversion of arms industries to those of civilian production.

The fund will be available to help spread information about methods of nonviolent action. It will also aid individuals and groups who are themselves suffering or in need of help, as a result of their nonviolent intercession for those under persecution or oppression.

Honorary presidents of the fund are two internationally known pacifists: the Brazilian Catholic Archbishop, Dom Helder Camara, and the French Protestant pastor, Jean Lasserre. The fund works closely with the boards of the World Council of Churches, the International Fellowship of Reconciliation and the Historic Peace Churches.

For more information write: Church and Peace, Rinstrasse 21, D6331 Schoeffengrund (near Wetzlar), Fed. Rep. of Germany.

Fellowship Magazine

How to Research Your Local War Industry

Which local companies have military contracts to produce weapons and other war products? Which firms are affiliated with one of the huge conglomerates such as ITT? How does one find out more about local defense contracts? Here are some suggestions.

Discovering the Local Military Presence

1. The best way to start finding out about local military contractors is to write NARMIC for a *list of contract awards* in your county for the last year. This will give you the names of local contractors, how much money was awarded to them, and what sort of work they are doing. Also available: lists of contracts awarded to particular *companies.* Send $4.00 to cover costs. (Note: because of the large number of requests received, priority must be given to local action/research projects and so they cannot guarantee to service requests from individuals for information only.)

2. You can also write the Pentagon for a copy of *Department of Defense Prime Contractors Which Re-*ceived Awards of $10,000 or More for your state. This publication is issued annually for each state by the Deputy Comptroller for Information Services, Office of the Secretary of Defense, Washington, D.C. 20301 at a price of $2.00 to $8.00 depending on the size of your state. Each state report includes the prime contractors which received awards of over $10,000 during the fiscal year (October 1 to September 30). The corporations are listed by city, together with the total dollar amount of contracts for each corporation and the total for each city. No information is given about the nature of the contracts.

(Note: Military agencies award *prime contracts* to companies which will then often award *subcontracts* to other firms for parts and supplies needed to fulfill the contract. You should keep an ear open for news of subcontracts awarded to local firms; these are often very important but are usually much harder to track down than prime contracts.)

3. Once you have narrowed your research down to a particular company, you should find out whether it is a subsidiary of a larger corporation. You will need to know this because most sources list contracts only under the name of the parent corporation. Consult *Moody's Industrial Manual* or *Standard Corporation Descriptions* for indexes of parent corporations and their subsidiaries.

4. Check the corporation section of the *Wall Street Journal Index* or the *F & S Index of Corporations and Industries* (available in large public libraries and university libraries). These indexes generally list military contracts over $1 million, along with a wealth of background articles on other aspects of the companies' activities.

5. Your *local newspaper* is likely to carry announcements of new defense contracts awarded to local firms. Besides examining the paper regularly, you may be able to consult clipping files at your local library or even at the newspaper's offices. Friendly relationships with reporters can open up possibilities too. Sometimes the press can get information that you can't get yourself.

6. Another important source of information is your *U.S. Senator or Representative* in Washington. Write to his or her office, asking for a list of all government contracts held locally by the company in which you are interested. Many Senators and Representatives are very conscientious and thorough in supplying information to interested citizens.

7. You may be able to get to know *people who work for the corporation* who will be willing to supply information. Careful, patient effort is needed in making these contacts, and you must be sensitive to the personal situation of those involved.

8. A word of caution: Even though you find listings of contracts recently awarded to a particular corporation, the firm may claim that it no longer manufactures such weapons. Because the time needed to complete contracts varies widely and indexes may not appear until long after the contract is awarded, it may be difficult to

prove that a company is still making a certain item. You should also recognize that in many cases a particular company does not make an entire weapon but only a part of it (for instance, the metal parts of a bomb). To avoid this problem, consider focussing your campaign on the munition as an example of the general nature of the military work of the corporation and also their willingness to accept or consider future contracts.

9. If there is a *military base* near you, write the base's Public Information Officer for information on its history, mission, and current activities. Find out how many people are stationed there and what role their work plays in the overall military scheme of things. Visit the base some day when it is open for public tours. Get to know soldiers, officers, and civilian employees and find out what life on the base is like.

10. Research on *arms exporters* presents special problems. if you suspect that a company in your community is selling weapons abroad, and need assistance in tracking it down, write NARMIC for further information.

Background Sources on Corporations

General descriptions of corporations can be found in *Moody's Industrial Manual* or in *Standard Corporation Descriptions*. These include only those corporations that are listed on the stock exchanges. You can find one or the other of these sources at your local public library or at a university library. Here you can find a description of the products manufactured, a list of the corporate officers, plant locations, subsidiary firms, information on recent major contracts, and a brief history of the corporation. Both have indexes that give the parent firms of subsidiary corporations. Since the main purpose of these manuals is to assist investors, most of the information is financial data on the corporations: the corporate balance sheets and ratings of their securities.

If the company is too small to be listed in *Moody's Industrial Manual* or in *Standard Corporation Descriptions*, try *Dun and Bradstreet Million Dollar Directory*

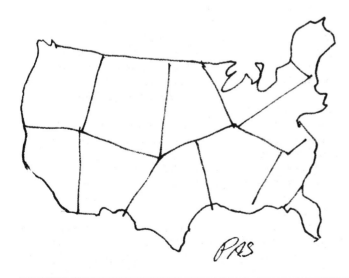

(for larger corporations) or *Dun and Bradstreet Middle Market Directory* (for smaller companies). These two directories list most corporations including even modest sized ones, together with their addresses, products manufactured, and names of officers and directors. They also have a geographical index and a general index of products where you can look up which corporations are in your town and what they manufacture.

Finally, if the corporation in which you are interested is not listed in any of the sources above, try *Thomas Register of American Manufacturers*. It even has listings for companies that are not publicly owned. Volume 7 of *Thomas Register* lists companies, giving their addresses and brief descriptions of their main products.

Write for the corporation's annual report. It is usually available free from the corporation or can be located in a good business library. Frequently annual reports give useful information about the subsidiaries, products, officers and directors, sales divisions, plant location, and finances of the company. Annual reports are produced mainly for public relations and should be read with a critical eye. The format is usually slick and glossy with lots of pictures—good copy for leaflets.

If you are after biographical information about a corporation's officers and directors, check *Who's Who in America* and the various regional Who's Whos. *Poor's Register of Corporations, Directors and Executives* is useful for learning the various corporate boards of directors to which a particular individual belongs.

State and Local Directories

Every state publishes an industrial directory, listing most firms in the state, even small companies. The listings are normally by county and will sometimes indicate whether a firm is locally controlled or managed from the outside. State Industrial Directories Corp. also publishes industrial directories for most states. Its directories list companies by county, with a company index at the end, and indicate the number of employees, plant location, names of directors or local managers, and types of products manufactured. Your local telephone book, especially the "yellow pages", is a valuable research tool. Your local Chamber of Commerce may have brochures which will give a good overview of the local economy. Your state capital maintains files of information on corporations in the state, including official papers which the corporations are required to submit.

Other Useful Sources of Information

1. NARMIC publications: "The New Generation of Nuclear Weapons" (15¢). Map series, "The Military-Industrial Atlas of the United States": No. 1, nuclear warhead facilities and contractors—no. 2, nuclear weapons accidents—no. 3, makers of the new generation of nuclear weapons—no. 4, ammunition manufacturers and exporters—no. 5, top 100 defense contractors with annual sales and principal plants (10¢ each).

"Atoms for Peace—Atoms for War?", 4-page fact sheet (15¢). "Arming the Third World," 8-page fact sheet (15¢). "Meet Your Local Merchant of Death," a state-by-state list of munitions manufacturers and exporters ($1). Add 20 percent postage on all orders. Write for literature list.

2. Issued annually and available free from OASD (Comptroller), Directorate for Information Operations and Reports, Department of Defense, Washington, D.C. 20301: "One Hundred Largest Defense Contractors and Their Subsidiary Corporations"; "Five Hundred Contractors Receiving the Largest Dollar Volume of Military Prime Contract Awards for Research, Development, Test and Evaluation"; "Prime Contract Awards by State"; "Educational and Non-profit Institutions Receiving Military Prime Contracts of $10,000 or More for Research, Development, Test and Evaluation Work."

3. *NACLA Research Methodology Guide* ($2.00 postpaid from NACLA, 151 W. 19th St., New York, N.Y. 10011). *Peace Conversion,* special issue (30¢ from Win magazine, 503 Atlantic Ave., Brooklyn, N.Y. 11217). *Open the Books: How to Research a Corporation* ($4 plus 40¢ postage from Midwest Academy, 600 W. Fullerton Ave., Chicago, Ill. 60614). *Corporate Action Guide* ($2.50 from Michael Reisch, Corporate Action Project, 519 Ardaph Lane, Pueblo, Co. 81005). *The Corporate Examiner* ($25/year from Interfaith Center for Corporate Responsibility, 475 Riverside Drive, New York, N.Y. 10027).

4. "Disarmament Action Guide"; "Human Rights Action Guide"; "Unemployment: Fallout of the Arms Race" (10¢ each from Coalition for a New Foreign and Military Policy, 120 Maryland Ave. NE, Washington, D.C. 20002).

NARMIC, March 1979

narmic

national action/research on the military industrial complex

Although NARMIC receives the bulk of its funding from the American Friends Service Committee, a substantial part of NARMIC's operating expenses must be raised from outside contributions. NARMIC membership is a way of helping this crucial research and educational effort to continue. NARMIC members receive periodic mailings of new publications and their contributions help support NARMIC's work. Categories are: $1,000 organizational, $500 associate, $100 sustaining, $25 supporting, $10 individual membership.

Checks may be made payable to NARMIC/AFSC. Contributions are tax deductible.

NARMIC • 1501 Cherry Street • Philadelphia, PA 19102 • (215) 241-7175

SCHOOLS NEED PEACE STUDIES

by Fran Donelan

Often people trying to gain the same kind of access to students in schools which recruiters have are faced with the question of what they offer as an alternative. Information to counter or clarify what the recruiters are saying is one such alternative, but, more often, a sympathetic administrator or school board is looking for something more concrete which they feel will speak to a need in their schools.

In this time of escalating violence and callousness on the part of students toward each other and staff in schools, schools seem more receptive now to an offering of education geared to helping schools with this problem. In many school systems the introduction of Junior ROTC is seen as a means to improve discipline. This also needs to be challenged. Do we need to put uniforms on teachers and give them license to physically and verbally abuse students to bring order to the classroom? Just imagine such a school system.

Peace Studies is a possible answer and can take many forms. There is always the possibility of designing a course in conflict resolution in co-operation with the Human Relations staff in the school. Their job usually begins after violence has taken place, and many of them would welcome help from outside to prevent such acts.

There are many books and manuals available, both inside and outside the school curriculum; teachers all over the country are already using these resources themselves, but it is important for those of us concerned about militarism in education to realize that sympathetic teachers may feel very isolated in schools where the administration is pro-military. My experience is that the pro-military or JROTC school presents teachers with a set of problems they might not otherwise have.

For example, during the Iranian situation an English teacher was confronted by an Air Force JROTC cadet saying that the Iranians were like animals and didn't value life because of their religion, that they didn't believe like us and looked forward to dying. The teacher, who is Jewish, was appalled. Was this attitude much different from what the Nazis told students about the Jews? The student said that he had heard this said about the Iranians in a discussion in JROTC class.

The U.S. Department of Education's social studies guidelines state clearly that students should become adept at problem-solving and decision-making, with an understanding and appreciation of cultural and ethnic differences. So a curriculum should allow for the "we are all people" theme or one that emphasizes the interdependency and responsibility of us all.

A unit on peace heroes could be offered, with the emphasis not on the uniqueness of such people, but on their humanity, their integrity, and the roots of their concerns. Such a unit would include not only Martin Luther King, but local individuals who are practicing alternatives to violence—such as people who work in

centers for battered women and soup kitchens. Every community contains such people, and the school system is often eager to include the community element in their curriculum.

Another possible direction for a Peace Studies unit is the idea of Careers in Peace—presenting the various organizations and agencies working in the community and the world for alternatives to violence as sources of jobs for students. For example, every community has United Way agencies and groups working independently to help people in the community. The Food Stamp Hotline, Drug Hotline, Meals on Wheels,

daycare centers . . . the list is endless. A presentation can be made on the types of skills needed, types of jobs various groups have, training and volunteer possibilities, and the necessary higher education needed to fulfil certain job expectations. Most students and counselors never consider these agencies seriously when counseling or thinking about work; this gives the person presenting the unit an opportunity to raise consciousness about how one's values and attitudes are related to choice of work.

Finally, the draft and conscientious objection represent issues very crucial to students, and presentation of information on these issues is made easier through the use of audio-visual materials. There are also units on the draft and many other written resources available from members of the Taskforce on Recruitment and Militarism. (Addresses of TFORM member groups are available on request from CCCO.)

These are only a few ideas for positive input into the schools. Let us know about yours.

Fran Donelan is a staff member at the Middle Atlantic Region office of the American Friends Service Committee, 317 E. 25 St., Baltimore, MD 21218.

CCCO Notes

A Checklist of Nuclear Books

Compiled by Joann Davis and Wendy Smith

Fear books. Books that deliver disquieting messages about radiation leaks and environmental poisons and bombs so powerful they could ultimately destroy the human race. Most of us have a hard time escaping these horrors on the nightly news and in the morning papers. Do we really want to read about them in our leisure time?

Publishers hope so. There has been a notable increase in the number of nuclear books, with many titles (almost 30% of those listed) slated for publication later this year. Of the approximately 130 books described here, more than 80% have been published since 1980. Even taking into account publishers' habitual consignment of slow-selling titles—and books about nuclear matters often fall into this category—this still indicates considerable growth.

The growth in titles is all the more remarkable, given the attitude of those publishing them. Daniel Moses, editor-in-chief of Sierra Club Books, voiced the feelings of many when he recently told *PW*, "Editors and publishers don't expect to sell a lot of books on this topic; it's not a commercial enterprise. I think they genuinely feel an obligation to inform the public on this issue, to make books available."

This sense of responsibility certainly accompanies publication of one of the most important nuclear books to appear this spring: "The Fate of the Earth," Jonathan Schell's three-part *New Yorker* article. Explaining Knopf's decision to rush Schell's work into book form by April, editor-in-chief Robert Gottlieb recently said, "This is the most important and urgent subject of our time. We want as many people as possible to read about it as quickly as possible."

An Offer You Can't Refuse

In keeping with that sentiment, Knopf decided at a recent promotion meeting to reduce the book's price from $13.95 to $11.95. Acting independently, the Book-of-the-Month Club has embarked upon a similar course of action. Through an unusual royalty agreement with the publisher and author, BOMC will be offering "The Fate of the Earth" to its members at cost, an unprecedented action. "I've been saying in our editorial meetings for some time that we had to find a book about nuclear holocaust that people would read," senior vice-president and editor-in-chief Gloria Norris told *PW*. "When the Schell book came in, I felt it was so important that we had to make it available to our readers at as low a cost as possible."

Pocket Books editor-in-chief Martin Asher felt similar conviction in deciding to publish the mass market original, "Nuclear War: What's in It for You?" ($2.95) by Ground Zero, a nonpartisan nuclear educational group. Asher met Ground Zero executive director Roger C. Molander last fall, on the day Egyptian president Sadat was assassinated.

"Everyone was feeling very shaky about the state of the world that day," Asher recalled, "and Molander and I spoke about his experiences as Kissinger's assistant during the SALT negotiations, and about what's happening now. We're both fathers of young sons, and we talked about our concern for them and their future."

"Nuclear War: What's in It for You?" will be published as the official tie-in for Ground Zero Week, April 18 to April 25. Seminars and speeches designed to alert Americans to the dangers of nuclear war will be held during this period in 110 major cities and 200 small towns hosting events and discussion groups, according to Molander. Pocket Books is demonstrably committed to using Ground Zero Week to get its book into the hands of consumers: "Nuclear War" is Pocket's lead title for April, and will have a 100,000-copy first printing.

Although nuclear war and weaponry have been the objects of particular scrutiny in recent months, other aspects of nuclear technology are also covered in the checklist below. Nuclear power is the single largest category, and books about the 1979 Three Mile Island accident are numerous enough to merit their own section. In addition, several titles explore the impact of nuclear power plants—and nuclear weapons—on the environment and public health. Books on various aspects of nuclear strife—the arms race, nuclear war, nuclear weapons and how to survive a nuclear attack—are so legion that they had to be divided up into four separate categories.

A number of titles seek to remind readers that nuclear power is often intimately connected with the military use of fissionable materials. Although the vast majority of books either argue against the use of nuclear power or raise serious questions about its safety, a few titles favor the technology—often militantly so.

Does Anybody Care?

Given the fact that publishers themselves acknowledge the iffy sales record of books on this subject in the past, the question naturally arises: does anyone want to read about this? Is the subject of a possible nuclear holocaust, or even an accident at a nuclear

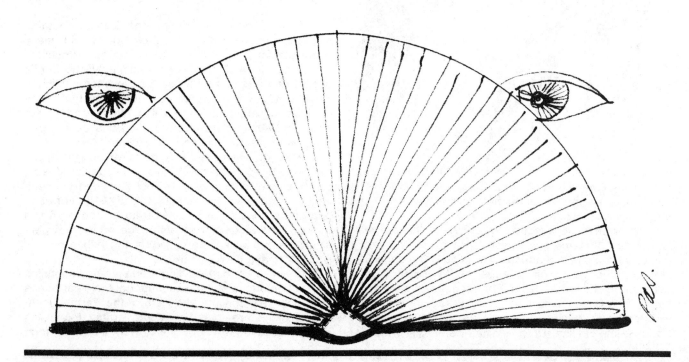

power plant, just too threatening for most people to deal with?

Publishers Weekly solicited the opinions of booksellers on this question. As for publishers, they point to a number of recent events: the tremendous stir caused by Schell's article ("I don't know of any other piece of writing that's generated this much alarm and attention," said Moses, who compared it to Rachel Carson's "Silent Spring"); the growing public skepticism toward the claims of high technology in general and nuclear power in particular; increased grassroots political activity; and the growing involvement in the disarmament issue of such religious organizations as the Lutherans and the Catholic Church.

"We're all frightened by this subject and don't want to read about it," said Gottlieb, "but the moment comes when major issues can't be denied. It happened with civil rights, it happened with Vietnam, I think it's happened now with this subject." Martin Asher shares Gottlieb's view. "It's like Vietnam," he said. "It seemed that the war was so big, and we were very small. But that's the great thing about this country: if people scream loud enough and long enough about an issue, they can change things."

Nuclear War

Allanheld, Osmun (81 Adams Dr., Totowa, N.J. 07512). **The Effects of Nuclear War.** Office of Technology Assessment, U.S. Congress. Examines the social, economic and physical effects of a nuclear war, including its short- and long-term repercussions. $9.95. 1980.

Ballinger. **Life After Nuclear War.** Arthur M. Katz. Challenges the belief that it would be possible to recover from a nuclear war, examining the effect of a nuclear attack on society. $14.95 paper. April 1982. (Hardcover $27.50. January 1982.)

Knopf. **The Fate of the Earth.** Jonathan Schell. This reprint of a three-part *New Yorker* article looks at the consequences of a major nuclear attack: blast waves, mass fires, crop destruction, alteration of the globe's climate and atmosphere, global epidemics and more. $11.95. 50,000 first printing. April 1982.

Hiroshima. John Hersey. The famous account of six people who survived the 1945 atomic attack. 100,000 copies in print. $7.95. 1946.

Oelgeschlager, Gunn & Hain. **Nuclear Radiation in Warfare.** J. Rotblat. Looks at the biological effects of a nuclear war and discusses attacks on civilian power stations, terrorist activities and other warlike uses of nuclear radiation. $20. 1961.

Children of Hiroshima. Arata Osada. Collects the firsthand accounts of people who were schoolchildren in Hiroshima on August 6, 1945. $9.95, cloth $22.50. 1981.

Penguin. **Nuclear Nightmares: An Investigation into Possible Wars.** Nigel Calder. Outlines the four most likely routes toward nuclear disaster and looks at what nuclear weaponry is and how it's supposed to work.

30,000 first printing; $3.95 paper. June 1981.

Pocket Books. **Nuclear War: What's in It for You?** Ground Zero. Examines the history of weapons development, possible scenarios for nuclear war and the consequences of a nuclear exchange. A Special Release. $2.95 paper. April 1982.

Quartet Books (dist. by Charles River Books). **Nagasaki 1945.** Tatsuichiro Akizuki. An eyewitness account by a doctor of the events after the bomb was dropped on Nagasaki, detailing the medical problems that followed the attack. 50,000 first printing. $5.95 paper. April 1982.

W. H. Smith. **Nuclear War: The Facts on Our Survival.** Peter Goodwin. Discusses policies of deterrence, explaining different types of nuclear weapons and their effects, and looks at the pros and cons of evacuation and sheltering units. $5.95, cloth $9.95. September 1981.

Times Books. **Russian Roulette: The Superpower Game.** Arthur Macy Cox. A former State Department and CIA member looks at the danger of accidental nuclear war, offering a proposal for the avoidance of nuclear war. $16.95. June 1982.

University of Chicago Press. **Apocalypse: Nuclear Catastrophe in World Politics.** Louis René Beres. Contemplates the ways in which a nuclear war could start and depicts the consequences. $6.95 paper. March 1982.

The Final Epidemic: Physicians and Scientists on Nuclear War. Edited by Ruth Adams and Susan Cullen. Various essays present the medical consequences of a nuclear attack, an analysis of the nuclear arsenals of the world, etc. $4.95 paper. February 1982.

Viking. **Nuclear Nightmares: An investigation into Possible Wars.** Nigel Calder. (See Penguin, above.) $10.95. August 1980.

The Arms Race/Disarmament

Avon/Discus. **The War Machine: The Case Against the Arms Race.** James Avery Joyce. Calls U.S. policy of nuclear deterrence "a criminal exercise in military suicide" and argues for an end to the arms race. $3.95 paper. August 1982.

Beacon Press. **Day Before Doomsday: An Anatomy of the Nuclear Arms Race.** Sidney Lens. Tells of the race for supremacy from Hiroshima through the present and criticizes American nuclear arms policy. $6.50 paper. December 1978.

Brethren Press (dist. by Caroline House). **The Idea of**

Disarmament: Rethinking the Unthinkable. Alan Geyer. Analyzes historical disarmament patterns and suggests options for the future. $11.95, cloth $17.95. March 1982.

Farrar, Straus & Giroux. **The Baroque Arsenal.** Mary Kaldor. Asserts that modern armaments are remote from military and economic reality. $14.95. September 1981.

W. H. Freeman & Co. **Progress in Arms Control? Readings from Scientific American.** Introductions by Bruce M. Russett and Bruce G. Blair. Examines arms control problems in relation to international relations, foreign policy and national security. $9.95, cloth $18.95. 1979.

Oelgeschlager, Gunn & Hain. **World Armaments and Disarmament: The SIPRI Yearbook 1981.** Stockholm International Peace Research Institute. Describes quantitative and qualitative changes in the world's armaments and analyzes efforts to control the build-up. $50. June 1981.

Paulist Press. **Nuclear Disarmament: Key Statements from the Vatican, Catholic Leaders in North America and Ecumenical Bodies.** Edited by Robert J. Heyer. Collects important church statements on the moral issue of disarmament. $7.95 paper. May 1982.

Quartet Books (dist. by Charles River Books). **The War Machine: The Case Against the Arms Race.** James Avery Joyce. (See Avon, above.) $14.95. 1981.

Random House. **National Defense.** James Fallows. Outlines the priorities the author believes must be established to develop a reliable and affordable defense system; the technical realities of nuclear weaponry and the risks of nuclear attack are explored. $12.95. 1981.

St. Martin's Press. **The Balance of Military Power.** Lt. Col. D. M. O. Miller, Col. William V. Kennedy, John Jordan and Douglas Richardson, foreword by J. M. A. H. Luns. Compares the weapons and capabilities of NATO and Warsaw Pact nations, with an entire section devoted to nuclear weaponry. $24.95. February 1982.

Seabury Press. **Rumors of War: A Moral and Theological Perspective on the Arms Race.** Edited by C. A. Cesaretti and Joseph T. Vitale. Explores the political, economic and moral ramifications of the arms race. $6.95 paper. March 1982.

The Risk of the Cross: Christian Discipleship in the Nuclear Age. J. Christopher Grannis, Arthur J. Laffin and Elin Schade, foreword by Henri J. M. Nouwen. Presents the authors' rejection of the arms race within the context of the Gospel. $4.95 paper. May 1981.

Unipub. **Obstacles to Disarmament and Ways of Overcoming Them.** United Nations Educational. Scientific and Cultural Organization. Explores international, legal and diplomatic aspects of disarmament. $17 paper. 1981.

Study on All the Aspects of Regional Disarmament. United Nations. Surveys past and present regional disarmament efforts, evaluating the regional approach. $17 paper. 1981.

University of Wisconsin Press. **Nuclear Proliferation: Breaking the Chain.** Edited by George Quester. Addresses the question of both nuclear weapons and reactors in a collection of articles. $6.95 paper. April 1981.

Viking. **Nuclear Illusion and Reality.** Solly Zuckerman. Argues that it is still possible to curb the stockpiling and refining of nuclear weapons. 20,000 first printing; $10.95. April 1982.

Yale University Press. **Controlling the Bomb: Nuclear Proliferation in the 1980's—A Twentieth Century Fund Report.** Lewis A. Dunn. Reviews the history of the nuclear age, identifies the countries most likely to obtain the bomb, and proposes policies to help the U.S. contain the bomb's spread and deal with a nuclearized world. $6.95, cloth $21. April 1982.

The Nuclear Power/Weapons Link

Addison-Wesley. **Nuclear Almanac: Confronting the Atom in War and Peace.** Edited by MIT faculty members, prologue by Henry Steele Commager. Reports on the nuclear issues of today: arms control, nuclear waste, nuclear arsenals and more. $14.95. September 1982.

Friends of the Earth. **Energy/War: Breaking the Nuclear Link.** Amory B. and L. Hunter Lovins. Argues that nuclear power spreads nuclear weapons and makes necessary the continued dependence of America on foreign oil. $10. Fall 1980.

Harper & Row. **Energy/War: Breaking the Nuclear Link: A Prescription for Non-Proliferation.** Amory B. and L. Hunter Lovins. (See Friends of the Earth, above.) $4.95 paper. May 1981.

Oelgeschlager, Gunn & Hain. **Nuclear Power and Nonproliferation: An Interdisciplinary Perspective.** Wiliam C. Potter. Provides description and analysis of the nuclear power/proliferation debate and assesses alternative strategies for nonproliferation. $25. March 1982.

Internationalization: An Alternative to Nuclear Proliferation? Edited by Eberhard Meller. Addresses the controversy between the U.S. and its European allies over the development of fast breeder reactors, stressing such factors as military security and politics. $22.50. 1980.

Sierra Club Books. **Nukespeak: Nuclear Language, Visions and Mindset.** Stephen Hilgartner, Richard Bell and Rory O'Connor. Argues that the government and nuclear power industry, which are closely linked, have used a "linguistic filter" to defuse the public's anxiety about nuclear power and weapons over the years. Price not set. September 1982.

Universe Books. **The Politics of Uranium.** Norman Moss. Discusses the conflicts over this rare and strategic metal used both to create electricity and to make bombs. $13.95. April 1982.

Nuclear Weapons

Autumn Press. **Nuclear Weapons: Report of the Secretary-General.** Contains the text of a report prepared by an international panel for a special United Nations session on disarmanent scheduled to open June 7. $7.95, cloth $12.95. September 1981.

Pergamon Press. **Born Secret: The H Bomb, *The Progressive* Case and National Security.** Explores the impact of the U.S. government's attempt to prevent publication of a magazine article about designing an H-bomb. $17.50. 1981.

Random House. **The Secret That Exploded.** Howard Morland. Offers a portrait of the nuclear weapons industry while recounting the author's search for the H-Bomb formula and the government's attempt to suppress its publication in the *Progressive* magazine. $13.95. 1981.

Unipub. **Comprehensive Study on Nuclear Weapons.** United Nations. Examines the trends in technological development of nuclear weapons systems and analyzes various theories about nuclear war. $13. 1981.

Nuclear Power

Ace. **The Health Hazards of Not Going Nuclear.** Dr. Petr Beckman. Argues that nuclear power is far safer than either coal or oil as a source of energy. $2.50 paper. September 1980.

American Tech. **Nuclear Power in Industry.** Leo A. Meyer. Describes in simplified terms the use of nuclear materials in industry, schools, medicine and research. $8. 1974.

Committee For Nuclear Responsibility (P.O. Box 11207, San Francisco, Calif. 94101). **An Irreverent, Illustrated View of Nuclear Power.** John W. Gofman. A group of "independent thinkers" and artists combine forces in this volume issued by a nonprofit organization. $3.95 paper. 1979.

Crane, Russak. **The Necessity for Nuclear Power.**

Geoffrey Greenhalgh. Analyzes trends in world energy demand and argues that nuclear power is an essential source for energy. $19. 1981.

Dell/Laurel. **Nuclear Power: The Unviable Option.** John J. Berger, introduction by Dr. Linus Pauling. Aims to translate technical and scientific information about nuclear power into prose accessible to the general reader, arguing that nuclear power is dangerous and expensive. $2.50 paper. 1977.

Facts on File. **The Encyclopedia of the Nuclear Age.** Barry J. Smernoff. Analyzes terms, theories, concepts, technology and events related to nuclear power. Price not set. December 1982.

Atomic Energy and the Safety Controversy. Grace M. Ferrara. Surveys the domestic and international discussion over health and technological hazards posed by the use of nuclear energy. $19.95. 1978.

Freemen Institute (P.O. Box 31776, Salt Lake City, Utah 84131). **The Nuclear War.** Eric N. Skousen, foreword by Edward Teller. Asserts that nuclear energy is safe and essential to continued American economic growth. $7.95 paper. December 1981.

Golem Press (Box 1342, Boulder, Colo. 80306). **The Health Hazards of Not Going Nuclear.** Petr Beckman. (See Ace, above.) $5.95 paper. 1976.

Harcourt Brace Jovanovich. **The Nuclear Question.** Ann E. Weiss. Discusses the benefits, dangers and development of nuclear power in a book aimed at young adults. $10.95. June 1981.

Heinemann Educational Books (4 Front St., Exeter, N.H. 03833). **How Safe Is Nuclear Energy.** Alan Cottrell. Explains how nuclear energy works, what the hazards are and how dangers can be countered. Advertising. $6 paper. November 1981.

Energy or Extinction. Fred Hoyle. Argues in favor of nuclear power as a source of energy and political protection. $3.95 paper. 1979.

Morrow. **Time Bomb: Understanding the Threat of Nuclear Power.** Corinne Browne and Robert Munroe.

Says that the threat of nuclear disaster is very real and must be fought. $11.95. November 1981.

Nichols Publishing. **Nuclear Power in Perspective.** Eric Addinall and Henry Ellington. Describes what nuclear power is and examines the arguments for and against its use in a nontechnical manner. $22.50. December 1981.

Norton. **Nuclear Power: Both Sides, The Best Arguments for and Against the Most Controversial Technology.** Edited by Michio Kaku and Jennifer Trainer. Experts on both sides discuss such issues as radiation, waste disposal, reactor safety and more in 21 essays. Price not set. September 1982.

Penguin. **Nuclear Power.** Walter C. Patterson. Surveys the development of nuclear power and describes the technology and how it works. $3.95 paper. 1976.

Pergamon Press. **Transitional Energy Policy 1980–2030: Alternative Nuclear Technologies.** Hugh B. Stewart. Contends that traditional nuclear planning is an inappropriate response to the world's energy requirements for the next 50 years. $12.50, cloth $30. 1981.

Nuclear Energy: An Introduction to the Concepts, Systems, and Applications of Nuclear Processes. Raymond L. Murray. Now in its second edition, this work covers the oil shortage, problems in the nuclear industry and public opposition to nuclear power. $15, cloth $39. October 1980.

Solar vs. Nuclear: Choosing Energy Futures. Secretariat for Futures Studies, Stockholm, Sweden. Examines the prospects for replacing fossil fuels with solar or nuclear energy. $18, cloth $43. February 1980.

Nuclear Safety. MMR Williams Nuclear Engineering Department, Queen Mary College, London. Collects articles on nuclear safety covering such topics as international cooperation, risk assessment and reliability. $18.50 paper. 1979.

Second Chance Press/The Permanent Press. **Cover Up: What You *Are Not* Supposed to Know About**

PAS

Nuclear Power. Karl Grossman. The single best-selling title for this publisher in its hardcover edition. $11.95. November 1980. Paperback: $8.95. June 1982.

Ticknor & Fields. **Nuclear Stakes: Race to the Finish?** Dervla Murphy. An Irish travel writer explores the nuclear power industry in a book prompted by the Three Mile Island incident. $12.95. May 1982.

University of California Press. **A Guidebook to Nuclear Reactors.** Anthony V. Nero, Jr. Provides information on basic reactor features, environmental interaction, plant emissions and the potential for accidents. 15,000 copies in print. $11.95, cloth $35. 1979.

University of Michigan Press. **Nuclear Power: Technology on Trial.** James J. Duderstadt and Chihiro Kikuchi. Offers a discussion of the issues in language designed for lay readers. $8.50, cloth $16. November 1979.

The Anti-Nuclear Movement

Crossing Press. **Grass Roots: An Anti-Nuke Sourcebook.** Edited by Fred Wilcox. Shows 15 ways readers can combat the nuclear industry and includes a list of U.S. antinuclear groups. $6.95, cloth $14.95. 1980.

Harper & Row. **Non-Nuclear Futures: The Case for an Ethical Strategy.** Amory Lovins and John Price. Discusses the technical, ethical, social, environmental, economic and political considerations of energy development. $3.95 paper. May 1980.

Judson Press. **Peace in Search of Makers.** Edited by Jane Rockman. Compiles papers presented during the Reverse the Arms Race convocation held in New York City at Riverside Church. $5.95 paper. 1979.

Monthly Review Press. **Protest and Survive.** Edited by E. P. Thompson and Dan Smith, foreword by Daniel Ellsberg. Contains an appeal to Americans (the book was originally published in England), a plan for a nuclear-free Europe and more. 25,000 copies in print; $4.95 paper. September 1981.

Norton. **Nuclear Witnesses: Insiders Speak Out.** Leslie J. Freeman. Workers in the nuclear industry—physicists, construction workers, uranium miners, test bomb veterans and others—talk about the health hazards and dangers that led them to oppose the industry they worked in. $5.95 paper. April 1982. ($16.95 cloth, published September 1981.)

Pantheon. **The Anti-Nuclear Handbook.** Stephen Croall, illustrations by Kaianders. Details the risks involved in building nuclear power plants and the dangers of nuclear waste, in a comic book format. $3.95 paper. June 1979.

South End Press. **No Nukes: everyone's guide to nuclear power.** Anna Gyorgy et al. Describes the inner workings of nuclear plants, chronicles the rise of opposition to the reactors and looks at the alternatives. $10, cloth $15. January 1979.

Twayne Publishers. **The Anti-Nuclear Movement.** Jerome Price. Gives a history of the movement, showing how it grew to its present size and influence and looking at its subgroups; environmentalists, scientists and direct-action groups. Price not set. November 1982.

Vision Books (St. Mary, Ky. 40063). **The Hundredth Monkey.** Ken Keyes, Jr. Summarizes data on the dangers of nuclear radiation and argues that a worldwide peace movement can reverse the current arms race. $2 paper. February 1982.

Survival Guides

Dial Press. **Life After Doomsday: A Survivalist Guide to Nuclear War and Other Major Disasters.** Bruce D. Clayton. Provides information for a family to prepare for and survive a nuclear holocaust, including advice on shelters, food, energy, equipment, group psychology and more. $8.95 paper. February 1981.

Macmillan/Collier. **The Nuclear Survival Handbook: Living Through and After a Nuclear Attack.** Barry Popkess. Tells what happens when the bomb drops and gives instructions for living in the aftermath. $5.95 paper. Fall 1982.

New Century Publishers. **How to Survive a Nuclear Disaster.** Thalif Deen and Col. Earl S. Browning. Advice on how to stockpile food, store water, find medical supplies, find a suitable shelter and more. $12.95. January 1982.

NWS Research Bureau (dist. by Caroline House). **Nuclear War Survival Skills.** Cresson H. Kearney, foreword by Dr. Edward Teller. Makes available the civil defense strategies of the scientists at the Oak Ridge National Laboratory. $9.95 paper. April 1981.

Paladin Press. **Life After Doomsday: A Survivalist Guide to Nuclear War and Other Major Disasters.** Bruce D. Clayton. (See Dial, above.) $19.95. February 1980.

Stein and Day. **Survive the Coming Nuclear War: How to Do it.** Ronald and Dr. Robert L. Cruit. Covers the main effect of nuclear weapons, home shelter designs, food and water storage, evacuation plans and more. $14.95. April 1982.

Health and Environmental Impact

Enslow Publishers. **Radiation: Waves & Particles/Benefits and Risks.** Laurence Pringle. Discusses the risks of low-level radiation, saying that it causes genetic damage and cancer. $8.95. June 1982.

Greenpeace/Center for Investigative Reporting (Fort Mason, Bldg. E, San Francisco, Calif. 94123). **Nuclear California.** Edited by David E. Kaplan. An anthology of reports on the social and environmental impact of nuclear technology on California. $5.95 paper. May 1982.

Pergamon Press. **Nuclear Energy and the Environment.** Essam E. El-Hinnawi. Assesses the environmental impact of the nuclear fuel cycle and how this will affect the future development of nuclear power. $56. June 1980.

Playboy Press. **Human Debris.** Lawrence White. Doc-

uments the occupational hazards faced by workers in nuclear power industries. $13.50. August 1982.

Putnam. **Countdown Zero.** Thomas H. Saffer with Orville E. Kelly. In 1980, coauthor Kelly died from cancer caused by radiation exposure to which some 250,000 U.S. servicemen were exposed from 1945 to 1962; this book examines U.S. military participation in nuclear weapons testing. $15.95. May 1982.

Sierra Club Books. **Radiation and Human Health.** Dr. John W. Gofman. Collects studies on the effects on humans, arguing that there is no safe level of radiation. $29.95. October 1981.

Radioactive Waste

Oelfgeschlager, Gunn & Hain. **Equity Issues in Radioactive Waste Management.** Edited by Roger Kasperson and Robert W. Kates. Analyzes major ques-

tions in this area, identifying various technical options and exploring areas of public choice. $25. May 1982.

Random House. **Radwaste: A Reporter's Investigation of a Growing Nuclear Menace.** Fred C. Shapiro. Examines the possibilities for safe and permanent containment of nuclear wastes that can remain lethal for as long as 240,000 years. $13.95. November 1982.

University of California Press. **Radioactive Waste from Nuclear Power Plants.** Thomas B. Johansson and Peter Steen. Looks at the Swedish government's 1980 decision to close down all existing nuclear power plants by the year 2010. $15.95. 1981.

Three Mile Island

Crossing Press. **Voices from 3-Mile Island, The People Speak Out.** Robert Leppzer. The personal accounts of people who live within a five-mile radius of the nuclear power plant differ greatly from the reports of the Nuclear Regulatory Commission, says the publisher. $3.95, cloth $10.95. 1980.

The New York Academy of Sciences (Box 5075, FDR Station, New York, N.Y. 10150). **The Three Mile Island Nuclear Accident: Lessons and Implications.** Edited

by Thomas H. Moss and David L. Sills. Describes the accident and explores the questions of environmental contamination, dissemination of information to the press and society's reaction to the event. $66. 1981.
Norton. **The Warning: Accident at Three Mile Island.** Mike Gray and Ira Rosen. Gives a step-by-step account of what happened at the plant before, during and after the 1979 accident. $14.95. June 1982.
Penguin. **Three Mile Island: Thirty Minutes to Meltdown.** Daniel F. Ford. Explains how the accident happened, how it was handled and what these events mean for the future of nuclear power. 25,000 first printing; $5.95 paper. March 1982.
Pergamon Press. **Report of the President's Commission on the Accident at Three Mile Island: The Need for Change: The Legacy of TMI.** John G. Kemeny. Contains the full text of the report. $27, cloth $35. December 1979.
Random House. **Three Mile Island.** Mark Stephens. The author served on the Presidential commission that investigated the accident and here retells the story of the nation's worst nuclear accident. $11.95. January 1981.
Sierra Club Books. **The People of Three Mile Island.** Robert Del Tredici. Photos and text explore the personal experiences of the people who lived near the plant. $7.95 paper. November 1980.

History and Strategy

American Nuclear Society (555 N. Kensington Ave., La Grange Park, Ill. 60525. **The Atomic Complex: A Worldwide Political History of Nuclear Energy.** Bertrand Goldschmidt. Explores the use of the atom from the first production of nuclear weapons through the 1981 Israeli attack on an Iraqi reactor. Price not set. Spring 1982.
FERMI-1: New Age for Nuclear Power. Edited by E. Pauline Alexanderson and Harvey A. Wagner. Documents the beginnings of nuclear power in 1945, the "atoms for peace" years and the history of the first functional nuclear power plant in the U.S. through 1972, when it was decommissioned. $27.80. 1979.
Cambridge University Press. **Nuclear Power and Non-Proliferation: The Remaking of U.S. Policy.** Michael J. Brenner. Discusses the ways the U.S. has dealt with the problem of nuclear weapons proliferation since 1974. $24.95. 1981.
The Nuclear Revolution: International Politics Before and After Hiroshima. Michael Mandelbaum. Looks at the way nuclear weapons have affected the alliances and strategies of nations. $8.95. cloth $29.95. 1981.
The Nuclear Question. Michael Mandelbaum. Examines the development of American military strategy and the arms limitation struggle witin the Soviet Union. $6.95, cloth $19.95. 1979.
Coward, McCann & Geoghegan. **Nuclear Culture: Living and Working in the World's Largest Atomic**

Complex. Paul Loeb. Portrays the people who live and work on the Washington State Hanford Nuclear Reservation. $14.95. April 1982.
E. P. Dutton. **The Bomb.** Sidney Lens. Traces the steps leading to the development of the atomic bomb, looks at the creation of complex weapons and delivery systems, and examines the different eras of atomic weapons including possibilities for the future. $11.50. May 1982.
Harper & Row **The Greatest Power on Earth: The International Race for Nuclear Supremacy.** Ronald Clark. Explores the interplay between science, politics and technology in the history of the development of nuclear power. $14.95. May 1981.
Holt, Rinehart and Winston. **The Nuclear Barons.** Peter Pringle and James Spigelman. Looks at the international elite of scientists, technocrats and businessmen who have controlled nuclear power and weapons for some four decades. 15,000 copies in print. $16.95. September 1981.
Houghton Mifflin. **The Killing of Karen Silkwood: The Story Behind the Kerr-McGee Plutonium Case.** Richard Rashke. Tells of the controversial nuclear contamination case that ended when Silkwood was killed in a car crash. $11.95. March 1981.
International Scholarly Book Services (P.O. Box 1632, Beaverton. Ore. 97075). **Worlds Within Worlds: The Story of Nuclear Energy.** Isaac Asimov. Explains the scientific concepts of nuclear reactions to the lay reader. $5.95, cloth $8.95. 1980.
Johns Hopkins University Press. **Strategic Thought in the Nuclear Age.** Edited by Laurence Martin. An international group of expoerts examine various aspects of strategy and defense in this collection of essays. $6.95 paper. September 1981. (Hardcover $18.50. 1980.)
Knopf. **The Winning Weapon: The Atomic Bomb in the Cold War 1945–1950.** Gregg Herken. Examines how American diplomats tried, but failed, to make the U.S. nuclear monopoly work to their advantage in negotiating with the U.S.S.R. $15.00. 1980.
A World Destroyed: The Atomic Bomb and the Grand Alliance. Martin J. Sherwin. Discusses the diplomatic and military role of the bomb during World War II. $12.95. 1975.
Macmillan. **Nuclear Power: From Physics to Politics.** Laurence Pringle. Surveys the history of the development of nuclear power in the U.S. in a book designed for young adults. $7.95. 1979.
Regnery Gateway. **Survival and Peace in the Nuclear Age.** Laurence W. Beilenson. Uses the lessons of history to prescribe a plan for U.S. military preparedness and civil defense. $10.95. October 1980.
Summit Books. **Who Killed Karen Silkwood?** Howard Kohn. Documents Silkwood's efforts to expose what she believed to be safety and health violations at the Kerr-McGee nuclear power plant and looks at the investigation surrounding her death. $8.95, cloth $14.95. November 1981.
Times Books. **The Islamic Bomb: The Nuclear Threat**

to Israel and the Middle East. Steve Weissman and Herbert Krosney. Studies the nuclear arms contest in such countries as India, Israel, Iraq, Libya and Pakistan. $15.50. January 1982.

Unipub. **The Swedish Public and Nuclear Energy: The Referendum 1980.** United Nations University. Studies the Swedish referendum in light of party politics and traces the formation of public opinion during the campaign that occurred two years ago. $5 paper. 1980.

University Books (a division of G. K. Hall). **Studies in Nuclear Terrorism.** Edited by Martin H. Greenberg and Augustus R. Norton. Collects essays analyzing terrorism on the national and international level, covering both individual and group threats. $24.95. 1979.

University of Alabama Press. **Nuclear Strategy in a Dynamic World: American Policy in the 1980s.** Donald M. Snow. Analyzes the nature of the nuclear system and looks at the stability and philosophy of the deterrence system. $12.95, cloth $25. January 1981.

University of California Press. **Kennedy, Khrushchev, and the Test Ban.** Glenn T. Seaborg with the assistance of Benjamin S. Loeb, foreword by W. Averell Har-

riman. Tells of the author's tenure as head of the Atomic Energy Commission and his involvement in the Limited Test Ban Treaty. $16.95. December 1981.

University of Oklahoma Press. **Innovations in Energy: The Story of Kerr-McGee.** John S. Ezell. Chronicles the history of the company's development of energy resources and includes an account of the Karen Silkwood case. 15,000 copies in print. $19.95. December 1979.

University of Wisconsin Press. **Nuclear Reactor Safety: On the History of the Regulatory Process.** David Okrent. Looks at the history of light water reactor safety, revealing the inner workings of the regulatory process. $29.50. June 1981.

Vintage. **The Winning Weapon.** Gregg Herken. (See Knopf, above.) $7.95 paper. February 1982.

Westview Press. **Science, Politics, and Controversy: Civilian Nuclear Power in the United States, 1946–1974.** Steven L. Del Sesto. Traces the evolution of civilian nuclear power and analyzes the commercialization of nuclear energy. $12, cloth $26.50. 1979.

Fiction

Ashley Books. **The Nuclear Catastrophe.** Bett Pohnka and Barbara C. Griffin. A minor earthquake jams the controls of a Southern California nuclear power plant, which then explodes. $12.95. 1977.

Delacorte/Seymour Lawrence. **"The Nuclear Age."** Tim O'Brien. The author of "Going After Cacciato" offers a comic novel spanning five decades of American life since the birth of the bomb. Price not set. 1983.

Dodd, Mead. **When Sirens Scream.** Robert E. Rubinstein. A teenage boy whose father is a state representative finds himself caught up in the problems caused by living near a nuclear power plant in a novel for readers aged 12 and up. $7.95. April 1981.

Out of Print

The Accident. Dexter Masters. This novel, based on a real-life occurrence at Los Alamos in 1946, tells of a physicist who is exposed to deadly amounts of radiation when a hazardous experiment he's working on goes awry. Published by Knopf in 1955 and reissued in a second edition in 1965, the book is currently out of print. The author recently revised the novel, dropping some of the historical background to make it "leaner and starker," and is currently seeking a publisher for a new edition. The book came to *PW's* attention through a letter from Richard Magat, former director of publications at the Ford Foundation and a Visiting Fellow at Yale, who was an early admirer of the book and hopes that today it can serve as "a reminder that thoughtful, articulate people were thinking and worrying about the profound social and political issues raised by the new genie even as it was being uncorked."

Publishers Weekly

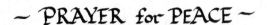

~ PRAYER for PEACE ~

Lead me from Death to life,
    from Falsehood to Truth.
Lead me from Despair to Hope,
    from Fear to Trust.
Lead me from Hate to Love,
    from War to Peace.
Let Peace fill our Heart, our World, our Universe.

~ · ~ ∷ ~ · ~

Mother Teresa of Calcutta
Westminster Abbey, London
Hiroshima Day, August 6, 1981

Of several minds: *Thomas Powers*

THE BOMB BIBLIOGRAPHY
BOOKS THAT HELPED MY THINKING

THE LITERATURE on nuclear weapons is vast, but much of it is written in a cautious, professional tone with one eye on job opportunities in the Pentagon. The result is a body of writing meticulous in scholarship and rigorous in analysis, but blinkered by the twin assumptions that things had to work out this way, and are well in hand. I'm not sure whether the first is true or not; the second strikes me as being willfully, even perversely, hopeful. Following are some of the books that helped me form my own views.

John Hersey, *Hiroshima* (Alfred Knopf, 1946). A brilliant short account of six people who survived the first nuclear weapon used in war, and of some of their friends, neighbors, and colleagues who did not. Reading it, one marvels at Truman's effrontery in describing Hiroshima as "a military target."

Samuel Glasstone, *The Effects of Nuclear Weapons* (U.S. Department of Defense, Third Edition 1977). A detailed technical treatise, with a handy "Nuclear Bomb-Effects Computer" — a sliderule-like device — in a pocket at the back. The emphasis is on what bombs do to things, not people.

Ruth Adams and Susan Cullen, *The Final Epidemic* (Educational Foundation for Nuclear Science, 1982). A collection of papers, mostly by scientists, on the medical, social, and ecological effects of nuclear war. This book will explain why a house in the country with a stock of canned goods in the basement is not enough. The emphasis is on what bombs do to people, communities, and the natural world—not things.

Stanislaw Ulam, *Adventures of a Mathematician* (Scribners, 1976). The best of the many memoirs of the Manhattan Project, which built the first bomb. Ulam captures the wartime cast of mind which allowed scientists to concentrate on the fascinating problems at hand. After the first Russian bomb was detonated in 1949, Ulam writes, "the general question was 'What now?' At once I said that work should be pushed on the 'super' " — the H-bomb.

Martin J. Sherwin, *A World Destroyed* (Knopf, 1975). As World War II drew to an end, Churchill asked, "What are we going to have between the white snows of Russia and the white cliffs of Dover?'' Sherwin persuasively argues that Hiroshima was at least partly the result of Truman's hope the bomb would make Stalin easier to handle.

Gregg Herken, *The Winning Weapon* (Knopf, 1981). By the end of 1950 the United States was firmly committed to nuclear weapons as the backbone of our military forces. Herken documents why this happened, and how the Joint Chiefs of Staff planned to use the bomb in the event of war.

C. Wright Mills, *The Causes of World War III* (Simon & Schuster, 1958). ''This disgraceful Cold War is surely a war in which we as intellectuals ought at once to become conscientious objectors.'' But with few exceptions, the intellectuals all went to work for the Department of Defense.

George Kistiakowsky, *A Scientist at the White House* (Harvard University Press, 1976). Kistiakowsky was Eisenhower's science advisor during the last years of his administration. He kept a fascinating diary recording his running battle with the Pentagon, which always wanted more of everything.

John Prados, *The Soviet Estimate* (Dial, 1982). Lawrence Freedman, *US Intelligence and the Soviet Threat* (Westview, 1977). What we knew about Russian military programs, and when we knew it. In retrospect it's clear we were ahead all the way, but repeatedly feared the Russians were about to streak ahead. The trouble is that it takes ten years to build a weapons system, but we can't know what the Russians will be doing that far down the road. The result is planning based on worst-case analysis.

Herman Kahn, *On Thermonuclear War* (Princeton University Press, 1960). Still the best introduction to the if-we-do-this, then-they'll-do-that school of strategic analysis. How to use fear of Armageddon as a politico-military tool. Kahn is the Homer of the scenario, and his approach is still the basis for Pentagon war games. Most of these show that *any* use of nuclear weapons leads to *heavy* use.

Barbara Tuchman, *The Guns of Au-gust* (Macmillan, 1960). We're not likely to see 1939 again; 1914 is what ought to worry us now. A principal cause of World War I was tight mobilization schedules which inexorably brought armies to frontiers where the best defense was an offense. What was the war about? It's hard to say. Europe had been preparing for war for thirty years, and eventually they had it.

Solly Zuckerman, *From Apes to Warlords* (Harper & Row, 1978). Zuckerman was at the heart of the WW II controversy over strategic bombing policy, a fierce and rational opponent of attacking cities. ''What [D.M.] Butt was particularly anxious to know was the ratio of casualties per ton of bombs in areas with different housing densities.'' Strategic bombing enthusiasts were on the run, until Hiroshima.

Sun Tzu, *The Art of War* (Oxford University Press, 1963). Clausewitz wrote, ''To introduce into the philosophy of war a principle of moderation would be an absurdity — war is an act of violence pushed to its utmost bounds.'' The Chinese military thinker Sun Tzu, who wrote in the fourth century B.C., took the opposite view. ''For to win a hundred victories in a hundred battles is not the acme of skill. To subdue the enemy without fighting is the acme of skills. Thus, what is of supreme importance in war is to attack the enemy's strategy . . . those skilled in war subdue the enemy's army without battle. They capture his cities without assaulting them and overthrow his state without protracted operations.''

Herbert Scoville, *MX: Prescription for Disaster* (MIT Press, 1981). ''The MX is a prime example of a nuclear war-fighting weapon that can lead us closer to the catastrophe of an atomic holocaust.'' Scoville provides a fine introduction to the current debate over strategic policy.

He argues that the MX would invite attack in a crisis, because it is accurate enough to threaten Soviet missiles.

Daniel O. Graham, *Shall America be Defended?* (Arlington House, 1979). A former director of the Defense Intelligence Agency argues that Russia, detente and SALT have led the U.S. down the garden path. ''The chance of war increases when aggressive powers like the Soviet Union build more and better weapons than peaceful countries such as the U.S.''

Gerard Smith, *Doubletalk: The Story of SALT I* (Doubleday, 1980). ''I had once heard President Eisenhower say that wars have a dynamic of their own. I believed that weapons design also had a dynamic of its own.'' Smith headed the delegation which negotiated the SALT I agreement with Russia, a three-year ordeal recounted here in fascinating detail. Smith laments the failure to ban MIRVs, multiple warheads which are now threatening to upset the strategic balance. We were ahead in MIRVs — for the moment — and didn't want to lose an ''advantage.'' Now Russian MIRVs threaten every American strategic weapon in a known location. Smith is both pithy and humane. ''Recently I was asked to lecture on the moral use of nuclear weapons. I declined. I knew of none.''

J.F.C. Fuller, *Armament and History* (London: Eyrie & Spottswoode, 1946). A professional soldier and military historian, Fuller concluded in 1946 that nuclear weapons changed everything. ''. . . the whole idea of maintaining peace through the power to destroy is unadulterated madness.'' Inevitably, he said, the bomb will be married to the rocket. ''Warfare will then take on a Krakatoan aspect.''

Thomas Pynchon, *Gravity's Rainbow* (Viking, 1973). The title refers to the arc of a missile in flight. This is a serious attempt to examine what modern war does to modern man. It is long and difficult to read. It treats the missile as the dominant fact of human history. It is amusing in parts. It might be described as the history of the next war, written in advance. THOMAS POWERS

Who wins if we have a nuclear war? NO ONE!

Who wins if we avoid nuclear war? PEOPLE!

"Each of our strategic submarines can destroy 160 Soviet cities. . . .No one can say we are not very powerful militarily. Now it's very difficult and somewhat embarrassing for military men to accept the fact that we have no defense against Soviet missiles and that Soviets have no defense against our missiles. We can destroy the Soviet Union even though they destroy us first. There are no winners in a nuclear war."
Rear Admiral Gene R. La Rocque, U S Navy (Ret)

War Without Winners is a film about people . . .

American people and Russian people.

Auto workers bomb assemblers, ballerinas, fruit vendors, space museum tour guides, and retired government officials.

War Without Winners is people expressing their fears, thoughts and hopes about the future in an age of nuclear weapons that can incinerate civilization in minutes.

"Can you imagine if they use the weapons we have? We'd destroy each other."

Man on the street

"If war ever came, everything would be destroyed. Of course, nothing would become of me. And all I'm hoping for is to dance."

Soviet ballerina

"I think the man on the street ought to be darn well concerned about how to prevent these extremely and uniquely destructive weapons from being used."

Dr. Ray Cline
Former CIA Deputy Director
for Intelligence

"Either we have to learn to live with the Russians, or we and the Russians will die at about the same time. And I am all for living."

Dr. George Kistiakowsky
Former Scientific Advisor to
Eisenhower, Kennedy and
Johnson

U.S. - 9500

USSR 5000

STRATEGIC NUCLEAR WEAPONS - 1979

"Not in one single nuclear weapons category have the Soviets demonstrated technological superiority. We have more strategic nuclear weapons than the Soviet Union. But you never hear this because the myth of U.S. inferiority is being spread to try and panic the public."

Dr. Herbert Scoville
Former CIA Deputy Director
for Science and Technology

"In the councils of government we must guard against the acquisition of unwarranted influence whether sought or unsought by the military industrial complex."

Dwight D. Eisenhower
Former U.S. President and General

"It's a chump's game. You can spend additional billions and the best you can hope for is that you won't be much worse off in national security. . . That's why arms control is in the interest of both sides."

Paul Warnke
Former Assistant Secretary of
Defense & SALT negotiator

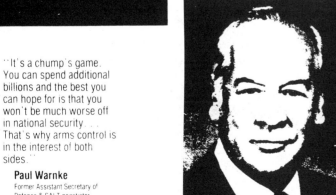

"The greatest issue of our age is nuclear war and our survival."

B.K. Gorwitz
Brigadier General, U.S. Army, Ret.

War Peace Film Guide

by John Dowling

World Without War

Video Tapes, Films, Slide Shows

"An Evening for Peace" (30-minute, videotape, ¾ inch cassette from Riverside Church Disarmament Program, 490 Riverside Drive, New York, New York 10027. Purchase: $30).

Highlights of December 7 event at Riverside Church with Dom Helder Camara, Olaf Palme, Studs Terkel, Vinnie Burrows, William Sloane Coffin, Cora Weiss, and the Bread and Puppet Theater.

"Dark Circle" (80 minute, 16 mm color. Contact The Independent Documentary Group, Judy Irving, Chris Beaver, 394 Elizabeth Street, San Francisco, CA 94114 (415) 824-5822).

Shot on location . . . , the film interweaves dramatic personal stories with rare footage of the secret world in which the Bomb is manufactured, tested, and sold.

"Day After Trinity" (90-minute film. Rental or purchase—contact: Pyramid Films, 2901 Colorado Avenue, Santa Monica, CA 90404 (213) 828-7577).

On J. Robert Oppenheimer and the atomic bomb.

"Eight Minutes to Midnight" (60-minute film. Color. Rental—contact: Direct Cinema Limited Library, P.O. Box 315, Franklin Lakes, New Jersey 07417 (201) 891-8240. For more information contact: Direct Cinema Limited, P.O. Box 69589, Los Angeles, CA 90060 (213) 656-4700).

Stirring portrayal of Dr. Helen Caldicott's tireless efforts to expose the nuclear industry in both its "peaceful" and its warlike activities; She takes us through the plutonium cycle from Navajo uranium mines to Three Mile Island, demonstrating the dangers of the nuclear era.

"Every Heart Beats True" (20-minute slide show/filmstrip with cassette narration from Packard Manse Media Project, Box 450, Stoughton, MA 02702. Purchase—$53/$24, rental—$12/week).

Thought-provoking program on Christian responses to the draft and registration; traces the history of the Church's position on war and peace. Excellent for draft-age audiences.

"Ground Zero at Bangor" (28-minute, 16mm color film from Religious Broadcasting Commission, 356 Post-Intelligencer Bldg., 521 Wall Street, Seattle, WA. Rent: $25. Sponsored by Northwest United Presbyterians through the Major Mission Fund).

Explores the emotional debate between advocates of disarmament and military superiority. Includes scenes from protests at the Bangor Trident Submarine Base.

"John, Mary, MIRV and MARV: The Arms Race and the Human Race" (15-minute slide show with cassette narration from Institute for World Order, 777 UN Plaza, New York, New York 10017. Purchase—$30, Rental—$7).

Imaginative treatment of the desire to be "Number One" and the folly and danger of using such categories in the nuclear era.

"Paul Jacobs and the Nuclear Gang" (60-minute film, free to borrow from Riverside Church Disarmament Program, 490 Riverside Drive, New York, New York 10027).

Emmy Award-winning film detailing the health effects of nuclear weapons production and testing on the surrounding community. A gripping portrayal of the human costs of the arms race. Eye-opener to government lying.

"Peace in Search of Makers" (30-minute slide show with cassette narration from Riverside Church Disarmament Program, 490 Riverside Drive, New York, New York 10027. Purchase—$60, Rental—$15).

Analysis of disarmament from a scientific and theological perspective with William Sloane Coffin, Richard Barnet and others commenting on the history of the arms race since Hiroshima and the prospects for reversing it.

The Disarmament Program is an educational, action-oriented effort, integral to the ministry of the Riverside Church. Through study, public forums, conferences and newsletters, we encourage religious people and others to work for peace. We assist young men and their families facing registration for the draft; we provide textbooks on disarmament for colleges and seminaries; we involve members of the congregation and the community in programs to study the impact of the arms race on our lives; we offer speakers, films, slide shows, and printed materials to people across the country. We study American foreign policy and its relationship to the arms race, and we encourage efforts to prevent war and preserve peace.

"War Without Winners" (30-minute film from Center for Defense Information, 122 Maryland Avenue, NE, Washington, D.C. 20002. Purchase—$350, Rental—$50).

Probably the most widely shown film on the nuclear arms race. Best thing available for the unconvinced. Documented. Conversations with American and Soviet citizens.

Nuclear Gang

Paul Jacobs and the Nuclear Gang is a moving and powerful social documentary about the US government's attempts to suppress information about the health hazards of low level radiation. The film covers exposure to atomic fallout by civilians around the government's Nevada test site in the 1950's and early 60's, the soldiers who were participants in the nuclear bomb tests and the problems today facing workers on the government's nuclear facilities at Hanford, Washington and Portsmouth, New Hampshire and the civilian population who live downwind from the Rocky Flats, Colorado nuclear plant. It's also about Paul Jacobs, political activist, filmmaker and journalist, who was one of the first to expose the government cover-up. Paul died in January 1978 of a rare form of lung cancer which the doctors believe he contracted investigating the story of 1957.

New Time Films Inc.
1501 Broadway, Suite 1904,
New York, New York 10036,
(212) 921-7020
Telex 620511
Rental $75—sale $750

Concord Films,
201 Felixstowe Road,
Ipswich, Suffolk, England
Tel. 0473-76012
15£ plus carriage and VAT

The World at War

Available from the Peace Pledge Union is a large (23″ X 16″) poster/wall chart entitled World at War. By showing two maps of the world, one with the major arms exporting countries in blue and the other with countries that have been at war at any time since 1945 in red, it vividly illustrates the world's north/south division.

The poster costs 20 pence (plus 10 pence p&p), with a discount for large orders, and is available from the Peace Pledge Union, 6 Endsleigh Street, London WC1 (Tel. 01-387-5501).

Peace News

Audio-Visual Materials

Freeze the Arms Race Slide Show—"Anatomy of the Arms Race" slide show was developed for a peace education program in Washington, DC. It describes the effects of nuclear weapons, examines the arsenals of the superpowers, looks at new strategies and the new weapons being developed and concludes with an appraisal of the Freeze proposal. 70 slides and a script. Cost: $45. Order from: Center for Peace Studies, Georgetown University, 2 O'Gara, Washington, DC 20057, (202) 656-4240.

Nuclear War and You: the Effects of Nuclear Weapons on Residential Structures—A two-and-a-half-minute 16mm silent film, and a descriptive guide, prepared for the Federation of American Scientists Nuclear War Education Project. Dramatic footage from the 1953 Nevada tests showing houses blasted by nuclear explosions. Draw a couple of circles on a map of your city and show this film. Your audience will no longer view nuclear war as an abstract concept. Cost: $15. Order from: Nuclear War Graphics Project, 100 Nevada Street, Northfield, MN 55057.

Nuclear War Graphics Package—130-slide package. Color slides on Hiroshima and Nagasaki, nuclear tests, the principles and production of nuclear weapons, the destructive capacity of modern nuclear weapons systems, U.S. and Soviet delivery systems, strate-

gic defensive systems, the arms race, proliferation, nuclear war scenarios and "can nuclear war be prevented?". An indispensable tool for educators and activists who wish to give illustrated talks on nuclear weapons, the arms race and nuclear war. Cost: $12. Order from: Nuclear War Graphics Project, 100 Nevada Street, Northfield, MN 55057.

The Threat of Nuclear War—A slide show originally prepared for the November 11, 1981 Union of Concerned Scientists Convocation. Included are 60 slides which were chosen from the Nuclear War Graphics Package, a tape-recorded narration, the script and a guide containing information about the slides. This 21-minute slide show is an excellent introduction to a discussion of the prospect of nuclear war. Cost: $10. Order from: Nuclear War Graphics Project, 100 Nevada Street, Northfield, MN 55057.

New Anti–Militarism Resource—The engrossing Vietnam documentary *Hearts and Minds* is now available for purchase at your local home video store for about $50.

The Nuclear Weapons Freeze Clearing House

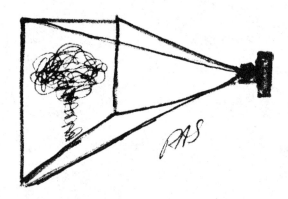

Anti-War Museum

A committee has been set up in Vienna to make plans for an International Anti-War Museum designed to attract attention beyond Austria, in order to awaken public opinion on the appalling violence endured during war, past and present. Plans include a permanent exhibition as well as temporary ones on specific issues, cultural gatherings and open forums, archives, a library, and film shows. For further information contact Joseph Peschon, BP 208 L-Luxembourg, or Michael Huffer, Kreuzbergstrasse 93, D-663 Saarlouis 3, FGR.

International F.O.R.

Some Anti-War Novels

Joseph Heller, *CATCH-22*

Erich Maria Remarque, *ALL QUIET ON THE WESTERN FRONT*

Dalton Trumbo, *JOHNNY GOT HIS GUN*

Jaroslav Hacek, *THE GOOD SOLDIER SCHWEIK*

Leo Tolstoy, *WAR AND PEACE*

Ernest Hemingway, *FAREWELL TO ARMS*

John Dos Passos, *THREE SOLDIERS*

Robert Stone, *THE DOG SOLDIER*

Among the Best Films

All Quiet on the Western Front	1930
The Grand Illusion	1937
Best Years of Our Lives	1946
Paths of Glory	1957
Dr. Strangelove	1964
Fail Safe	1964
Seven Days in May	1964
Americanization of Emily	1964
Bedford Incident	1965
Beach Red	1967
Patton	1970
Catch-22	1970

Marine Films

What Price Glory	1926
Flight	1929
Wake Island	1942
Guadalcanal Diary	1943
Sands of Iwo Jima	1949
Halls of Montezuma	1950
Battle Cry	1955
The D.I.	1957
Beach Red	1967
Boys in Company C	1978
Coming Home	1978
The Great Santini	1980

Vietnam

The Green Berets	1968
Limbo	1973
Rolling Thunder	1977
Heroes	1977
Coming Home	1978
Who'll Stop the Rain	1978
Go Tell the Spartans	1978
Boys in Company C	1978
Hair	1979
The Deer Hunter	1979
Apocalypse Now	1979
Rumor of War	1980
The Stunt Man	1980
Don't Cry, It's Only Thunder	1981

Films: Anti-War/Anti-Military

The Big Parade	1925
What Price Glory	1926
Wings	1927
All Quiet on the Western Front	1930
The Grand Illusion	1937
Sergeant York	1941
Paths of Glory	1957

World War II Films—significant, made during the war

Wake Island	1942
Bataan	1943
Air Force	1943
Destination Tokyo	1944
Thirty Seconds Over Tokyo	1944
Story of G.I. Joe	1945
They Were Expendable	1945
Walk in the Sun	1946

World War II Films—significant, made after the war

Sands of Iwo Jima	1949
Battleground	1949
Twelve O'Clock High	1949
Halls of Montezuma	1950
From Here to Eternity	1953
The Caine Mutiny	1954
Battle Cry	1955
The Enemy Below	1957
The Longest Day	1962

Korea

One Minute to Zero	1952
Retreat Hell	1952
Bridges at Toko-Ri	1954
Pork Chop Hill	1959
War Hunt	1962
Inchon	1982

Age of the Combat Spectacular

The Longest Day	1962
Battle of the Bulge	1965
Patton	1970
Tora! Tora! Tora!	1970
Catch-22	1970
Midway	1976
A Bridge Too Far	1977
Inchon	1982

Compiled by Lawrence Suid

Total Ban on War Toys Enforced in Sweden

The Swedish government has recently begun enforcing a total ban on war toys. Last year, shops started a voluntary ban, but the government has now banned all such toys by all routes, including mail order. Exceptions are items relating to pre-1914 traditions such as cowboy and Indian toys and "adult hobby" model kits, although the packaging of these must not display gory battle scenes.

There have been voluntary curbs on the sale of war toys in West Germany, as well. At the annual International Toy Fair recently held in Nuremberg, one organizer remarked: "You will have to look hard to find anything resembling a war toy."

Fellowship, *July-August 1980*

SAYING NO AND SAYING YES

by Steve Gulick

Conscientious objection to war is most commonly equated with military conscription and the decision by individuals to seek approval from the state to be excused from military "service" and do civilian work instead.

This is only the very narrow definition of conscientious objection allowed by the U.S. government. This official definition notwithstanding, conscientious objectors have taken actions ranging from refusing to register at all to refusing to perform "alternative service" to refusing induction.

At age sixteen or so I was struck by the phrasing offered by the government: ". . . conscientiously opposed to participation in war in any form." Although gramatically speaking there is only one interpretation, I read it in two ways: "war in any form" and "participation . . . in any form." How else, I wondered, may I be supporting war besides "serving" in the military? What aspects of my lifestyle, what products that I use, what actions that I habitually take—which of these may contribute to war without my knowing it? And what other conditions and situations may be root causes of war, violence, and human misery and may be conditions I can do something about? Pretty heavy questions for a sixteen-year-old, but nonetheless vital and vital, moreover, that sixteen- and sixty-year-olds seek the answers and live accordingly.

That is beyond the scope of this short article. Indeed, for me, it is the ongoing struggle of my lifetime. I want to focus here on an action that almost all adults must face: paying taxes which increasingly are spent for war and oppression.

Often the stumbling block for those who want to stop paying for war is how to do it, not why to, but, before outlining some how-tos, let me touch on three why-tos.

- Refusing to pay taxes for war helps individuals live in harmony with their beliefs; is personally empowering as resisters realize that they can control their own lives and stand firm in the face of government threats; and is a clear stand against war and for peace.
- Individual resisters find strength and support in the nationwide "community" of resisters. (there are contacts in at least 28 states and the District of Columbia).
- Resisted war taxes can be used in community self-development, education, social change, and peace projects—either by direct donation or by deposit in one of the at least 19 alternative funds nationwide which either lend or grant money. This helps make real the stand for peace and social justice.

There are a variety of steps one can take to begin stopping payment for war. I will simply outline some of them here.

- Send a protest letter along with the 1040 form—file and pay under protest.
- Stop paying the federal excise tax on the telephone bill. This is a tax associated with war since the First World War and can be refused by informing the phone company of one's action.
- Refuse a token amount of any tax due at tax time.
- Refuse a larger amount or a percentage or all of the tax due.
- Stop withholding or a percentage of it from one's paycheck by claiming more allowances or exemptions on the W-4 form filed with one's employer. (Note that this should be consistent with whatever one does on the 1040 form; also the employer is obliged to send to IRS a copy of any W-4 form which claims more than 9 allowances or claims exemption if the employee earns more than $200 per week. Otherwise the employer is supposed to accept any unaltered W-4 at face value. Of

course, a sudden change in the W-4 form can be considered "altered.")

- Reduce one's tax liability on the 1040 by claiming a "war crimes deduction" under miscellaneous on Schedule A; by increasing one's tax-deductible contributions; by taking on more dependents; and so on.
- Refuse to file a tax return (after having stopped withholding).
- Reduce one's income; live more simply; live below the taxable income level, but let the government know why.

Not everyone is able to do any given action, but everyone can do one or another of the above. Clearly some violate the law or regulations, but in general the consequences are not as harsh as they appear on paper.

Rather than say "oh, I can't do that," one can say "which action helps me live more in line with my beliefs and which *can* I do"? Some ask "which *must* I do"?

For more information or for a copy of the nationwide listing of war tax resistance counselors, centers, and alternative funds, send a stamped, self-addressed envelope and 25 cents to Philadelphia War Tax Resistance, 2208 South St., Philadelphia, PA 19146. (For the how-to guide *People Pay for Peace,* send $2 plus 40 cents postage.)

CCCO Notes

The Job of the
Peacemaker Is TO STOP WAR ·
TO PURIFY THE WORLD ·
TO GET IT SAVED FROM POVERTY AND RICHES ·
TO HEAL THE SICK · TO COMFORT THE SAD ·
TO WAKE UP THOSE WHO HAVE NOT YET FOUND GOD ·
To Find God TO CREATE JOY
AND BEAUTY
In Everything & In WHEREVER
YOU GO ·
& Everyone

MURIEL LESTER

When, Lord, did we ever see you hungry?

"The arms race can kill, though the weapons themselves may never be used . . . by their cost alone armaments kill the poor by causing them to starve."

Vatican statement to the United Nations, 1976

"The use of the modern technology of war is the most striking example of corporate sin and the prostitution of God's gifts."

Lambeth Conference of Church of England bishops, 1978

"The General Assembly urge Her Majesty's Government progressively to reduce the economic dependence of Britain's armament industry on foreign sales, to disband sales promotion agencies including the British Defence Sales Organisation and Millbank Technical Services Ltd, and to convert part of that industry to peaceful means."

Kirk of Scotland resolution, 1978

"They shall beat their swords into ploughshares and their spears into pruning-hooks; nation shall not lift up sword against nation, neither shall they learn war any more. But they shall sit every man under his vine and under his fig-tree; and none shall make them afraid."

Micah 4:3-4

The only purpose of weapons is to kill, and when Britain sells arms it is selling death. But the arms trade kills people indirectly, too. Most of the arms sold by Britain and the other arms suppliers go to developing countries where there is a desperate need for agricultural, educational, medical, and social welfare programmes.

People are starving . . . but their governments spend scarce resources on arms . . . and the British government, through its Defence Sales Organisation, encourages poor countries to buy even more arms.

The Campaign Against Arms Trade is a coalition of peace and internationalist groups working for an end to Britain's involvement in the arms trade, and for the conversion of military industry to peaceful production. It is supported by religious bodies, church leaders, and thousands of ordinary people who don't want Britain to remain a merchant of death.

The Lambeth Conference of Church of England bishops "called on Christian people everywhere to protest in whatever way possible at the escalation of the sale of armaments of war by the producing nations to the developing and dependent nations".

Work with the Campaign Against Arms Trade for a better, more peaceful world, where people are neither hungry nor afraid.

Peace for All Seasons

illustrated by Javan Stackley

NEBRASKA SPRING

Scarlet sky, edged in endless flowering quince,
I scream for you. Scandalous the threats
to sacrifice you; sacrilegious the schemes
to consider altering this inexpressible beauty.
A murderous scherzando (faster, faster)
plummets you to sarcophagus.
A lethal misplaced multiplexor,* a scathing
vengeful fingertip, scavenging defense contracts,
endless plots for plutonium triggers—
all these, my sacred scarlet sky,
my sacramental quince, all these conspire
against your safe conduct to another season.
Where is sanctuary for Creator's sad sandpiper?

Here is my sackclothed song. What is my last task?
Must I also keen for you? Will there be only scarabs?

*The 46C dime-sized computor chip that triggered the alarm system in 1980. See article by
Richard Thaxton in *Progressive*, August 1980. The Pentagon concedes that since 1968 there have
been at least thirty-two "broken arrows"—the military term for serious nuclear mishaps.

DAFFODILS WILL ALWAYS TAKE MY BREATH AWAY

Tremulous trumpets bowing
to my new longing—
evoking introspection.

Golden filigree of life—
spring for my winter
in brilliance and clarity.

Daffodils, yes, daffodils:
capsulized sunshine,
God's nonpareil work of art.

THE MISSILE OF FIRTH

Dateline 5 November 1980, *Lincoln Nebraska Sun:* "Firth
Co-op Acquires Atlas Missile Site—Intends Fuel Storage"

1961-1965: Active Duty
Who can tell of the missile of Firth?
A ninety-foot bullet hid in the earth
for four years waiting, prepared to give birth
to death to some of the people on earth.

1965-1979: Abandonment
Who can tell of the missile of Firth?
A fourteen-year lovers' lane laced now by mirth.
Love of all sorts where there had been dearth.
Fear bowed to love at the missile of Firth!

1980: Re-creation
Who can tell of the missile of Firth?
Now fuel can be stored in its tanks of much worth—
thousands of gallons safely under the earth!
A practical use for the silo of Firth.

19??: Hope
Who can tell of the missiles of Earth,
circling it 'round, gripping its girth?
Swords into plowshares would be of more worth.
Take the example of the missile of Firth!

LISTENING TO THE HIBAKUSHA* IN LINCOLN, NEBRASKA

Dateline 15 February 1981, *Sunday Journal and Star:*
". . . much of Nebraska would be in the front lines
should the unthinkable—a nuclear war—occur."

I was twenty-eight years old,
studying at home that day,
holding my baby.
My wife was shopping.
I heard the B-29,
and then the whole sky flashed
a bluish-white color.
The shock wave came.
Everything was complete darkness
when I opened my eyes.
I was lying flat,
still holding my child.
I heard people screaming for help.
Breakfast fires had been burning,
and these spread
When I found my wife
I handed her the baby
so she could feed it.
Her breasts were burned.
It was painful for her,
but she fed our baby.

The sin must not be repeated.

I was twenty years old
when the bomb fell.
On the third day after the bomb
black rain fell.
We were a mile from the center •
and the wind was in our favor.
. . . After two years I got married.
When I got pregnant I was afraid
because of radiation.
My husband said the baby was
a blessing.
I made up my mind to deliver
the child.
He died of lukemia at one year
and two months.
I realized that bitterness
should be directed to the bomb,
not to the American people.

The sin must not be repeated.

My husband
was one of the U.S. officers
who entered Nagaskai for
"clean up."
He was given no protective clothing.
He drank contaminated water.
When he came home, we began
our family.
Three of our seven children
were abnormal at birth.
In 1967 my husband developed
blood clots in his leg.
Incisions from amputation
wouldn't heal.
He is fifty-eight now.
He looks very, very old.

The sin must not be repeated.

I was forty-four on 6 August 1945.
I was at home
when the blinding flash came.
I went to look for my daughter.
I found her near the river where
many had come to cool their burns.
I heard her last words there.
I now live in a nursing home
for A-bomb survivors.
I tell my story for all humanity.

The sin must not be repeated.
Recorded by
Muriel Thiessen Stackley
Japanese for "sufferers from radiation" (pronounced: hee-BA-kush-a)

SING A SONG OF PEACE-MAKING

Sing a song of peace-making,
doing what you can.
Tell the world there's food for all—
for child! woman! man!

Sing a song of meat-canning;
rumble out the sound.
Every kind of Mennonite—
let goodwill abound.

Sing a song of Henderson—
fourteen thousand cans.
Hungry folks around the world
are holding out their hands.

Sing a song of Milford—
an annual giving thanks.*
Sharing food's a better way
than sending out the tanks.

Sing a song of peace-making,
doing what you can.
Tell the world there's food for all—
for child! woman! man!

*Meat-canning takes place in Milford, Nebraska,
every year during the week of Thanksgiving

Muriel Thiessen Stackley

LINDA'S GRANDMOTHER

Working on her treadle machine,
September to December in '73,
she sewed 108 kimonas and 36 quilts
for God and MCC

Plagued with hardened arteries,
her mind was no longer clear.
But she could surely make these things
for hundreds of babies to wear.

Her daughter once bought her two bolts of cloth,
fifty to sixty yards each.
"It doesn't take long and they're sewed up again,"
she said—a memorable speech!

Hundreds of diapers she sewed in her time
(twenty-seven inches square).
"No fancy work for me," she said.
"*That* just sits in the drawer."

Working on her treadle machine
for many of her years, seven and eighty,
she sewed a warm, strong, band of love
for God and MCC.

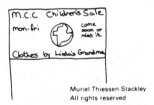

Muriel Thiessen Stackley

Suggested uses: postcards, place mats, greeting cards.

"WARS ARE POOR CHISELS FOR CARVING OUT PEACEFUL TOMORROWS.... WE MUST PURSUE PEACEFUL ENDS THROUGH PEACEFUL MEANS" MARTIN LUTHER KING

photo by Bob Fitch

"The ultimate weakness of violence is that it is a descending spiral, begetting the very thing it seeks to destroy. Instead of diminishing evil, it multiplies it. Through violence you may murder the liar, but you cannot murder the lie, nor establish the truth. Through violence you murder the hater, but you do not murder hate. In fact, violence merely increases hate...Returning violence for violence multiplies violence, adding deeper darkness to a night already devoid of stars. Darkness cannot drive out darkness; only light can do that. Hate cannot drive out hate: Only love can do that."

Martin Luther King Jr.

The Fellowship of Reconciliation, Nyack, New York

Do not listen to voices which speak the language of hatred, revenge, retaliation.

Do not follow any leaders who train you in the ways of inflicting death. LOVE LIFE, respect life in yourself and in others.

POPE JOHN PAUL II

UNITED STATES ACADEMY FOR PEACE AND CONFLICT RESOLUTION

As we begin the 1980's, creation of the United States Academy of Peace and Conflict Resolution is nearer than ever — now, when the need is greater than ever. Congress has considered the establishment of such an Academy and determined that the idea warranted definitive study by a National Commission. The U.S. Peace Academy Commission, funded in late 1979, has one year in which to decide whether such an Academy is needed, and if so, to recommend how and where it should function.

THE NATIONAL PEACE ACADEMY CAMPAIGN

The National Peace Academy Campaign (N-PAC), a membership-supported organization, has a single objective — establishment of the United States Academy of Peace and Conflict Resolution. Its members are convinced of the need for such an Academy and are working toward that goal. They believe that the Academy could both teach the affirmative use of conflict resolution techniques and sponsor, coordinate and conduct research in this vital field. They believe that third-party mediation has been proven effective in both domestic and international conflict situations, and that the state of the art has reached a level which warrants widespread application and concerted research.

OBJECTIVES OF THE ACADEMY

N-PAC believes that a United States Academy of Peace and Conflict Resolution could provide a sustained source of trained and experienced individuals who could:

- Employ cost-effective alternatives to force and violence in the resolution of conflict.
- Effect the sensible resolution of community, minority and environmental disputes.
- Curb terrorism and diminish community disruption attendant to violence.
- Protect personal safety and individual security.
- Improve economic stability.
- Spot developing international conflicts and resolve them *before* they erupt into violence.
- Lower international tensions and reduce the threat of catastrophe from today's weapons.

National Peace Academy Campaign
1625 Eye Street, N.W., Suite 726
Washington, D.C. 20006 (202) 466-7670

TRAINING, RESEARCH AND PLACEMENT

While the Commission will make the official recommendation concerning the Academy structure and operation, N-PAC suggests that a United States Academy of Peace and Conflict Resolution *could:*

- Be both federally and privately funded under Federal sponsorship, as are the Smithsonian Institution and the Corporation for Public Broadcasting, both of which function as largely autonomous, non-profit corporations. As such, a United States Peace Academy would become the prime example of a major nation committing its resources to training individuals in non-violent means of resolving conflict.
- Emphasize practical training involving "in the street" conflict resolution techniques plus advanced-level subjects including a multi-disciplinary curriculum of behavioral science, social science and mediative studies.
- Teach conflict resolution techniques applicable to both international and domestic conflict situations, at pre-emptive, crisis, and post-crisis stages — thus complementing diplomatic and international relations training in which traditional graduate schools specialize. This is essential, since the mediation skills required in conflict resolution differ significantly from the advocacy skills required of the professional diplomat.
- Offer a two-year masters program and internship period, as well as mini-courses and special short seminars for private citizens, business managers and employees, government employees, civic leaders, military personnel and law enforcement officers.
- Provide graduates the opportunity to move on to useful positions of their choice with community groups, the Federal government, non-governmental organizations, local, state and municipal agencies corporations and domestic and international organizations which aid in the instruction and delivery of conflict resolution services. In such positions graduates could serve to defuse potential conflict before it erupts into violence.

The United States has four military academies and five war colleges devoted to maintaining peace by armed force. Isn't it time we had at least one national institution dedicated to creating the conditions of peace by affirmative means?

WAR RESISTERS LEAGUE

Guide To War Tax Resistance

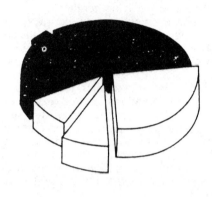

Everything You Wanted To Know About War Tax Resistance, But Were Afraid To Ask the IRS

This *Guide* is a comprehensive, up-to-date sourcebook on war tax resistance. The 17 chapters and the 40 photos, graphics, and charts, plus the index all provide a handy reference, whether you are a war tax resister, counselor, or just curious about resistance.

Besides the detailed chapters on the hows, why, and consequences, the *Guide* gives a thorough history of war tax resistance in America from 1673 to the present. There are inspiring accounts of 16 people who have experienced IRS harassment or have been jailed for their resistance, and some who have refused taxes for decades (up to 40 years) without an IRS collection.

The *Guide* is 128 pages long in an 8½" x 11" format, enclosed within a three-color perfect bound cover. Each book costs $6, plus $1 for postage and handling.

CONTENTS

War Resisters League, 339 Lafayette Street, New York, NY 10012

Church Refuses to
Take Pay for IRS

AMES, Iowa (AP)—St. Thomas Aquinas Roman Catholic Church has told the Internal Revenue Service it will not garnish the wages of a member of the church's staff who is refusing to pay federal taxes.

Tom Cordaro, a lay minister for the church, did not pay $828 in income taxes from 1979 and 1980, saying it would violate his religious beilefs to support the nuclear arms race.

Last week the parish council told the IRS it had decided not to deduct the amount owed from Cordaro's pay, and now the IRS may sue the church for the money if the council does not reconsider, according to the Rev. Patrick Geary, parish administrator.

In a letter to the IRS, Geary said the parish is "not a tax collecting agency and . . . we see underlying moral implications we have not had time to sufficiently explicate."

The South Bend, Indiana, Tribune, *February 2, 1982.*

Paying for War

God and Caesar, a newsletter published by the Commission on Home Ministries of the General Conference Mennonite Church, is for "serious sharing and mutual encouragement in discerning and doing the will of God in response to Caesar's demands for money for military purposes."
God and Caesar
Box 347
Newton, KS 67114

The 1981 edition of the *Handbook on Nonpayment of War Taxes* put out by Peacemakers is now available. It has sections on reasons for not paying war taxes, ways of nonpayment, regulations on filing, personal experiences, listing of war tax resistance counselors, centers, and alternative funds, and many other items. It is available at Peacemakers, Box 627, Garberville, CA 95440, and from Rod Nippert, Rt. 1, Box 90-B, Amesville, OH 45711. Prices postpaid are $1.50 single copy, $5.00 four copies, $50.00 fifty copies. Prepayment is preferred but they will send quantities without payment if every effort is made to pay them back. Anyone who cannot afford the price may ask for a free copy.

The *Newsletter,* published by Betty Johanna, War Tax Resistance, 331 17th Ave. East, Seattle, WA 98112, publishes an annual tax resistance issue.

You can also write **World Peace Tax Fund**, 2111 Florida Ave, NW, Washington, D.C. 20008.

God and Caesar

By Way of Introduction . . .

The history of nonviolent struggles for freedom and justice is a long and distinguished one, but it is little known. Probably most Americans vaguely associate nonviolent action with Martin Luther King, Jr., and perhaps with Mahatma Gandhi. If they think about it at all, they think of it as quaint, quixotic, quasi-religious or spiritual, and applicable only in those situations in which it has already occurred.

How many people know that nonviolent action was used successfully against the Nazis in World War II? That in Latin America, where violent revolution seems to be the order of the day, governments have been completely overthrown through popular nonviolent action? That here in the U.S. the United Farmworkers Organizing Committee, under Cesar Chavez, is successfully carrying on a revolutionary struggle through nonviolent means? Or that in India, where organized nonviolent action was supposed to have died with Gandhi, a popular revolutionary movement based on Gandhian principles has already touched tens of thousands of Indian villages?

Why is it that we know so little about these and other instances of radical nonviolent action? One reason is that we all suffer from a cultural addiction to violence as the only means of bringing about radical change. This addiction is most evident in our history books. Gandhi once remarked, "History is really a record of every interruption of the even working of the force of love or of the soul . . . interruption of the course of nature. *Satyagraha* (translated as 'the force born of truth and love' and as 'nonviolent resistance'), being natural, is not noted in history."

Our cultural addiction to violence is also evident in our mass media, which rarely reports anything which happens gently; the media is primarily interested in guns and flames. And, unfortunately, we consumers of the mass media have been conditioned to take notice of little else ourselves.

Finally, as Devi Prasad points out with reference to the *Gramdan* movement in India, ". . . man has lost faith in himself as an individual. Therefore, he fails to see revolution being carried out by ordinary people like himself, especially a revolution without bloodshed."

Disregarded History

NORWAY, 1942

"But what would you do about enemies like the Nazis? Could they really be opposed effectively by nonviolent means?"

The answer to this question is that during World War II there *was* considerable nonviolent resistance taking place on various scales in a number of countries, but especially important in the Netherlands, Denmark, and Norway. The Norwegian teachers' resistance is one of the most important of these resistance campaigns.

During the Nazi occupation, the Norwegian fascist "Minister-President," Vidkun Quisling, set out to establish a fascist Corporative State modeled after Mussolini's Italy, selecting teachers as the first "corporation." For this he created a new teachers' organization with compulsory membership. A compulsory fascist youth movement was also set up.

The underground called on teachers to resist. Between 8,000 and 10,000 of the country's 12,000 teachers signed their names and addresses to the text circulated by the underground, addressed to Quisling's Church and Education Department, saying they could not take part in the fascist education of youth and concluding: "I cannot regard myself as a member of the new teachers' organization."

The government threatened them with dismissal and then closed all schools for a month. Teachers held classes in homes. Despite censorship, news of the resistance spread. Tens of thousands of letters of protest from parents poured into the government office.

After the teachers defied the threats, about 1,000 male teachers were arrested and sent to concentration camps. Children gathered and sang at railroad stations as teachers were shipped through in cattle cars. In the camps, the Gestapo imposed an atmosphere of terror intended to induce capitulation. On starvation rations, the teachers were put through "torture gymnastics" in deep snow. Only a few gave in; "treatment" continued.

The schools reopened, but the remaining teachers told their pupils they repudiated membership in the new organization and spoke of a duty to conscience. Rumors were spread that if these teachers did not give in, some or all of those arrested would be killed. After difficult inner wrestling, the teachers who had not been arrested almost without exception stood firm.

Then on cattle car trains and overcrowded steamers, the arrested teachers were shipped to a camp near Kirkenes, in the far north of Norway. There they were kept in miserable conditions, doing dangerous work.

Their suffering, however, strengthened morale on the home front and posed problems for the Quisling regime, to the point that Quisling, visiting a school near Oslo, ranted and raved and screamed at the teachers, so loudly that it was heard in the schoolyard, "You teachers have destroyed everything for me!" Fearful of alienating Norwegians still further, Quisling finally ordered the teachers' release. Eight months after the arrests, the last teachers returned home to triumphal receptions.

Quisling's new organization for teachers never came into being, and the schools were never used for fascist propaganda. After Quisling encountered further difficulties in imposing the Corporative State, Hitler ordered him to abandon the plan entirely.

BERLIN, 1943

In the midst of the Second World War, in the capital of the Third Reich, toward the end of the Nazis' program of annihilation of Europe's Jews, a final round of arrests of Jews took place. Heinz Ullstein, one of the men arrested, describes the nonviolent protest that followed which, in the end, was completely successful:

The Gestapo were preparing for large-scale action. Columns of covered trucks were drawn up at the gates of factories and stood in front of private houses. All day long they rolled through the streets, escorted by armed SS men. . . . On this day, every Jew living in Germany was arrested and for the time being lodged in mass camps. It was the beginning of the end.

People lowered their eyes, some with indifference, others perhaps with a fleeting sense of horror and shame. . . . From the vast collecting centers to which the Jews of Berlin had been taken, the Gestapo sorted out those with "Aryan kin" and concentrated them in a separate prison in the Rosenstrasse. No one knew what was to happen to them.

At this point the wives stepped in. Already by the early hours of the next day they had discovered the whereabouts of their husbands and, as by common consent, as if they had been summoned, a crowd of them appeared at the gate of the improvised detention center. In vain the security police tried to turn away the demonstrators, some 6,000 of them, and to disperse them. Again and again they massed together, advanced, called for their husbands, who despite instructions to the contrary showed themselves at the windows, and demanded their release.

For a few hours the routine of a working day interrupted the demonstration, but in the afternoon the square was again crammed with people, and the demanding, accusing cries of the women rose above the noise of the traffic. . . .

Gestapo headquarters was situated in the Burgstrasse, not far from the square where the demonstration was taking place. A few salvos from a machine gun could have wiped the women off the square, but the SS did not fire, not this time. Scared by an incident which had no equal in the history of the Third Reich, headquarters consented to negotiate. They spoke soothingly, gave assurances, and finally released the prisoners.

CZECHOSLOVAKIA, 1968

Czechoslovakia in 1968 waged a nonviolent war of resistance against Soviet invasion which seems in the end to have been lost. But we learn from lost military wars and we can learn from lost nonviolent wars.

Soviet leaders expected that the massive invasion of Czechoslovakia by more than half a million troops in August 1968 would overwhelm the Czech army and succeed in installing a puppet regime within four days. Faced with the obvious futility of military resistance, Czech officials ordered their army to remain in the barracks. Alexander Dubcek and other Czech leaders, whose reforms were the reason for the Soviet invasion, were kidnapped by the Soviet KGB (State Police). Then, without preparations or training, the population undertook nonviolent resistance. Totally improvising under highly unfavorable circumstances, they prevented the installation of a collaborationist government for a full eight months, until April 1969. Although their troops were distributed throughout the country, the Soviet government was forced to release and negotiate with the very reformist government they had set out to replace.

Resistance began in the early hours of the invasion. Employees of the government news agency refused orders to issue a release stating that certain Czechoslovak leaders had requested the invasion. President Ludvik Svoboda, under house arrest, courageously refused to sign a document presented him by the conservative clique. Finally, through the clandestine radio network, it was possible to convene several official bodies, and these opposed the invasion. The Communist Party officials and government ministers who were left issued statements that the invasion had begun without their knowledge and that it had not been "requested." The National Assembly went on to demand "the release from detention of our constitutional representatives . . . in order that they can carry out their constitutional functions" and the "the immediate withdrawal of the armies of the five [Warsaw Pact] states."

The clandestine radio network played a crucial role during the first week, calling one-hour general strikes,

requesting rail workers to slow the transport of Russian tracking and jamming equipment, and discouraging collaboration among the Czechoslovak State Police (many of whom worked actively with the resistance). It argued the futility of acts of violence and the wisdom of nonviolent resistance. It instructed students in the streets to clear out of potentially explosive situations and cautioned against rumors. Through the radio, different levels of resistance and different parts of the country were kept in steady communication. With many government agencies put out of operation by Russian occupation of their offices, the radio also took on certain emergency functions (such as finding people to bring in potato and hops harvests) and provided vital information (ranging from assuring parents that their children in summer camps were safe to reporting meager news of the Moscow negotiations).

Militarily totally successful, the Russians now faced a strong political struggle. They had expected the situation would be so well under control within three days that invading troops could then be withdrawn. When this did not happen, serious logistical and morale problems began to develop among the invading troops. On the third day following the invasion, Soviet leaders agreed that President Svoboda would fly to Moscow for negotiations. Svoboda refused to negotiate until Dubcek and other kidnapped leaders joined the discussions. In four days a compromise was worked out. This left most of the leaders in their positions, but called for the party to exercise more fully its "leading role" and left Russian troops in the country. Certain reform-minded leaders and reforms were also sacrificed.

The compromise, called the Moscow Protocol, created severely mixed feelings among the people, and for a week the population refused to accept it. Even when they did, the remarkable fact remained that, despite a military victory under which negotiations should not have been required or expected, the Soviet Union had been forced to allow the Czech leaders to return to their positions and to keep major parts of the reforms. These were maintained until April 1969 when riots at the Aeroflot offices, a break in the nonviolent discipline possibly instigated by *agents provocateurs,* were used as an excuse by the Russians to replace the Czech leadership. It can be argued that the Soviet's ultimate success resulted more from the collapse of resistance by the government and Party than it did from any intrinsic weakness in the means of resistance.

The leadership capitulated—but only after holding out for eight months, with no preparation or training, compared with an estimate that the well-prepared and equipped Czech army could have held out for four days. Had unprepared military struggle against such odds held off the Russians for eight months it would have been hailed by the West as victory even in defeat, with courage and historical significance comparable to the Thermopylae.

Sources: Gene Sharp, The Politics of Nonviolent Action, *(Bos-*

ton: Porter Sargent, 1973); Sharp, Nonviolent Action as a Substitute for International War, Bulletin of Peace Proposals *(Oslo: Universiteitsforlaget)* Vol. 9, No. 4, 1978; and Sharp, Non-Military Defense, Peace News *(London),* 3 April 1981.

POLAND, the 1980s

A new chapter is being written in the history of civilian defense by the people of Poland. The activities of the independent trade union Solidarity set off a chain of events changing the life and spirit of the Polish people and transforming their society. The workers' unlikely symbols were the cross, the image of the pope, and the national flag, reflecting that from the beginning more than simple economic rights were at stake. Using strikes, sit-ins, and demonstrations—the weapons of nonviolence—Solidarity began a process of change that neither its own government nor the Soviet Union, with all its military power, has been able to stop.

One can't predict the final outcome—whether the Soviet Union will feel driven to invade Poland out of fear of the breakdown of the Warsaw Pact, the basis of its defense. Faced with that possibility, Solidarity in April [1981] prepared instructions for the population, mimeographed and widely distributed, which amount to a plan for civilian-based defense: news of an invasion would be spread using every possible means, including church bells, car horns, and sirens; highway signs, street names, house numbers, etc. would be taken down; the invaders would be given false information and delayed by other means; food producers would make it difficult to feed the invading troops; alternative strike committees would replace arrested Solidarity leaders; and so on. Leaflets warned the people of the sorts of repression that might occur and promised the Soviet Union that an intervention would be "extremely costly," because the Polish people were prepared to resist, even if it required great sacrifices.

One wonders to what extent it is the prospect of such resistance that has prevented an invasion so far.

The Soviet Union has surely not forgotten the eight months of civilian resistance by an *unprepared* population in Czechoslovakia in 1968. In any case, one thing is clear: The unarmed Polish movement is wielding a power whose potential has yet to be fully developed.

Reprinted from IFOR Report, June 1981

THE FUTURE

Most people have been totally unaware of the long history of nonviolent conflict resolution employed in response to aggression, tyranny, genocide, and oppression—a history dating back to 494 B.C.

Recently, however, the increased use of violence as a means of solving conflicts on both domestic and international levels, along with the threat of nuclear war, has led to the investigation and documentation of alternatives to violence by historians and educators. Research has uncovered a vast history of the use of such alternatives, unrecorded in most history books, which has used a wide variety of methods, including economic boycotts, sit-ins, protest marches and parallel governments. These methods have proven effective not only to convert opponents but, more importantly, to destroy the power of dictators.

Lack of knowledge about this greatly underdeveloped technique has meant that each time people have engaged in nonviolent conflict resolution they have had to improvise anew. As one historian has put it, the question and the challenge now before us is, "With education, research and training, will we eventually be capable of destroying a Nazi-type system by nonviolent means?"

For more information about Nonviolent Defense, how it has been used in the United States, and how individuals can further *alternatives to violence* in their own communities, write: *Fellowship of Reconciliation (FOR)* Alternatives to Violence, Youth Action, Box 271, Nyack, NY 10960. Contributions to cover the cost of these materials ($1) and to help educate about *alternatives to violence* may be sent to the same address.

Twenty Suggestions for Teaching Peace to Children in the Home

If, as most educators agree, the home is the most important place where peace values are taught, how does the home go about doing this? Where do I, a parent, go for help when I see my son solving a problem by what looks to me like violent methods? How do I teach peace to my children?

My survey of the literature on peace education of the historic peace churches—Mennonite, Brethren, Friends—and from other sources written during the past 30 years unearthed a surprising number of practical suggestions on teaching peace to children. These, however, have never before been brought together in one place and were not readily available to parents and other adults when they needed them most.

The suggestions I found in these sources on how to teach the values of peace and nonviolence to children can be grouped into four divisions. The first have to do with the atmosphere of the home:

1. Cultivate a good homelife.

Stephanie Judson, writing in *A Manual on Nonviolence and Children,* believes there are five elements that must be cultivated in a home where children will learn to be peacemakers: a) affirmation of each other; b) sharing of feelings, information, and experience in order to learn to understand others; c) a supportive community that allows people to work together on problems; d) practical experience for children on different ways to solve problems; and e) a sense of enjoying life together. A home where these are experienced develops in children a sense of well-being and wholeness, one that contradicts the feelings of helplessness and powerlessness that pervade the modern world.

2. Join a parent support group.

If parents would provide the proper kind of environment for their children, they themselves should have resources available to help them work through problems and deal with frustrations. A support group of other parents can be one of the best such resources.

"This support approach creates an atmosphere which nurtures an individual's ability to work creatively on problems," says *A Manual on Nonviolence and Children.* "Being appreciated and affirmed, whether at home, in a meeting, or in a classroom encourages people to discuss problems openly; it also provides an empowering sense that the problems can be solved without permanent physical or emotional damage to anybody involved in the conflict. When parents have an opportunity to draw on this nonviolent atmosphere themselves, they are far more likely to create and model it for their children."

3. Provide a good example.

Adults need to *be* the kind of persons they want their children to become. Unless parents believe an ideal important enough to incorporate it into their own lives, it is doubtful whether they will be able to teach it to their children.

Much of the literature on teaching peace values to children emphasizes the need for parents to be good role models. How they handle conflict in the home, how they react to it in the community, and how they relate to a violent world have tremendous teaching influence on the children in their lives.

One study of conscientious objectors in World War II found that encounters with a dynamic role model—minister, teacher, or community figure—often in early teens, was the most critical influence in having a young man become a conscientious objector.

4. Help children experience forgiveness.

To be encouraged to become peacemakers, children need to experience forgiveness from their parents when they make mistakes. They must also be helped to forgive others who wrong them. It is only as they learn to exercise and accept forgiveness that children can acquire the knowledge they need to become reconcilers in the conflict situations they meet later in life.

Another group of suggestions on how to teach peace values to children have to do with things parents should avoid bringing into the home:

5. Don't buy war toys.

Much of the literature of the past 30 years with regards to peace education has been concerned with the effect of war toys in peacemakers' homes.

"Although war games may be normal for growing youngsters and should not be forcibly prohibited, they should be discouraged through the encouraging of more constructive games and activities which are more creative and exciting," wrote Edith Graber in a General Conference Mennonite publication soon after World War II. "Special war toys, such as tanks, toy soldiers, etc., do not appear to be justifiable for any reason."

Leland Miles, writing in the December 12, 1961 issue of *The Mennonite,* said: "Toy soldiers, whether marching or fighting, do the same thing for a child that beer does for the American Legionnaire—they cast a romantic glow over the thud of lead in flesh, and make war a harmless little game of epaulets, salutes, gold-striped trousers, and pleasant jeep rides. In an age which features the most hideous weapons of all time, any parent who does not make every conceivable effort to dispel such a glow assumes a dreadful responsibility for the future."

Other writers mention the danger of war toys establishing behavior patterns and values children will follow as adults, and of making war more acceptable as a pattern of life for the child.

In short, with reference to parents in peace churches buying war toys for their children, the sources agree: *don't.*

6. Avoid entertainment glorifying violence.

Whether it be movies, television, or radio programs, the peace-loving family will shun entertainment based on violence or accepting violent solutions as a way of

life. "For most children, it's got to be difficult to interpret why Mom and Dad react so emotionally to a local shooting but sit and watch the same thing on TV with no show of emotion," says one writer.

7. Curb backyard fighting.

A way to teach peace values to children is to work with them on handling the conflicts that erupt during their play. One mother offered this solution for the fighting and bullying that occurred in her neighborhood: she outlawed fighting in her backyard and made it a rule that whoever tried to start one had to leave. If fights had to occur, they were to be outside her yard and without her children. She hoped that gradually the children would realize that differences can be settled in ways other than physical violence.

Other parents may not want to adopt such a legalistic approach. But they must be at least be interested in helping their children solve conflicts in nonviolent ways. A "hands off" or "boys will be boys" approach also teaches children something about how conflict should be handled.

8. Deemphasize possessions.

Much conflict in the world is about who owns what. Toning down the need for possessions will take away much of this source of conflict. Eberhard Arnold of the Society of Brothers suggests that children without an attachment to possessions will have less to want to defend and fight for. To parents he says "[Children] should see that we are completely detached from the things people usually own and that all rights of disposal mean nothing to us." With such an example children will be less inclined to stick up for their own "property rights," Arnold believes.

9. Tone down war expectancy

Worries and doom predictions can be self-fulfilling. So can expectations about war. One writer believes that wars may occur more readily when people expect them to happen. Parents help their children to be peacemakers by not teaching them that war is inevitable in the future.

Other practical suggestions for teaching peace values to children detail more positive things parents can do in the home:

10. Talk about war and peace.

Parents should not only act. They should talk about peace and what it means, war and what it does, and what is happening both in the worlds of their children and on the international scene that involves conflict. Not only does this defuse the subject for children, but it also gives them a perspective on what attitudes to take toward these situations.

11. Stress cooperative play.

"In our Western world, we have overstressed competitive activities vocationally and many other ways," says a Church of the Brethren leader. "Our competitive sports probably do not make for peace-mindedness—there is too much feeling about winning over some other person or group. Cooperative players in an orchestra make better music than competitive players." A spirit of cooperativeness also less likely leads to conflict than one of competition.

12. Tell stories.

For children to become peacemakers, they need to have a sense of belonging to a history of peacemakers. Parents can give them this sense by telling them stories both from the Bible and from their heritage.

One young Mennonite parent recalls: "When I was eight, World War II ended, so bombing drills are only a dim memory for me. I do recall hearing graphic stories of war-time suffering told by Mennonites and Brethren in Christ conscientious objectors. I doubted my ability to die for my nonresistant beliefs but never questioned that true faith in Christ demanded this if put to the test."

Stories can help children see peacemaking as being as heroic as making war. Too much of history glorifies the warmaker as hero. Hearing stories about peace heroes can help them see that often peacemaking takes even more moral courage than waging war. These stories can also help them realize that peace can be just as much a cause for which to live—and die—as is war.

Many stories about peace are available in books published by the peace churches and others. While these are invaluable in teaching peace to children, yet they can never supplant the actual hearing of peace stories from parents and other adults who have "been there."

13. Cultivate imagination.

Children have a wealth of imagination that needs to be directed. That imagination can help them identify with other people and what life must be like for them. Other persons are hard to classify "enemies" when one is able to put oneself into their shoes.

Imagination should also be encouraged for solving conflict situations. Children should be taught to handle conflict in their lives through attempting various solutions. One writer even suggests setting up a court in the backyard when solutions can't be reached in other ways.

14. Encourage autonomy.

Children need to be encouraged to be persons of their own. The willingness of parents to stand back and let their children experiment on their own and think for themselves appears to be equally important with warmth in the development of creative peacemakers.

This autonomy gives a child not only a sense of competency but also one of social responsibility.

15. Emphasize what it is that creates violence.

Not only must children be taught not to use violence as a solution for their problems, they must also be led to see that sometimes they can create violence in others while they apparently remain nonviolent.

If conflict is not handled creatively, it can develop into violence in others. Children are adept at this: they will not fight themselves but they will provoke a playmate to fighting so that he or she gets punished.

"To be prepared to be peaceful citizens of the world of the twentieth century, American children are going to have to be taught to recognize when they are provoking another person or nation to violence," writes Barbara Stanford in *Peacemaking: a Guide to Conflict Resolution for Individuals, Groups, and Nations*. "They will have to learn to take responsibility not only for fighting first or shooting the first missile, but also for creating the conflict which led to violence, or refusing to deal with the conflict before it became so desperate that it led to violence."

16. Have an abundance of peace materials in the home.

Peace-oriented art, photos, and literature of all types say something to a child when readily available in the home. When a child wants something to do or something to read, one of the options should be a source that deals with peace.

Still other things a parent can do to cultivate peace values involve a family with individuals and organizations outside the home:

17. Cultivate friendships with other peacemakers.

Parents need to seek out other families who believe in peace as a way of life and cultivate friendships with them. As children learn to know and become friends with the children of other peacemakers, these primary group relationships help them to develop their own peacemaking behavior.

18. Provide international experiences.

An appreciation for the way of peace comes as children are acquainted with others from a variety of cultures. Parents can invite visitors from various nationalities into their homes to interact with the family. As children learn to know people with a variety of customs and cultures, violence becomes less an alternative for settling problems with people who are different.

19. Support projects that express concern.

Families seriously committed to peace should make it a point to work with Mennonite Central Committee, Church World Service, the American Friends Service Committee, or other organizations in special projects to help others. In this way children also become aware of others and have a sense of relating to them.

20. Send peace cards and letters.

Peacemaking parents should write their concerns to their legislators, both locally and nationally. At the same time that it reminds politicians of nonviolence as an option, children also see their parents acting on a belief that means a great deal to them, one of the most

effective ways that peace education takes place.

J. Lorne Peachy, How to Teach Peace to Children, *1982, Herald Press, Scottdale, Pennsylvania*

If You Learn Nothing Else . . .

The late President Woodrow Wilson of Princeton University said that the purpose of education was to make the young as unlike their elders as possible. I address myself to the young here, in the hope of making them unlike their elders.

I am a geriatrician by profession—a student of old age. I have been studying the old for more than seventy years, and I flatter myself that I know all about them. On the basis of my studies I am able to inform you that their consuming passion is not avarice, or resentment, or despair. Their consuming passion is the fear of death.

They used to love war, in which the young did all the dying while the old lived it up on the fat of this bulletproof land. All of a sudden they show up in their thousands, in their tens of thousands, to protest. Against war? Not on your tintype. They protest against *nuclear* war—the kind that kills them and not just you.

The issue, my young friends, is not nuclear war. The issue is war. It wasn't nuclear war that killed more and more millions of young men every succeeding century. It was the old-fashioned kind of horse-and-buggy war in which the young did all the dying.

As long as war was nonnuclear, your elders preferred to see you dead than red. But they themselves would rather be anything than dead. So now they crusade against war—*nuclear* war. Don't let them divert you from the issue. Don't say No to nuclear war. Say No to war. Say No to being sent off by your elders to kill as many young men as you can who have never offended you and who are under the same injunction to kill you. . . .

A historian of antiquity said that his people fell under tyranny because they did not know how to pronounce the word No. The Russians are not accustomed to saying No. Neither are we. If we can bring ourselves to say No, our example may move the Russians. It's a slim chance—maybe one-tenth of 1 per cent. But a one-tenth of 1 per cent chance is one-tenth of 1 per cent better than no chance at all. War is no chance at all.

The old moralists are all saying that nuclear war is immoral. The old holy men are all saying that nuclear war is unholy. Do they mean that *non*nuclear war is moral and holy? You bet they do. They have always spread their blessing on it. They always will, unless by saying No you convince them that it is war that is immoral and unholy.

The purpose of education is to make the old as much like the young as possible. Go forth and educate.

Milton Mayer, speaking in April 1982 at Monterey, California Peninsula College

Global Issues

- The arms race issue is integrally linked with other issues which threaten human survival. The Center for Defense Information is a project of the FUND FOR PEACE, a non-profit institution which addresses not only military issues, but also the inequities in the world economic system, the imbalance between population growth and world food supply, systematic assaults on basic human rights, abuse of intelligence agencies within the U.S., and environmental deterioration and waste of scarce natural resources. Write for a brochure to the Fund for Peace, 1995 Broadway, NY, NY 10023, (212) 580-8635.

- For information on world security and global education send $1 to WORLD FEDERALISTS ASSOCIATION, 1011 Arlington Blvd., Arlington, VA 22209, (709) 524-2141.

- To help people conceptualize the often abstract images of world law, the WORLD SERVICE AUTHORITY has established a "functioning" mock global security system. Write WSA, National Press Building, Suite 440, 529 14th Street, N.W., Washington, DC 20045, (202) 638-2662.

- GLOBAL PERSPECTIVES IN EDUCATION serves teachers, professors & administrators with information, a newsletter, a national consultant resource bank, and *Global Perspectives Resource Directory*, 218 East 18th St., NY, NY 10013, (212) 475-0850.

- Many colleges have peace studies courses, and a campaign is underway to establish a United States Academy for Peace and Conflict Resolution. NATIONAL PEACE ACADEMY CAMPAIGN, 1625 Eye St., N.W., Suite 726, Washington, DC 20006, (202) 466-7670.

The momentum of the arms race is so powerful that it is easy to get discouraged. Nuclear war is practically inevitable in the next 20 or 30 years if the present military trends continue.

But current trends are not going to continue! Millions of citizens around the nation and our planet are beginning to mobilize against the arms race to assure world security and survival. Today the U.S. can have no national security without world security. Just as we've established a system for the State of Texas to settle a dispute with Alabama in court, not in war, so we must move toward a system of world security in which disputes between nations can be handled without resort to suicidal nuclear war.

Credit: CDI

More Resources

Alternative to War: The Peaceful Settlement of International Disputes—by Dr. Keith D. Suter. Published by the International League for Peace and Freedom, Australia Section. An optimistic book, welcome in an era of doomsayers. It details methods, tried and still-to-be-tried, for the peaceful resolution of international confrontation. Contact: WILPF, Australia Section, P.O. Box 35, Fairfield, Victoria, Australia 3078. 112p, $5.95.

World Military and Social Expenditures, 1981—by economist Ruth Leger Sivard. Provides documented statistical information on the components of global militarization that have pushed arms budgets to $550 billion a year. Contact: Ruth L. Sivard, World Priorities, 3013 Dunbarton Avenue, N.W. Washington, D.C. 20007. 44p, $4 per copy.

The International Bill of Human Rights—The first paperback publication of this bill. Includes the Universal Declaration on Human Rights, the Covenants on Civil and Political Rights and on Economic, Social and Cultural Rights. Also, contains a brief history of this fundamental document. Contact: Entwhistle Books, Box 611, Glen Ellen, CA 95442. $3.25 paper; $9.95 cloth. 160p.

Sharing Global Resources: Toward a New Economic Order—40 minute slideshow or filmstrip with cassette tape, documentation, study/action guide. Slideshow $50; filmstrip $45; Spanish language slideshow $50; rental $10/wk; script 50¢; as separate purchase—Study Action Guide $1; Documentation $3. Contact: NARMIC, American Friends Service Committee, 1501 Cherry Street, Philadelphia, PA 19102.

Peacemaking and the Community of Faith: A Handbook for Local Congregations by John Donaghy ($3.00; $2.00/10-49 copies; $1.00/50 or more); **Dunbar's Breman: A Morality Play** in One Act on the Use of Tactical Nuclear Weapons by James Stegenga ($1.00; 90¢/10-19 copies; 85¢/20 or more); **New Abolitionist Covenant** (30¢; 10¢/100); **World Peace Pledge, World Peace Prayer** post card, **Economic Conversion, Reversing the Arms Race** (10¢; 5¢/100). Plus 20% postage. From: Fellowship of Reconciliation, Box 271, Nyack, NY 10960.

The **Student/Teacher Organization to Prevent Nuclear War** (S.T.O.P. NUCLEAR WAR) is a growing, nationwide network of high school students and educators dedicated to informing their communities about the dangers of the nuclear arms race, the imminent threat of nuclear war, and the concrete actions which young people, with the guidance of teachers, can take to reverse this march to an all-encompassing holocaust. **S.T.O.P. News** focuses exclusively on programs and resources appropriate for high schools and youth groups. S.T.O.P. NUCLEAR WAR , Box 232, Northfield, MA 01360, 413-498-5311 ✕418.

Makers of the New Generation of Nuclear Weapons—details the prime contractors and subcontractors benefitting from Reagan's plan to "improve" our strategic triad. Includes a description of the latest plans for the B-1 bomber, MX, Cruise, Pershing and Trident Missiles. Cost is 50¢ each or $10.00 per 100. Contact: NARMIC, 1501 Cherry Street, Philadelphia, PA 19102, 215-241-7175.

Makers of the Nuclear Holocaust—A Guide to the Nuclear Weapons Complex and Citizen Action is the inside story on the politics of the nuclear weapons program. Includes directory of organizations actively working for economic conversion. 24 pages. ($1.25; 10-100 at 75¢/copy; 101+ at 60¢/copy). Plus 15% postage. Contact: Rocky Flats/Nuclear Weapons Facilities Project, FOR, Box 271, Nyack, NY 10960, 914-358-4601, or AFSC, 1660 Lafayette, Denver, CO 80218, 303-832-4508.

Educational and Organizing Packet—produced by the Gray Panthers to help you get organized and fight back against cuts in social services. Cost $15.00 per packet. Contact: Gray Panther Project Fund, 3635 Chestnut Stret, Philadelphia, PA 19104.

WILPF T-Shirts: Royal blue T-shirts with dove in white encircled by Women's International League for Peace and Freedom. Men's T-shirts in S-M-L. $7.50 each, $6.50 each for 10 or more. Order from Southern Indiana WILPF, PO Box 1832, Bloomington, IN 47402.

Invisible Violence—Proceedings of the National Citizens' Hearings for Radiation Victims (April 10-14, 1980). Contains testimony of nuclear workers, atomic veterans, residents exposed to atomic fallout, uranium miners and others. $3.00 per copy, $2.50 each for bulk orders of 20 or more. Contact: NCRV, 317 Pennsylvania Avenue, SE, Washington, DC 20003.

Making the Abolition of War a Realistic Goal by Gene Sharp—A fifteen page article proposing *civilian based defense*—that is, prepared protest, non-cooperation and disruptive intervention as a nonviolent strategy by which citizens can discourage or thwart either internal usurpation or invasion and occupation. Contact: Institute for World Order, 777 UN Plaza, NY, NY 10017, 212-490-0010. Single copy, $1.00; 5-25 copies, 75¢ each; 26 or more copies, 50¢ each.

Speeches from the April 25, 1981, rally and teach-in at the General Dynamics Shipyard, Groton, Connecticut protesting the Trident Submarine and in support of a mutual US-USSR Nuclear Weapons Freeze. This handsome booklet contains pictures, facts and speeches and is available for $2.50 per copy. Contact: Connecticut Coalition for a Nuclear Arms Freeze, c/o American Friends Service Committee, RD#1, Box 494, Voluntown, CT. 06384, 203-376-4098.

The Plutonium Connection—Turn On A Light, Build A Bomb—a new, 20 minute slideshow exposing the proposed plans of the Reagan Administration to use spent fuel from commercial nuclear reactors to build nuclear bombs. The slideshow is only being sold—at a cost of $75.00 a copy. Contact: Organizing Mec Project, 514 10th Street, NW, Washington, DC, 202-462-9100.

Grappling With The Last Epidemic: The Medical Response To Nuclear War—another new slideshow developed at Brown University to teach medical students and physicians about the public health threat of nuclear war. Available for purchase or rental; 30 minutes. Contact: International Physicians for the Prevention of Nuclear War, 635 Huntington Avenue, 2nd floor, Boston, MA 02115, 617-738-9404.

Draft Resistance and Counseling Manual—published recently by the Washington, DC Area Military and Draft Law Panel. This is a comprehensive manual covering the complete Military Selective Service Act, the Justice Department Prosecutorial Discretion Guidelines and lots more. Cost is $25.00 for individuals and $35.00 for institutions, plus $3.00 for postage. Contact: WAMDLP, c/o DC Chapter of the National Lawyers Guild, 2000 P Street, NW, Suite 612, Washington, DC 20036.

Resources for Understanding the Arms Race. Sources of information on the economic effects of military spending:

Council on Economic Priorities, 84 Fifth Ave., New York, NY 10011, (212) 691-8550. CEP publishes a host of studies on the economic impact of military spending, on economic conversion, and on military industries; as well as studies on other economic issues. CEP publishes 3-6 Studies or Reports annually and 8-12 Newsletters. Studies include "The Economic Impact of the MX Missile." Newsletters include, "The Defense Department's Top 100."

Institute for Defense and Disarmament Studies, 251 Harvard Street, Brookline, MA 92146. IDDS is a research and public education center on military forces and disarmament. Write to order: The *American Peace Directory,* with names and addresses of 2,000 national and local peace groups, and for *The Price of Defense* by The Boston Study Group, detailing the possibility of as much as a $50 billion cut in military spending.

Employment Research Associates, 400 S. Washington Ave., Lansing, MI 48933. Publishes studies of employment and other effects of military spending, and of the effects of economic conversion. Most recently see, Marion Anderson, "Converting the Work Force: Where the Jobs Would Be," $3.00 single copy. Other studies: "The Empty Pork Barrel," "Bankrupting America: Tax Impact of the Military Budget."

NARMIC, National Action/Research on the Military Industrial Complex, 1501 Cherry Street, Philadelphia, PA 19102, a project of the American Friends Service Committee which produces a wide range of useful resources on the military and on human rights. NARMIC will provide information to local organizers on military contracts in particular communities or on particular companies. See their recent map of companies involved in production of the new generation of nuclear weapons.

National Center for Economic Alternatives, 2000 P Street, N.W., Washington, DC 20036. Directed by economists Gar Alperovitz and Jeff Faux, the Center produces reports on a number of economic issues, including inflation and, in the past, economic conversion: See Philip Webre, *Jobs to People,* an unpublished report on conversion.

Center for Defense Information, 122 Maryland Ave., NE, Washington, DC 20002. CDI publishes the *Defense Monitor,* a monthly analysis of military issues. Past *Monitors* have considered the military budget, the MX, cruise missiles, U.S. military policy in the Persian Gulf, and the overall balance of power between the United States and the Soviet Union.

The Brookings Institution, 1775 Massachusetts Ave., N.W., Washington, DC 20036. Publishes a number of studies on military affairs from a generally "liberal" perspective, as well as an annual book called *Setting National Priorities* which reviews the federal budget, including the military budget.

American Enterprise Institute for Policy Research, 1150 17th Street, N.W., Washington, DC 20036. AEI is a politically conservative think tank, and it provided a number of bureaucrats for the Reagan Administration, but many of its publications provide good information, and its researchers are thoughtful and moderate. See "The FY 1981-1985 Defense Program: Issues and Trends," $2.50.

Government agencies:

Arms Control and Disarmament Agency, U.S. Department of State, Washington, DC 20451. Publishes information on disarmament treaties, ongoing negotiations, non-proliferation and other arms control issues. It also occasionally does studies of aspects of the military balance. Annually it publishes *World Military Expenditures and Arms Transfers.*

Department of Defense has a couple of major information offices. The Washington Headquarters Service Directorate of Information, Room 4B 938 Pentagon, Washington, DC 20301, distributes a number of reviews of Pentagon contracts, bases, personnel, etc. Write for a list of publications and an order form— particular reports can often be obtained free by calling and asking for the reports by name, (202) 697-3182. Other information on military issues can be obtained from the office of Public Correspondence: Staff Assistant for Public Affairs, OASD/PA, Room 2E 777 Pentagon, Washington, DC 20301, or call (202) 697-5737.

U.S. Government Accounting Office, Document Handling and Information Services Facility, P.O. Box 6015,

Gaithersburg, MD 20760. The GAO reviews the general efficiency of government administration and particular procurement programs. It is a good source of authoritative critiques of Pentagon programs. Write for the *Monthly List of GAO Reports,* which includes an order

form—a single copy of any GAO report is free.

Congressional Budget Office, Office of Intergovernmental Relations, House Annex #2, 2nd and D Streets, S.W., Washington, DC 20515. The CBO is an agency of Congress established to review the budgetary implications of various programs. Budget issue papers consider a host of narrow issues, but also very broad strategic analyses. Write for a list of publications. All CBO publications can be received free.

Department of Energy nuclear weapons budget:

Nuclear Weapons Facilities Project, FOR/AFSC, 1660 Lafayette St., Denver, CO 80218. A joint project of the American Friends Service Committee and the Fellowship of Reconciliation, this project coordinates activities to convert nuclear weapons production facilities to socially useful production. Write for information about projects around the country. An organizing packet is available for $1.50.

National Citizens' Hearings for Radiation Victims, 317 Pennsylvania Ave., S.E., Washington, DC 20003. This organization focuses on radiation hazards from the nuclear industry, nuclear weapons tests, etc.

Environmental Policy Center, 317 Pennsylvania Ave., S.E., Washington, DC 20003. A research and lobbying organization which focuses on the hazards of the nuclear industry in general, including some emphasis on the nuclear weapons industry.

Lobbying and membership organizations working on national priorities:

Americans for Democratic Action, 1411 K Street, N.W., Suite 850, Washington, DC 20006. ADA is a national membership organization of liberal activists, many of whom work in the Democratic Party. ADA coordinates a large coalition of domestic groups on federal budget issues.

American Friends Service Committee (AFSC), national office: 1501 Cherry Street, Philadelphia, PA 19102. AFSC works to build informed resistance to war and militarism and to advance non-violent action for change. Area offices stress conversion and dependency on defense spending.

Business Executives Move for New National Priorities, 901 Howard Street, Baltimore, MD 21201. An organization of more than 2000 business men and women which opposes excessive military spending and works to promote economic conversion. Newsletter: *Newsnotes.* Reviews the military budget and the Department of Defense Annual Report.

Arms Control Association, 11 Dupont Circle, N.W., Washington, DC 20036. ACA is a non-partisan national membership organization dedicated to promoting public understanding and support for arms control and disarmament. Newsletter: *Arms Control Today,* $20 per year.

Clergy and Laity Concerned, 198 Broadway, New York, NY 10038. CALC is an interfaith organization dedicated to religious, political action for peace and justice. Local chapters are active on priorities issues.

Committee Against Registration and the Draft (CARD), 201 Massachusetts Ave., N.E., Suite 111, Washington, DC 20002. CARD is a coalition of organizations which oppose reinstitution of the draft. They can provide information, speakers, and coordinate lobbying and local action.

Coalition for a New Foreign and Military Policy, 120 Maryland Avenue, N.E., Washington, D.C. 20002. The coalition unites 46 national religious, labor, peace and other groups to work on behalf of a non-interventionist and demilitarized U. S. foreign policy.

Central Committee for Conscientious Objectors, 2208 South Street, Philadelphia, PA 19103. CCCO provides excellent literature and information about the draft and conscientious objection.

Draft Action, 534 Washington Building, 1435 G Street, N.W., Washington, D.C. 20005. A cornucopia of information about anything pertaining to the draft and conscientious objection.

Council for a Livable World, 100 Maryland Avenue, N.E., Washington, D.C. 20002. The Council is a public interest group which raises funds for Senatorial candidates who work for arms control, and which lobbies on arms control and military budget issues. The Council provides facts sheets on congressional issues.

Federation of American Scientists, 307 Massachusetts Avenue, N.E., Washington, D.C. 20002. FAS is a lobbying organization with a membership of 6,000 scientists concerned with the role of science in society. They produce books and reports on a full range of arms control and disarmament issues. *Public Interest Group,* $25 per year.

Fellowship of Reconciliation (FOR), Box 271, Nyack, NY 10960. FOR is a pacifist organization committed to non-violent social change. It produces many pamphlets on non-violence and disarmament and publishes *Fellowship,* a monthly, costing $10 annually.

Friends Committee on National Legislation (FCNL), 245 Second Street, N.E., Washington, D.C. 20002. FCNL lobbies on foreign and domestic issues, including the military budget and national priorities. Publications focus on disarmament, the military budget; Con-

gressional voting records. *Washington Newsletter,* $15 per year.

IMPACT, 100 Maryland Avenue, N.E., Washington, D.C. 20002. IMPACT is a grassroots network of individuals motivated by religious or moral conviction to influence U.S. public policy on a number of foreign and domestic issues, including food policy, military spending and employment. It sends out a variety of action alerts and analyses at least once monthly. National membership is $7.50 annually. Where there are state networks, membership is $15.

Jewish Peace Fellowship (JPF), Box 271, Nyack, NY 10960. JPF members are religious and secular Jews from all traditions and all branches of Judaism who believe deeply that Jewish ideals and experience provide inspiration for a nonviolent way of life. Committed to nonviolent social activism and Jewish teachings, JPF is also concerned with the issue of conscientious objection. It publishes a wide range of literature plus a quarterly newsletter *Shalom* (membership is $15 annually; non-members pay $3 per year for newsletter).

International Association of Machinists. 1300 Connecticut Avenue, N.W., Washington, D.C. 20036. An international union which strongly supports economic conversion and produces resources on related issues. One study: "The Impact of Military Spending on the Machinists Union." Newsletter: *The Machinist.*

Jobs With Peace Initiative Campaign, 2990 22nd Street, San Francisco, CA 94110. Based on work organizing referenda on the military budget and national priorities in Oakland and San Francisco, this group can provide information and assistance to local groups interested in putting such initiatives on the ballot in their own communities or states. Organizing Packet, $5. Similar campaigns are active in Boston, Detroit, Chicago, Seattle and elsewhere.

Mid-Peninsula Conversion Project, 867 West Dana Street, Mountain View, CA 94041. One of the oldest and best established conversion projects in the country. Its 1978 study, *Creating Solar Jobs: Options for Military Workers and Communities,* $3.50, is a model research product. *Plowshare Press,* $6 per year, comes out every month and covers the arms race, the military budget and conversion. For information on other conversion projects, contact the Conversion Information Center at the Council on Economic Priorities (listed above).

Mobilization for Survival, 3601 Locust Walk, Philadelphia, PA 19104. MFS is a coalition of groups emphasizing grass-roots organizing and action on nuclear weapons, nuclear power, the arms race, and funds to meet human needs. Newsletter, *The Mobilizer,* $10 per year. Publishes numerous resource packets, posters, tee-shirts, buttons, etc.

National Council of Churches, Washington Office, 110 Maryland Ave., N.E., Washington, DC 20002. NCC is a national council of 32 major Protestant and Orthodox church denominations, and coordinates activity on a broad range of issues, including budget priorities.

Network, 806 Rhode Island Ave., N.E., Washington, DC 20018. A Catholic, multi-issue social justice lobby, which works on priorities, human rights and other issues. Publishes quarterly articles on disarmament and human rights.

New Directions, 305 Massachusetts Ave., N.E., Washington, DC 20002. A citizen's lobby on global issues, including the arms race and arms limitation, as well as aid to developing countries. Many of its issues bear on budget priorities.

Physicians for Social Responsibility, POB 144, 56 N. Beacon Street, Watertown, Mass. 02172. One of the major new groups that raised the issue of the nuclear arms freeze. Produced the very fine film "The Last Epidemic," which makes clear that there is no longer a viable activity called "war."

Riverside Church Disarmament Program, 490 Riverside Dr., New York, NY 10027. Provides speakers and resources for local disarmament education, particularly for the religious community. The *Riverside Disarmament Reader,* available for $15, is an invaluable compendium of articles for studying disarmament and the military. *Peace in Search of Makers,* $5.95, contains presentations from conferences at Riverside Church.

SANE, 514 C Street, N.E., Washington, DC 20002. SANE is a grassroots action and lobbying organization working on military conversion, disarmament, and the MX missile. Membership, $20, includes newsletter,

action alerts and issue analyses.

United Automobile, Aerospace, and Agricultural Implement Workers of America (UAW), 800 East Jefferson Ave., Detroit, MI 48214. International union that has worked actively on planned economic conversion and budget priorities. Now concerned above all with unemployment.

War Resisters League, 339 Lafayette St., New York, NY 10012. WRL is a national pacifist organization opposed to armaments, conscription and war. *WRL News,* published every other month, is free. *WIN* magazine is $20 per year.

Women's International League for Peace and Freedom (WILPF), 1213 Race Street, Philadelphia, PA 19107. WILPF is an international organization which emphasizes non-violent solutions to domestic and international problems. WILPF and its local chapters work actively on priorities and disarmament issues.

Women Strike for Peace, 145 South 13th Street, Philadelphia, PA 19107. WSP is an organization of women committed to disarmament under international controls. WSP and its local chapters work actively on banning nuclear testing and ending the arms race. National Legislative Office, 201 Massachusetts Ave., N.E., Washington, DC 20002.

And, for Human Rights Information. . . .

Amnesty International, (AI), 304 West 58th Street, New York, NY 10019. The respected AI, a worldwide organization, catalogues the state of freedom everywhere in the world. Best of all, it is more often than not fair and objective, sparing no nation. Its annual reports are indispensable.

Humanitas International, POB 818, Menlo Park, CA 94025. Headed by Joan Baez, this group also deals with liberty and respects no violator. Humanitas fearlessly condemns haters of freedom in both the communist and non-communist orbits.

And, two worthwhile publications. . . .

Human Rights Quarterly. A quarterly journal published by the Government and Politics Department, University of Maryland, College Park, MD. 20742. *HRQ* is connected to no particular ideology. A good example of its coverage was the excellent article by Richard Greenfield, "The Human Rights Literature of the Soviet Union," Spring 1982. Subscriptions are $16 per year from the Journals Division, The Johns Hopkins University Press, Baltimore, MD 21218.

Human Rights Internet Reporter. 5 times yearly. Publishes well-informed summaries from countries throughout the world. $35 per year. 1502 Ogden Street, N.W., Washington, D.C. 20010.

The Coalition for a New Foreign and Military Policy

BALANCE OF POWER

Professionals Organize to Prevent Nuclear War

by Terry Brown

In the past year, over half a dozen new constituency groups that focus exclusively on preventing nuclear war have sprung up in the Boston area. Some are local in scope, others hope to establish chapters around the country. The activities of some are described here in the hope that readers will join or start their own group or tell friends who might be interested in participating.

Business Alert to Nuclear War—Formed this summer, BANW has 50 members from all types of businesses. It sponsors a monthly series of dinners at which experts discuss the dangers of nuclear-weapon proliferation and explore ways to defuse the situation. This winter, it plans to offer a more in-depth, four-to-six week course.

The members feel that when the business community voices its concern about the arms race, it might have a sympathetic ear in pro-business Washington. They are particularly interested in attracting people who have not previously been involved in social change activities. "Nuclear war is bad for business," says president Alan Kay, reflecting BANW's practical approach. Contact: BANW, Box 7, Belmont, MA 02178, (617)253-1578.

Physicians for Social Responsibility—Committed to public and professional education on the medical hazards of nuclear technology, PSR directly links the expansion of nuclear weapons to the health effects that exist throughout the entire nuclear fuel chain. PSR has been holding well-attended symposia throughout the country on the medical consequences of nuclear war and has chapters in many areas. A recent Freeze endorser, PSR can provide speakers and films for public programs. Contact: PSR, P.O. Box 144, 23 Main St., Watertown, MA 02172, (617)924-3468.

Lawyers' Alliance for Nuclear Arms Control—Recently formed to educate lawyers, paralegals, and law students about the need for arms control. The Alliance has 150 members in Massachusetts and is forming chapters in other sections of the country. It is planning presentations at local law schools and regional and national conferences of lawyers to discuss arms control. Contact: LANAC, P.O. Box 9171, Boston, MA 02114, (617)277-0118.

Nurses Alliance for the Prevention of Nuclear War—This organization was formed last May. Its current membership is confined to Massachusetts, but it intends to become international. It is developing a newsletter and is planning programs for nurses, the first of which will be on 13 October. Contact: Elizabeth Johnson, 48 Addingon Rd., Brookline, MA 02146, (617) 739-1239.

Educators for Social Responsibility—This group grew out of the May Waging Peace Conference at Harvard. (See July Newsletter.) Its core membership is 41, but over 150 have been involved in meetings. It has three active committees which (1) collect and develop resources for use in classrooms; (2) recruit membership and do publicity: and (3) network with other groups, designing programs for educators. ESR can help other groups with bibliographies, curriculum development, and teaching methods. Contact: Bobbi Snow, ESR, Box 1041, Brookline Village, MA 02147, (617) 734-1111 Ext .335.

Student Network for Nuclear Disarmament—Started last summer by activists from Brown University and Hampshire College, SNND has spread to include over a score of colleges. The Network hopes to foster campus opposition to the nuclear arms race by sharing information and organizing ideas. It will participate in the Freeze conference at Hampshire College and the Union of Concerned Scientists 11 November Convocation. In the Boston area, faculty, staff and students from eight area universities formed the Intercollegiate Association Against Nuclear War. This year it will concentrate on the national Freeze petition drive. Contact: SNND at the Freeze Clearinghouse or Roseria Solerno, Boston College, McElroy 215, Chestnut Hill, MA 02167, (617) 969-0100.

High-Technology Professionals for Peace—Initiated with hope but without illusion, this organization has had considerable success raising the issue of nuclear war with engineers and computer programmers. Their Freeze petition was published in "Computer," a trade publication with a large circulation. An alternative employment agency, to find non-military work for engineers, has been established: and the group has held press conferences at arms bazaars and military-technology conferences. Contact: Warren Davis, Hi-Tech Professionals for Peace, 2161 Massachusetts Ave., Cambridge, MA 02140, (617) 332-9457.

Artists for Survival—an organization of professional artists formed in response to the escalating threat of nuclear war. The artists in the group hope to reach people emotionally through the language of art. They have had several exhibits in the Boston area, including their first in the Harvard Medical School Countway Library. Artists for Survival will arrange exhibitions of any size, appropriate to hospitals, schools, libraries, universities, business offices, galleries, etc. A major percentage of the proceeds from sales resulting from exhibitions will be donated to organizations working on the nuclear Freeze. Contact: Mitchell Kamen, Artists West, 144 Moody Street, Waltham, MA 02154, (617) 861-1653.

In the New England area, a valuable resource for the artist/peace community is **Communicators for Nuclear Disarmament**. This is an association of 150 artists, designers, film makers, writers, public relations and media professionals. It offers a full range of creative services to peace groups. Contact: (617) 923-8800.

More Alternatives:
More Books

The Iron Triangle: The Politics of Defense Spending—A major work written by Gordon Adams, Director of Research on Governmental Relations for the Council on Economic Priorities. Provides a detailed analysis of the lobbying efforts of eight defense corporations (Boeing, General Dynamics, Grumman, Lockheed, McDonnell-Douglas, Northrup, Rockwell International and United Technologies). Available from: Council on Economic Priorities, 84 5th Avenue, New York, NY 10011.

Effects and Dangers of Nuclear War—An educational exhibit from: John B. Massen, Northern California Division of the United Nations Association of the USA, 152 St. Francis Boulevard, Daly City, CA 94015, (415) 991-2080. 16-page booklet 50¢ ea., $22/100. Also 16 posters, 38″ x 25″ at $30.

Peace Library

American Peace Directory 1980, edited by Randall Forsberg is a comprehensive address-and-description list of 2,000 national and local peace groups including research centers, college and graduate programs and membership, activist lobbying groups, etc. Price: $5. Order from: Westview Press, 5500 Central Ave., Boulder, CO.

Directory of Peace and Conflict Programs is a list of organizations concerned in a major way with peaceful resolution of conflict among nations. Price: $2.50. Order from: Communications Institute, Academy for Educational Development, Inc., 680 Fifth Ave., New York, NY 10010.

Media & Methods for Your Church by Vernon Schmid provides a quick and convenient group of media fundamentals. Price: $3.95. Order from: Contemporary Drama Service, Box 457, Downers Grove, IL 60515.

World Peace Directory 1980 is a useful pocket-sized listing of some 1,600 peace organizations and periodicals in more than 100 countries, with a brief description of their work. Price: $1. Order from: FOR, Box 271, Nyack, NY 10960.

Conscience and the Law: A Court Guide for the Civilly Disobedient by Bill Durland and Donna Baker is a useful resource and support tool for those involved in or considering civil disobedience. Price: $5. Order from: Center on Law and Pacifism, 300 West Apsley St., Philadelphia, PA 19144.

Pacificus Papers, a quarterly published by the Center on Law and Pacifism, contains action possibilities for persons refusing to pay war taxes. The Center has also published a tax refusal guide, **People Pay for Peace,** describing the options and steps for military tax resistance. Every step is clearly explained, as are the possible and probable IRS responses. Copies of **Pacificus Papers** are $1 each; the **People Pay for Peace** tax guide is $2. Write: Center on Law and Pacifism, 300 West Apsley St., Philadelphia, PA 19144.

Final Environmental Impact Statement for the MX Missile System Milestone II may be obtained free from: Civil Engineering Division, SAMSO/MNND, Norton AFB, CA 92409.

Earthscape: Transition Toward World Order is the most recent edition of Whole Earth Papers which seeks to "hold out a basis for hope at a time when images of pessimism and despair pervade." Price: $2.50. Order from : Global Education Associates, 552 Park Ave., East Orange, NJ 07017.

Neither Victims Nor Executioners by Albert Camus is a classic introduction to the values underlying work for a world without war. Price: $2.95. Order from: Seabury Press, 815 Second Ave., New York, NY 10017.

The Jewish Roots of Non-Violence. Where, how and why Judaism reveres peace. Price: $2. Order from: Jewish Peace Fellowship, Box 271, Nyack, NY 10960.

Peace Book Covers—alternatives to those distributed in schools by the armed forces—are now available. One cover says: Defend the World—Resist Militarism and the Draft; the other says: Work for Peace—Release Our Hostage Future. Measuring 17″ × 22″, they can be trimmed to fit most textbooks. Price: 10¢ each. Printed on heavy tan paper, in red and black ink. Order from: Mennonite Central Committee, 21 South 12th St., Akron, PA 17501.

To Study War No More—a Bibliography on War, Peace and Conscience. Price: $1.50. Order from: CCCO, 2208 South St., Philadelphia, PA 19103.

THE SWARTHMORE PEACE LIBRARY has the largest collection of peace material in the United States. Includes: photos, biographical material, history, books, pamphlets, etc., all on the subject of peace. An excellent resource. For information write: Swarthmore Peace Collection, Swarthmore, PA 19081.

Periodicals

The most comprehensive single magazine for people interested in peace activities and alternatives to seeing the world through gunsights is **Fellowship**. For information write: **Fellowship**, Box 271, Nyack, NY 10960. $10 for 1 year; $18 for 2 years; $26 for 3 years.

Peace Action News is a quarterly newspaper about nonviolent actions around the world.

It is published by Non-Violent Alternatives, the international service network founded by Dom Helder Camara with offices in Antwerp, Belgium. Dom Helder spoke often of his dream of a "multinational for peace," a worldwide concentration of nonviolent forces for liberation and justice.

The first concrete steps toward realizing his dream were taken as a result of a regional consultation organized by Pax Christi International and the International Fellowship of Reconciliation at Derry, Northern Ireland, in 1977, at which Dom Helder was the principal speaker.

The committee that followed up on that consultation by establishing Non-Violent Alternatives in Antwerp included Bishop Thomas Gumbleton of Detroit, Adolfo Perez Esquivel of Argentina, Father Elias Chacour of Israel, Ciaran McKeown of Northern Ireland, Etienne De Jonghe, International Secretary of Pax Christi, and Jim Forest of the Fellowship of Reconciliation.

Airmail subscription and rates from: Kerkstraat 150, B-2000 Antwerp, Belgium.

Disarmament Campaigns, the new international newsletter on actions against the arms race around the world, is in its second year of publication. This 20-30 page magazine meets an important peace need by establishing communication between disarmament groups in Europe, North America, Australia, and—to the degree possible—Eastern Europe.

It is published quarterly in Antwerp, Belgium, under the responsibility of an international editorial board.

Members of the board include Bruce Kent (Campaign for Nuclear Disarmament, England), Jim Forest (International Fellowship of Reconciliation), Erich Weingartner (World Council of Churches, Geneva), Christian Mellon (Mouvement pour une Alternative Non-Violente, France), Laurens Hogebrink (Inter-Church Peace Council, Netherlands), and Gerard Vanderhaar (Pax Christi USA).

An air-mail subscription from: **Disarmament Campaigns,** c/o Gerard Vanderhaar, 3554 Boxdale, Memphis, TN 38118. A sample copy is also available on request.

Nonviolence: Theory and Practice, a sixteen-page pamphlet by Dr. Gerard Vanderhaar, was published recently at the International Peace Center in Antwerp, Belgium, where he worked during his sabbatical last year. Dr. Vanderhaar, Professor of Religion and Peace Studies at Christian Brothers College and Chairperson of the Commission on Alternatives to Violence of Pax Christi USA, hopes the pamphlet will be a useful introduction to the meaning of non-violence. Copies are available from the author at: 3554 Boxdale, Memphis TN 38118.

Catholic Worker

If You Want to Know Even More

Bibliography on Peace Research in History, Blanche Cook (ed.), 72pp. 1969, ABC-Clio, O.P. A research guide for historians which includes archival holdings, current and out-of-print books, and peace organization record depositories. Emphasizes international relations, disarmament, nonviolence, and world law.

The Garland Library of War and Peace: A Collection of 327 Titles, Blanche Cook, Charles Chatfield & Sandi Cooper (eds.), 136pp. 1971, Garland, Free. An attractive catalogue of reprinted landmarks in thought about war and peace is available free. An introduction to neglected writings in Europe and the U.S. during the last 400 years. Included in the 328 volume collection are works by Dante, Erasmus, Croce, Grotius, Bentham, Kant, Tolstoy, and Norman Thomas. Some of these titles might have been left to mold, but overall, this is a most useful collection for a library.

Robert Woito, To End War *(N.Y. 1982)*

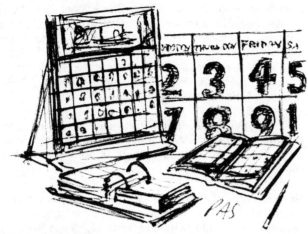

Calendars

Peace Diary, $5 (FOR, Box 271, Nyack, NY 10960).
Wall Calendar (World Without War, 67 East Madison, Suite 1417, Chicago, IL 60603).
Desk Calendar, $5 (War Resisters League, 339 Lafayette St., New York, NY 10012).
Calendar, $3.25 (Syracuse Peace Council's Calendar, 924 Burnet Ave., Syracuse, NY 13203).

Coalition for a New Foreign and Military Policy

Pornography

Nothing in human history is more obscene than the cool discussions of competing nuclear strategies by apocalyptic gameplayers. All sorts of scenarios are being put forward about the circumstances under which we would drop bombs on the Soviet Union and the Soviet Union would drop bombs on us, as though both countries were involved in nothing more than a super backgammon game. The strategists in both countries need to be reminded that they are not playing with poker chips but with human lives and the whole of the human future.

Norman Cousins   Saturday Review   December, 1981

Not Like Lemmings

All I ask is that, in the midst of a murderous world, we agree to reflect on murder and to make a choice.

Albert Camus, 1946

Not Worth It

There is no practical problem existing between nations whose importance is in any proportion to the tremendous losses which must be expected in an atomic war.

Albert Schweitzer

Role Model

As human beings, our greatness lies not so much in being able to remake the world—that is the myth of the "atomic age"—as in being able to remake ourselves.

Gandhi

Real Change

I do not believe in violence . . . hatred . . . or armed insurrection. They take place too quickly. They change the circumstances of people's lives without giving them time to adapt to the changes. It is useless to dream of reforming socio-economic structures . . . without a corresponding deep change in our inner lives.

Dom Helder Camara
Archbishop of Recife & Olinda, Brazil

The Meaning of "Peace"

Peace is a state of personal and social existence which is far more than mere absence of conflict. The world without war envisaged by our seers is warless because of its health, its wholeness, its intrinsic justice, its at-oneness with the universe. We have come to see human liberation, economic development and world peace as a dynamic triangular process.

Homer A. Jack in World Religion/World Peace

A Prayer for Peace

Attributed to St. Francis of Assisi

Lord, make me an instrument of Your peace.
Where there is hatred, let me sow love;
Where there is injury, pardon;
Where there is doubt, faith;
Where there is despair, hope;
Where there is darkness, light;
And where there is sadness, joy.
O, Divine Master, grant that I may seek not so
    much to be consoled as to console;
To be understood as to understand;
To be loved as to love;
For it is in giving that we receive;
It is in pardoning that we are pardoned;
And it is in dying that we are born to eternal life.

F.Y.I.

Doctors estimate that within 40 days after a major nuclear exchange, 90 percent of Americans would be dead . . . when you think about this, nothing else matters. It really doesn't matter whether we do well at work, whether we look after our children and give them good food, or we love each other or we live a good life. By our passivity we've allowed this to happen.

—*Helen Caldicott (Addressing 1981 Southampton, N.Y. anti-nuclear rally)*

If we assume that life is worth living and that we have a right to survive, then we must find an alternative to war. . . . Therefore I suggest that the philosophy and strategy of nonviolence become immediately a subject for study and for serious experimentation in every field of human conflict, by no means excluding the relations between nations.

Martin Luther King, Jr.

On my knees I beg you to turn away from the paths of violence and to return to the ways of peace . . . Violence only delays the day of justice. Violence destroys the work of justice. . .

I say to you, with all the love I have for you, with all the trust I have in young peoples: do not listen to voices which speak the language of hatred, revenge, retaliation. Do not follow any leaders who train you in the ways of inflicting death. Love life, respect life, in yourself and in others. Give yourself to the service of life, not the work of death. . . Violence is the enemy of justice. Only peace can lead the way to true justice.

Pope John Paul II
September 29, 1979
Drogheda, Ireland

To remember the past is to commit oneself to the future. To remember Hiroshima is to abhor nuclear war. To remember Hiroshima is to commit oneself to peace. To remember what the people of this city suffered is to renew our faith in humankind, in their capacity to do what is good, in their freedom to choose what is right, in their determination to turn disaster into a new beginning. In the face of the man-made calamity that every war is, one must affirm and reaffirm, again and again, that the waging of war is not inevitable or unchangeable. Humanity is not destined to self-destruction.

—*Pope John Paul II speaking to 100,000 people February 25, 1981 at Peace Memorial Park in Hiroshima*

And Good Russians, Too

"Good Germans" is the phrase historians use to describe a people who silently go along with their government's grand plans for military adventures. If the madness of World War III really is upon us, perhaps this is the era of Good Americans.

—*Colman McCarthy,* The Washington Post, *5/29/80*

Once Upon a Time . . .

by Richard M. Powell

Once upon a time, a Leader was beleaguered and at bay, scorned by his countrymen as totally wanting in the skills of leadership. Sorely beset, he cried out in desperation. "Wait!" he said. "Wait! If you will continue to let me lead I will give you something of great price, of great price truly!"

The people were unbelieving, since the Leader and those around him had never spoken the truth before. "What is it? What is this thing of great price?"

"A secret," answered the Leader. "A secret that will change your scorn of me to idolatry, a secret that will end your guilts and your frustrations, a secret that will make you feel whole again, and strong."

"If it is as you say," the people answered, "we will let you lead us again. Give us the secret."

"Let me lead and one thing more," said the Leader.

"And one thing more," they assented. "Now tell us the secret! Give it to us!"

"I will give you," said the Leader, "an Enemy. There he is; gaze upon him waiting to destroy you."

The people looked, and where nothing stood before they now saw him, and with one great voice they shouted, "Yes! Yes, we see him—our Enemy!"

And then were the people jubilant as the flags were unfurled and the bands began to play, and then did they know that they, the people, were blameless for the ills besetting their country, blameless for the emptiness they had felt inside—it was the Enemy, all along it had been the Enemy! "Lead us," they cried. "Lead us so that we can destroy our enemy!"

"First," the Leader reminded them, "you must give me one more thing."

"What is that?" they asked.

"You must give me," said the Leader, "your children."

CCCO notes

BARBARA DEMING

Poet and essayist; walker-for peace (Quebec to Guantanamo in 1963) imprisoned in Albany, Georgia, during the walk, from which came Prison Notes.

Some of you will ask a further question: If we abandon reliance upon military force—before international agreements have been signed—upon what alternative power can our country rely? The answer, I would say, is clearly the power of nonviolent resistance. And it seems to me an answer which we, as women, are peculiarly fitted to give. Gandhi once declared that it was his wife who unwittingly taught him the effectiveness of nonviolence. Who better than women should know that battles can be won without resort to physical strength? Who better than we should know all the power that resides in noncooperation?

—Letter to WSP, Liberation, *April 1963, included in* Revolution and Equilibrium, *Grossman Publishers*

By Way of Introduction . . . .

That the twentieth century is the bloodiest of all centuries in recorded history seems beyond doubt. That it may become even more destructive is chilling. One can recite the litany of horrendous acts of mass killing without much effort: the senselessness of the First World War, Stalin's brutalization of his own people, the Holocaust which systematically destroyed millions of Jewish men, women and children, Hiroshima and Nagasaki and a host of wars, small and large, all fought in the name of some cause.

The violence that spawned these crimes was doubtless a reflection in part of the sort carried out daily in all nations against the weak and helpless. When, however, it is sanctioned by the State then it becomes more menacing with the accompanying hatreds and lies, and the incessant calls for patriotism, sacrifice and the need to inflict unspeakable agonies on the enemy.

The concept of limited nuclear wars—that is, the untestable notion that we will drop a few here and there and they will do likewise—is both naive and misleading. In fact, nuclear strategists have no more idea of how it might all turn out than the rest of us do.

There are more important things than peace.

Alexander M. Haig, Jr., January 1981, during his confirmation hearing as Secretary of State before the Senate Foreign Relations Committee ★★★★

Change of Address?

The U.S. Postal Service plans to issue emergency change-of-address cards in the event of a nuclear attack.

WOR, [New York], March 15, 1982

Dr. Strangelove—Again

Dr. Eugene P. Wigner, Nobel Prize-winning physicist, urged that all secondary schools in the U.S. begin to organize courses on how to prepare for nuclear war. He told the American Civil Defense Association on October 10, 1981 that children should be "made aware that such a danger [of nuclear war] exists."

How do you win a nuclear war?

You have a survivability of command and control, survivability of industrial potential, protection of a percentage of your citizens and you have a capability that inflicts more damage on the opposition than it can inflict upon you.

George Bush, February, 1980

With greatly increased offensive and defensive preparations the United States could hold casualties in a nuclear war to 20 million, a level compatible with survival and recovery.

Colin Gray,
State Department Consultant,
"Victory is Possible"
Foreign Policy,
Summer, 1980

Mourn Now

Mourn now for the next war's dead,
weep now for the agony of the injured,
grieve now for the devastation of homelands.

Now is the time to mourn, to weep, to grieve,
now when tears can cleanse the future;
when war starts it is too late,
then we can only bury the dead,
shudder at the screams of the wounded,
grope through the ruins of our cities.

Mourn now in the streets and homes
where people live who allow war,
grieve now in the board rooms and factories
where the machines of death are made,
weep now in the halls of governments
whose actions lead relentlessly to war.

Now is the time to mourn, to weep, to grieve,
for the millions who will die,
while it still may not be too late.

Wallace Collett

Smart Kid

"Nuclear war is stupid. It should be
stopped. It's so quick. It can just wipe
out everything. I'm going to work on my
own project to show how bad nuclear war is."

Finnegan Small, 5th grader, Waltham, Mass. (The Justice, Brandeis University)

War

It kills.
It murders.
It terrorizes.
It fills the hearts of all with dread and horror.

People give birth to war.
They thirst for the dying blood of others.
It will not end until there is nothing left to destroy.

6th grade child, Anonymous

How do you survive a nuclear holocaust?

Everybody's going to make it if there are enough shovels to go around. Dig a hole, cover it with a couple of doors and then throw three feet of dirt on top. It's the dirt that does it.

Thomas K. Jones, Deputy Under Secretary of Defense for strategic nuclear forces, explaining how Americans can survive nuclear attack, Los Angeles Times, January 16, 1982

We're Number One!

Protected geographically by two huge oceans, on a continent that has never been invaded or even subjected to aerial attack, the (American) people suffer from a diminished reality-sense in which wars are always something which will happen "over there."

E.P. Thompson, British historian and a leader of the anti-nuclear campaign

To The Soviet Hawks

Madness=Those Soviet marshals and generals who still believe nuclear war is winnable.

Shalom

Where Is Herman Kahn Now that We Need Him?

Think-tank analysts can set levels of "acceptable damage" well up in the hundreds of millions of lives. . . . They are in an unreal world. In the real world of real political leaders—whether here or in the Soviet Union—a decision that would bring even one hydrogen bomb on one city of one's own country would be recognized in advance as a catastrophic blunder; 10 bombs on 10 cities would be a disaster beyond history; and 100 bombs on 100 cities are unthinkable.

McGeorge Bundy

Without Comment

It would be compounded folly to assume that better control of nuclear arms can result from a race to nuclear superiority. My reading of the Soviet experience—and I have met with every Soviet leader from Lenin to Brezhnev—indicates that Moscow will sacrifice what it takes to remain equal—as we will, too. The conclusion will not be superiority; the end will be an arms race without end.

W. Averell Harriman
Former Governor of New York
Former Ambassador to the Soviet Union

To Arms

We're in the midst of a world crisis caused by the surge of Soviet power since the collapse of our policy in Vietnam. To arrest the slide toward war, the U.S. and its allies must announce that they can no longer accept the situation in which they live by rules of the United Nations Charter governing the international use of force, while the Soviets and their allies violate them on an ever-larger scale.

Eugene V. Rostow, head of the Arms Control and Disarmament Agency, at the University of Idaho, April 3, 1981

Subversives

As the military power comes under scrutiny it will be reduced to asserting that its critics are indifferent to Soviet or ·Chinese intentions, unacquainted with the most recent intelligence, militarily inexperienced, naive, or afraid to look nuclear destruction in the eye. Or it will be said that they are witting or unwitting tools of the Communist conspiracy. In line with Secretary [of Defense Melvin] Laird's effort on behalf of the ABM (when he deployed from new intelligence an exceptionally alarming generation of Soviet missiles), a special appeal will be made to fear. A bureaucracy under attack is a fortress with thick walls but fixed guns.

John Kenneth Galbraith,
How to Control the Military,
© 1969, Doubleday & Co.

Medical Advice

"People are getting toughened about death," said Dr. Thomas C. Chalmers, Dean of the Mount Sinai Medical School. "They do not realize the prolonged suffering of nuclear attacks, with hundreds of people taking weeks to die, screaming to be shot, with no medical help available. Our whole concept of a civilized response to a tragedy is totally inapplicable."

March 20, 1981
The New York Times

Right or Wrong?

Both armed camps remain a menace to each other and to the rest of the world. Both are perpetually capable of going to war or intervening militarily (Vietnam, Afghanistan, etc.). Both need to be curbed when they reach for superiority or first strike capability.

W. Averell Harriman, former ambassador to Moscow and under-secretary of state, wrote in late 1981: "In our short time on Earth, we have a choice about the kind of world we leave behind. With nuclear weapons in our custody, our generation carries a heavy obligation. There will be no historian to record one day that we failed our watch."

Senator Daniel Patrick Moynihan wrote his constituents in late 1981: "How are we to think of civilization disappearing in an hour's time? Hard and carefully, that is how."

Honor Thy Mother and Thy Father

In a nuclear war, the overall cancer risk among survivors could be reduced if older people do jobs and eat food that could expose them to more radiation than younger people.

Drs. Kathy Gant and Conrad Chester,
Oak Ridge National Laboratory.
Newsday, *December 2, 1981*

The Peter Principle in Academia and Government

It's inaccurate thinking to say that the use of nuclear weapons would be the end of the human race. That's an egocentric thought. Of course, it's horrendous to contemplate, but in strictly statistical terms, if the United States used up all of its arsenal in the Soviet Union and the Soviet Union used up all of its against the United States it would not be the end of humanity. That's egocentric. There are other people on earth.

Zbigniew Brzezinski, quoted by Elizabeth Drew in The New Yorker, *1979*

RIVERSIDE CHURCH DISARMAMENT PROGRAM

490 Riverside Drive, New York, NY 10027, (212) 865-3883.

Founded by the anti-Vietnam War leader Reverend William Sloane Coffin and affiliated with the Riverside Church, the RCDP is a significant educational resource center, largely for the religious community. It emphasizes local organizing around such issues as opposition to a renewed draft, the uselessness of civil defense and support for a verifiable mutual nuclear freeze.

RCDP is also one of the six co-sponsors of the Peace Sabbath services whereby churches and synagogues throughout the country dedicate themselves to the struggle to avoid war. RCDP also serves as a national clearing house for information.

Director: Cora Weiss
Assistant Director: Rev. Michael Clark
Their publication: *Disarming Notes*
(newsletter free)

Personal Horoscope

Most of you will probably be involved in a nuclear war.

George Kistiakowsky, to an audience in Boston in 1981. Kistiakowsky was President Eisenhower's science advisor

CITIZENS FOR SPACE DEMILITARIZATION

There is only one national organization dedicated to a progressive analysis of space exploration and the space arms race — the San Francisco-based Citizens For Space Demilitarization (CFSD). Founded in the summer of 1979 by a dozen advocates of peaceful uses of space technology who were increasingly concerned about the dominance of space programs by military goals, CFSD has grown to 100 members across the United States. CFSD has sponsored public meetings in several major cities to publicize the space arms race, and the growing opposition to it. CFSD's membership includes professors, students, aerospace workers and technicians, and writers, editors, and publishers working in the aerospace press. A sprinkling of anti-nuclear, environmental and anti-war activists rounds out the roster. The group publishes the bi-monthly *Space For All People,* which is always full of articles analyzing military space systems and the politics of the space program, as well as an internal Membership Bulletin.

CFSD strives to establish working relationships with the increasingly-popular pro-space organizations, as well as with major groups opposing the arms race in general. The group's programmatic emphasis is support of arms control treaties, especially those to ban anti-satellite weapons and space laser weapons, and support of peaceful space exploration and development, especially projects involving international cooperation.

Citizens For Space Demilitarization
1476 California #9
San Francisco, CA 94109

Quiz

1. Do you agree that everyone "needs an enemy"? Do *you*? How far are the qualities which you detest in *your* enemy qualities which you yourself possess?
2. If nuclear wars are not likely to be waged for economic reasons, what are the possible reasons for wars of this kind—or indeed any kind at all—being waged?
3. Is there an obligation on the richer countries to help the poorer ones? How far should they imperil their own standard of living to do so? How far should their approval—or disapproval—of a regime (e.g., in Africa or the Middle East) govern their willingness to give?
4. Equally, how far have poorer countries a duty to ensure the efficient use of the aid they receive? Should this imply a willingness to accept supervision in the planning and spending of such aid?

Eric Baker. A Search for Alternatives to Violence *(London)*

Quiz

- What can religious bodies do to help establish a more just international economic order?
- What can the people of our religious groups do to help the nations avoid war, advance towards disarmament, and achieve an alternative to violence in the resolution of conflict?
- What can members of our religious traditions do to help families, neighborhoods, nations, and the world society protect and promote social justice and the dignity of the human person in community?
- What can our religions do to promote education for peace?
- How can we recover and strengthen the spiritual dimensions within our respective heritages, and bring them to bear on our work:
    a) to renew our particular community;
    b) to deepen our common fellowship; and
    c) to support our cooperative efforts for peace?

Quiz

1. Do you think we will have a nuclear war?
2. What can you picture in your mind's eye being destroyed that is most precious to you?
3. If you could imagine one million people doing something at the same time to stop the impending holocaust, what might that be?
4. If there were something you could do, with others, to stop the holocaust, would you do it?
5. Would you sign a petition calling for a nuclear freeze by the U.S. and the U.S.S.R. and go to others to ask them these same five questions?

Quiz

1. Should the U.S. and the U.S.S.R. continue to produce neutron warheads?

2. Do you feel more secure or more threatened by the nuclear arms race?

3. List the following categories of government spending in order of importance to you.
   (a) education, social services, health
   (b) military and defense
   (c) farming, regional development, mass transportation, the environment
   (d) space, taxation, foreign trade

Quiz

1. Do you feel secure with this country's military policies?

2. Should the U.S. match the Soviet Union in levels of armaments?

3. Should the U.S. surpass the Soviet Union in levels of armaments?

4. Should the U.S. and the Soviet Union sign a "no first strike" agreement banning first use of nuclear weapons?

5. Should the U.S. and the Soviet Union agree to freeze nuclear arsenals at current levels?

6. Should the U.S. and the Soviet Union agree to reduce current levels and move toward elimination of nuclear arms?

7. Were you in favor of supplying Saudi Arabia with AWACS and Sidewinder missiles?

8. Will deploying Cruise and Pershing missiles in NATO countries help prevent nuclear war in Europe?

9. Should the U.S. continue to sell weapons to Latin American, Asian, and African countries?

10. Should the U.S. continue to sell weapons to European countries?

11. Should the U.S. continue to maintain occupation troops in Germany and Japan?

12. Can the U.S. economy afford projected military spending of $1.5 trillion over the the next five years?

13. Do you believe the U.S. is the most powerful nation in the world?

14. Do you think a nuclear war will occur in the next ten years?

Center for Defense Information

The Fund for Peace

Quiz

Arms Race Survey

1. With our present nuclear stockpile, government officials estimate we can kill every Soviet citizen
   A) once
   B) 10 times over
   C) 40 times over
   D) 60 times over

2. Which nation has forged all of the major advances in the nuclear arms race?
   A) Soviet Union
   B) United States
   C) Both have led some advances

3. About 40% of our federal budget is used for military spending. How do large military budgets affect our economy?
   A) Stops unemployment
   B) Aids free enterprise
   C) Creates unemployment and inflation
   D) Lowers taxes

4. Over the next 5 years, the average family of four will spend at least how much on nuclear weapons programs?
   A) about $500
   B) about $1000
   C) about $5000
   D) about $8000

TEST YOURSELF!

Answers

1. c

   Dept. of Defense figures of U.S. missile destructive power show that we can now kill all Soviet citizens "40 times over". Such power is wasteful and nonsensical.

2. b

   The United States has taken an initiating role in all 9 major nuclear weapons developments.
   These are: Atom-bomb (US, 1945; USSR, 1950); H-bomb (US, 1955; USSR, 1955); A-bombs in Europe (US, 1954; USSR, 1957); nuclear missile subs (US, 1960; USSR, 1965); intercontinental nuclear missiles (US, 1965; USSR, 1970); highly accurate MIRV missiles (US, 1970; USSR, 1975); short-range attack missiles (US, 1975; USSR—); underwater long-range missiles (US, 1980; USSR—); First strike nuclear war strategy (US, 1980; USSR—).

3. c

   Military programs are capital intensive and cause unemployment. That is why major labor unions, like the Longshoremen (ILWU), Aerospace and Machinists (IAM), and Electrical Workers (UE) are calling for less military spending. Military spending also fuels inflation.

4. d

   The average family will pay about $8000 in taxes for nuclear weapons programs in the next five years.

Quiz

1. What is the value of British arms exports this year? Who said recently "it is not enough"?

2. What proportion of the world's arms trade goes to the Third World? What is Britain's share of this?

3. To which regions of the world is Britain the second-largest supplier?

4. Which of these countries export more arms

Answers

1. £1200 million according to the Defense Sales Organisation. Mrs Thatcher. *(Newsletters 44 & 45)*

2. Two thirds. Five per cent. *(SIPRI)*

3. South America (2nd to USA) and Central America (2nd to USSR) during 1975-79. *(SIPRI)*

4. USA, USSR and France. Italy and West Germa-

Q|A

than Britain? Belgium, Brazil, Czechoslovakia, France, Israel, Italy, South Africa, Sweden, Switzerland, USA, USSR, West Germany.

5. What are: the DSO? BAEE? RNEE?

6. How many countries were allowed to sign contracts for British arms in 1979?

7. Does Britain sell military equipment to the Warsaw Pact? Or to other communist countries?

8. Does the government prohibit the sale of British arms to countries with bad human rights records?

9. A British Aerospace "Hawk" ground attack/trainer aircraft costs about £3 million. How many people could be given a clean water supply for that amount?

10. How does the arms trade cause disability?

11. Which of the following does Britain *not* export? submarines, fighter aircraft, nuclear bombs, antiship missiles, armoured cars, rifles, leg irons, surveillance cameras, chemical weapons.

12. What are "grey area goods"?

13. Is there a company near you which makes arms for export?

14. How many people in Britain are employed directly in making arms for export?

15. If you had $1000 million to invest, which would generate more jobs: spending it on military projects, on housing, or on health?

16. Which company refused to consider alternatives to arms production proposed by its workers in 1976?

17. What will the DMA be doing at the Brighton Metropole from 12-14 May 1981?

18. What proportion of research in the British electronics industry is military-related?

19. What did the 1978 UN Special Session on Disarmament say about the arms trade? When is the next SSD?

20. What does your MP think about the arms trade?

Campaign Against Arms Trade
5, Caledonian Road, Kings Cross,
London N1 9DX England

ny export about the same as Britain. *(SIPRI)**

5. The Defense Sales Organisation, the British Army Equipment Exhibition, and the Royal Navy Equipment Exhibition, all part of Britain's arms sales drive. *(The DSO)*

6. Sixty-one. *(Factsheet 27)*

7. Yes, transport aircraft to Romania. Yes, to China and Yugoslavia. *(Factsheet 27)*

8. Only under pressure—e.g. the cancellation of a deal with El Salvador in 1978, and the 1974 embargo on arms for Chile (lifted in July 1980). *(Newsletter 43)*

9. One and a half million. *(Arming the World)*

10. Directly, through war casualties; indirectly through the diversion of resources from health and rehabilitation programmes. *(IYDP and You)*

11. Nuclear bombs, but British parts allowed Pakistan to acquire a nuclear capacity. *(Newsletter, "Arming the World" section)*

12. Items which have both civil and military uses, and whose export is therefore not controlled. *(The Repression Trade)*

13. Find out from *The Arms Traders.*

14. 75,000, according to the DSO. *(Choices leaflet)*

15. Health (139,000 jobs), housing construction (100,000 jobs), military (76,000 jobs). *(Choices)*

16. Lucas Aerospace. *(Lucas: an alternative plan)*

17. The Defense Manufacturers Association will be holding its Defense Components Expo. *(Newsletter 44)*

18. Well over half. *(A defense for arms?)*

19. It called for consultations among arms suppliers and recipients. 1982. *(Newsletter 45)*

20. Write and find out, or ask the CAAT office about his or her previous record. *(Newsletter 44)*

Armaments or disarmament? This and all other references above are available from CAAT.

CHILDREN'S LETTERS

To President Reagan...

Dear Mr. President,

I am only eleven and I want to get older, but at the rate the world is going I won't grow to be fifteen! I am worried about nuclear weapons. people (in high places) don't seem to know how we (the kids) feel. I hope you do now! Remember, I'm only a kid. Sincerely,

Signe Folsom
10 Blackwell St.
Montpelier, Vt
05602

President Reagan,

How can you say you're for peace when most of our economy, is going towards the military?

The citizens of this country would appreciate the U.S. much more if they all felt as if they could trust and respect their leaders. To get this trust and respect, you can't hold our lives in yours hands It would be foolish for the world's leaders to wast millions of lives for their own personal satisfaction and feeling of power

It's funny that you—the president know and care less about nuclear disarmament than a bunch of kids. Or maybe it isn't so funny...

Nelly Reifler
New York City

Dear President
Please stop making nuclear bombs.
I want to live! I don't want a war, anyway. Whats the use for a war? And it _always_ takes a long time to rebuild buildings. Sincerely
age (9½) Amy Sanford

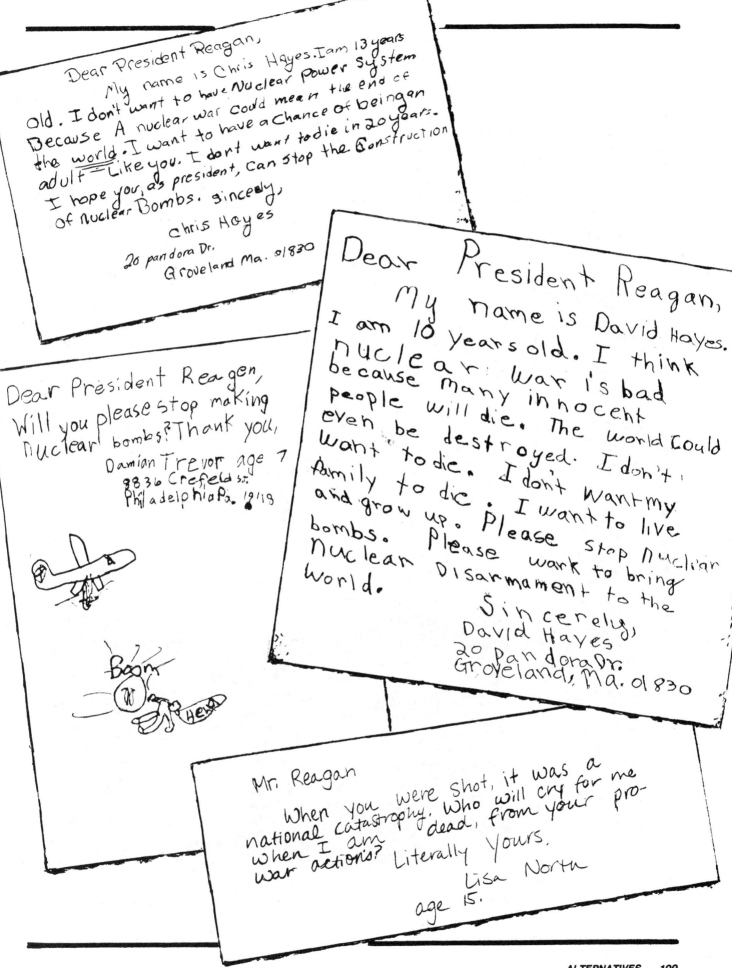

Dear President Reagan,
My name is Chris Hayes. I am 13 years old. I don't want to have Nuclear Power System Because A nuclear war Could mean the end of the world. I want to have a Chance of being an adult—Like you. I dont want to die in 20 years. I hope you, as president, Can stop the Construction of Nuclear Bombs. Sincerly,
Chris Hayes
20 pandora Dr.
Groveland Ma. 01830

Dear President Reagen,
Will you please stop making nuclear bombs? Thank you,
Damian Trevor age 7
8836 Crefeld st.
Philadelphia Pa. 19118

Boom
W
Head

Dear President Reagan,
My name is David Hayes. I am 10 years old. I think nuclear war is bad because many innocent people will die. The world could even be destroyed. I don't want to die. I don't want my family to die. I want to live and grow up. Please stop Nuclar bombs. Please work to bring nuclear Disarmament to the world.
Sincerely,
David Hayes
20 Pandora Dr.
Groveland, Ma. 01830

Mr. Reagan
When you were shot, it was a national Catastrophy. Who will cry for me when I am dead, from your pro-war actions? Literally yours.
Lisa North
age 15.

the vermont Vanguard Press

NEWS AND ARTS WEEKLY

JUNE 26-JULY 3 1981

VOL. IV, NO. 23

It's the spares that make profits

Constant 1980 $ bn

Spare parts

Original jet engine sales

1958 62 66 70 74 78 82 86 90

Source: Based on Rolls-Royce figures

Children Ask Reagan For Nuke-Free Life

PLAINFIELD

THOSE WHO ARGUE Against the escalation of the nuclear arms race often express concern for the "future of our children." Now the children are speaking for themselves.

The Children's Campaign for Nuclear Disarmament (CCND), a recently formed group, is conducting a letter campaign to organize children throughout the nation around the issue of nuclear disarmament. They are asking children to write letters to President Reagan expressing opposition to the nuclear arms race. The letters will be taken on Oct. 17 to the White House and presented publicly. Each letter will be read aloud; "each one is important," the Children's Campaign insists.

The six young women who founded the campaign have been friends since infancy and share an interest in political affairs and a desire to learn about the issues. In response to an apparent increasing threat of a world-wide nuclear holocaust, they met on May 18 to discuss plans for action.

The six organizers, between the ages of twelve and 22, are from New England – two from Boston, one from Maine, and three from Vermont – but are determined to have their message heard throughout the country.

"It is a matter of life and death," says Susan Rabin, a Vermont organizer. "We must not lose sight of this fact. The lives of innocent children are at stake.

"Kids can say things in a powerful and direct way," she says. "Adults get caught up in complications. They forget to think about fear of death. Everyone should be frightened."

A CCND statement being circulated says, "We are children who fear for the future of our world." CCND hopes "to have hundreds, maybe thousands of letters" by October. Children who want to participate may send letters to Children's Campaign for Nuclear Disarmament, Box 550, RD1, Plainfield, Vt., 05667. The letters should be "respectful and responsible," Susan Rabin explained. "We want to bring President Reagan over to our side, not to push him further away."

Campaign participants will take part in the Walk from Washington to Moscow (in Vermont) on Aug. 6 through 9.

– Aileen Lachs

JULES AND HELEN RABIN

Members of the Children's Campaign for Disarmament, from left: Nessa Rabin, 12; new member Becky Dennison, 11; Susan Rabin and Susan Dennison, both 15.

LISTEN TO THIS:

There IS an alternative to compulsory military service. If you have moral, ethical, or religious objections to participation in any war or military training, you can be a conscientious objector. One can be a CO regardless of one's religion: an agnostic or atheist can make a CO claim based on deeply held, personal beliefs. The Central Committee for Conscientious Objectors is an organization engaged in a nation-wide effort to inform people about Conscientious objection and related peace issues.

We are also registering conscientious objectors with our CO card. This card simply states: "Because of my beliefs about war, I am opposed to participation in the military." Should the draft be reinstated, and this is becoming increasingly likely, a CO card could provide important documentation of your status as an objector. For more information, write to:

CCCO
P.O.Box 15796
Philadelphia,
PA. 19103

CONSCIENTIOUS OBJECTOR STATUS, THINK ABOUT IT.

C. Maxwell Stanley   *International Citizen*

Many Americans find keeping up with international political and military events a difficult and complex undertaking. A few Americans actively pursue a greater understanding of these seemingly intractable issues, and, further, bring them in a practical form to the public's attention. One of the few is C. Maxwell Stanley.

Max and his wife Elizabeth (Betty), both native Iowans, established the Stanley Foundation in Muscatine, Iowa, in 1956 to encourage study, research, and education in the field of international policy with emphasis on world organization. The Stanley Foundation's primary activity is conducting conferences which bring together diplomats, policy-makers, academicians, and other experts to discuss world issues—present and future.

Among the conferences hosted by the Stanley Foundation are an annual conference on Strategy for Peace; United Nations of the Next Decade; and United Nations Procedures. The Foundation also produces conference reports, occasional papers, and "Common Ground," a radio series on world affairs.

Max Stanley, a general engineer from the University of Iowa who later received an M.S. in Hydraulic Engineering, became prominent in his field and founded Stanley Consultants, Inc., international consultants with world-wide contacts in engineering, architecture, planning, and management. Along the way, he had time to start an office furnishings business (now Hon Industries).

Since 1947, he has been a member of the World Federalists Association where he met Mrs. Arthur M. Young, Academy Founder/Chairman. Ruth Young recently noted, "I have for many years respected Max Stanley for his efforts and commitment to bringing about a more peaceful world. He has been a most generous supporter of the Academy from the very beginning and has much to do with the Academy's development."

Max has authored two books on global politics. His latest book, *Managing Global Problems* (December, 1979), focuses on issues moving the world community, including peace and security, human rights, economic order, development, international organization, and U.S. foreign policy. He wrote *Waging Peace* in 1956 which outlined a positive program for securing global peace and progress.

The Foundation also supports the monthly magazine, *World Press Review*, which excerpts and reprints materials from the press outside the United States. It is based in New York City and under the direction of Editor Alfred Balk.

"Fear, frustration, and anger are useless unless translated into action, for there will be no breakthroughs in these problem areas unless and until the leaders of nations bring them about. It is my sincere hope that our deliberations may strengthen the resolve of each one of us to press the leaders of this country to look to the future and develop a comprehensive strategy for peace." (Stanley at 22nd Annual Strategy for Peace Conference, October, 1981.) This resolve and commitment to peace define Max Stanley.

Max Stanley (left) presents Secretary-General Kurt Waldheim with a copy of the Stanley Foundation's report "The United Nations of the Next Decade" (1980).

WOMEN'S PEACE RESOURCES

Compiled by Josephine Rubin

The overview of the women's movement is incomplete without some understanding of their position on war/peace. The movement derives its position from the women's rejection of 'dominance' in all aspects of life and for this reason movement women have provided talent and energy in the advocacy of world peace. This list is an introduction for use in Peace Studies courses and Women's Studies courses because neither curriculae is complete without the other. It is useful as a guide for groups and individuals wishing to know more about the peace component of the movement. For convenience we have coded each entry to help you to locate the materials. For example: (B) means bookstore; (L) means Library; (P) means publisher and (A) means author.

J.R.

Andrea Hinding, Editor, Women's History Sources, indexed for peace, Bowker Publishing Company 1180 Avenue of the Americas, New York, N.Y. 1980. Price $175.00. (L) or (P)

U.S. Library of Congress, Washington, D.C. has the papers of Susan B. Anthony and Carrie Chapman Catt. (L)

The Gerritsen Collection, University of Kansas Library, Lawrence, Ka. contains the papers of Dr. Aletta Jacobs, Holland's first woman physician and convener of the Hague Congress of Women (L)

Proceedings of the Hague Congress of Women available for study at the Swarthmore Peace Collection, Swarthmore College, Swarthmore, Pa. and the Schwimmer-Lloyd Peace Collection, Manuscript Division, New York Public Library. (L)

The Garland Library on War and Peace, Edited by Blanche Weisen Cook, Charles Chatfield and Sandi Cooper consists of cloth-bound volumes of 200 basic writings most of which are out of print. Available as a nucleus of a peace library or as individual volumes. Send for catalogue to Garland Publishing Company, 136 Madison Avenue, New York, N.Y. 10016. (P)

Pioneers for Peace, history of the Women's International League for Peace and Freedom, updated, with introduction by Kay Camp. Paperback, $7.00 from WILPF, 1213 Race Street, Philadelphia, Pa. 10107. (P)

Mercedes Randall, **Improper Bostonian,** (Emily Green Balch) Thwayne Publishers, New York. (L)

Allan Davis, **American Heroine,** Life and legend of Jane Addams, Oxford University Press, 1973. (L)

Marie Louise Degen, **A History of the Women's Peace Party,** Garland Publishing Company, 136 Madison Avenue, New York, N.Y. (L)

Lella Secour, **A Diary in Letters 1915-1922,** Burt Franklin Inc. 235 East 44 Street, New York, N.Y. 10017 1980. (B) or (P)

For Biography of Rosika Schwimmer see **Fourth Supplement, Dictionary of American Biography.**

Edith Wynner and Georgia Lloyd, **Searchlight on Peace Plans,** E.P. Dutton New York, 1947. (L)

Edith Wynner, **Feminism and Militarism,** Spring 1980 2pp. Free 40 West 86 Street New York, N.Y. 10024 (A)

Women, War and Revolution, Edited by Carol R. Berken and Clara M. Lovett, Holmes and Meier, Publishers, 30 Irving Place, New York, N.Y. 10003. 1980. Extensive Bibliography. $14.95. (B)

Ruby Rohrlich, **State Formation in Sumer and the Subjugation of Women,** Feminist Studies, Vol 6 #1. Spring 1980. $5.00. Women's Studies Program University of Maryland, College Park, Maryland 20742. (B) or (P)

From Global Education Associates, 552 Park Avenue, East Orange New Jersey 07017 the following monographs from the series, **Whole Earth Papers**:

Josephine Rubin, **Women and Peace,** Spring 1978, Vol 1 No. 6. 70¢ Discount on orders over 9. (10pp)

Patricia Mische, **Women, Power and Alternative Futures,** Part 1 8pp. 60¢ Discount on orders over 9.

Patricia Mische, **Women, Power and Alternative Futures,** Part 2 8 pp. 60¢ Discount on orders over 9.

Betty Reardon, **The Child and World Order,** Reflections on International Year of the Child, 10pp. 70¢ Discount on orders over 9.

Lorenne Clark and Debra Lewis, **Rape, The Price of Coercive Sexuality** Canadian Women's Educational Press, Toronto (B) or (P)

Lorenne Clark and Lynda Lange, Eds. **The Sexism of Social and Political Theory** from Plato to Nietzsche, University of Toronto Press, 1979. $5.00 (B)

Lili Hahn, **Arms Control and Conversion to Peacetime Economy,** a 4 page program planner, prepared for Unitarian Universalist Women's Federation, 25 Beacon Street, Boston, Mass. $1.00. (P)

Ruth Leger Sivard, **World Military and Social Expenditures** for the years 1974, 76, 77 and 78 Price $2.50 each. For years 1979 and 80 price $3.50. Four earlier editions available to libraries at $6.00 the set. Order from World Priorities, Inc. Box 1003, Leesburg, Virginia 22075. (P)

Ruth Leger Sivard, **World Energy Survey,** $30. World Priorities, Box 1003, Leesburg, Virginia 22075. (P)

Hanna Newcombe, Director, Canadian Peace Research Institute and, with her nusband Alan, co-director of Peace Research Institute publishes **Peace Abstracts Journal** and **Peace Research Reviews Journal** by subscription only. A dozen books from PRI and 70 articles by Dr. Hanna Newcombe. List available from Peace Research Institute 25 Dundana Avenue Dundas, Ontario, Canada L9H 4E5.

Beverly Woodward, **Peace Studies and the Feminist Challenge,** in Peace and Change: A Journal of Peace Research, Vol 111, No. 4. Spring 1976. Reprints from author at 75¢ each. Box 38 South Boston, Mass. 02127. (A)

Beverly Woodward, **Non Violence and Global Transformation** Gandhi Marg. Journal of the Gandhi Peace Foundation 221-223 Deen Dayal, New Delhi, India 11002 Spring 1981. And, by Same author **The Abolition of War,** same journal, December 1980. (L) or (P)

Helen Caldicott, **Nuclear Madness,** Paperback, 1980 $5.00 (B)

ISIS, International Bulletin #15, **Nuclear Power and Militarization,** Via Della Pellicia 31, 00153, Rome, Italy. $3.00 (B) or (P)

WIN-NEWS, Fran Hosken, Editor, international coverage of movement events with articles. 187 Grant Street, Lexington, Mass. 02173. $15. yearly. (P)

WIRE Service, issues reprints of articles and addresses from women in third world countries. English and Spanish. Prices range from 50¢ to $2.50. WIRE Service 2700 Broadway Room 7, New York, N.Y. 10025 (P)

War, Peace Film Guide, John Dowling, a standard Reference. World without War Council, 67 E. Madison, Suite 1417 Chicago, Illinois, 60603. $5.00 (P)

World Peace News, concentrates on world government. Published 10 times a year, by subscription, $10.00. 777 United Nations Plaza, New York, New York 10017 (P)

For additional copies of Women's Peace Resources, send stamped self-addressed envelope to Global Educational Associates, 552 Park Avenue, East Orange New Jersey 07017.

Peace Brigades

Mark Shepard

The effort to abolish war has been blocked in part by an important obstacle: we need war. It is the only way we know to protect a large group of people against determined aggression, or to resolve severe conflicts. We will likely always face these situations. To abolish war, then, we must find alternative ways to handle them.

Happily, thinkers and activists have begun to face this challenge. They have gradually been developing two concepts that provide alternatives to war. One is nonviolent civilian defense (also known as "civilian-based defense," or "social defense"), in which populations offer nonviolent resistance to invaders. Though the concept still needs much formal development, spontaneous examples have occurred throughout history, as in the Czech resistance to Soviet troops in 1968.

The second concept is "peace brigades." Peace brigades are teams of unarmed civilians skilled in aggressive peacemaking through nonviolent means. They intervene as "third parties" in local, national, or international conflicts.

As with nonviolent civilian defense, peace brigade actions can be found throughout history. Development of the concept can be traced to Mahatma Gandhi. Gandhi first suggested the idea in 1922, as a way to

handle riots in Bombay; and again in 1938, when he first used the term "peace brigade."

The idea failed to take hold during Gandhi's lifetime, but was later revived by his acknowledged spiritual successor, Vinoba Bhave (pronounced Bah-vay). In 1957, Bhave founded Shanti Sena, the "Peace Army," to deal with riots in Indian towns and cities. At Shanti Sena's peak in the 1960s, its roster included several thousand active, part-time "Shanti Sainiks" (peace soldiers), mostly Gandhian rural development workers, both male and female. India's political turmoil in the mid-70s dealt Shanti Sena a staggering blow, from which the organization has never fully recovered. Still, the Gandhians continue their Shanti Sena activities, usually under other banners.

Most of India's riots are between Hindus and Moslems, with the dominant Hindus usually the main aggressor. (Nearly all the Shanti Sainiks are themselves Hindu.) These riots have sometimes left thousands of dead within a single city. Other riots have been started by political, ethnic, and student groups. Since riots and wars are in many ways alike, a look at Shanti Sena methods gives an idea how peace brigades might act in an international conflict as well.

When violence erupts, up to thirty or more Shanti Sainiks rush to the city by train, individually or in small groups, organizing themselves into teams. One team contacts local officials and community leaders. Sometimes the Sainiks will convince the leaders of rioting

communities to call for an end to the violence, or to open talks with the other side.

Most of the teams patrol violence-prone areas of the city, the Sainiks clad in their distinctive uniforms. They talk with people about their grievances, and encourage them to see the need for a return to peace. The presence of the teams discourages violence. But if violence breaks out, the teams will rush between opponents, shouting peace slogans, and absorbing blows from either side.

One team may have the special job of fighting rumors, which often play a large part in inciting violence. The Sainiks determine the facts in each case, then broadcast their findings through grassroots channels and the media. Riots are also fed by fear, so the Sainiks work hard to counteract it. Their presence can be reassuring to a neighborhood. Sometimes the Sainiks will quarter themselves among those who are afraid, and other times, among those they are supposed to fear. At times they will organize silent processions of locals through riot-struck areas.

Once the violence begins to subside, the Sainiks begin shifting to relief work: medical services, food and clothing supply, reconstruction of burnt homes, and clean-up jobs. This relief work often becomes the basis of efforts to reconcile opposing communities. In one city, for instance, the Sainiks convinced Hindus to give money to rebuild Moslem homes they had destroyed only a week earlier.

At times the Sainiks have launched into action when rising tensions have made rioting seem imminent. Shanti Sena has mounted major relief operations after natural disasters, and has aided Bengali refugees during the 1971 war between East and West Pakistan.

Shanti Sena has impressed nonviolent activists in other countries, some of whom have wanted to try the idea on an international level. In late 1961, a conference near Beirut, Lebanon brought together activists from around the world—including Shanti Sena leaders—to form the World Peace Brigade.

Though WPB in its brief life did not restrict itself to peacemaking, it sponsored at least one action in the Shanti Sena tradition. This was the Delhi-Peking Friendship March in 1963-64, following the brief 1962 border war between China and India. Organized mostly by Shanti Sainiks, it was an attempt to see whether the people of two opposing countries could bypass their governments and make contacts to promote peace.

The international team of seventeen marchers walked east from New Delhi, joined near each of its daily stops by hundreds or thousands of locals. The direct route of the marchers would have taken them across East Pakistan and Burma; but pressure from China on those governments denied them entry to either, forcing detours. They were finally refused entry at the Chinese border itself. But the march did seem to have helped calm the war fever in India.

In 1964, another action in India involved WPB and Gandhian activists. The Nagaland Peace Mission negotiated a ceasefire between the central government and tribal guerillas in far eastern India. An observers' team headed by Gandhian activists then helped maintain the truce without serious incident for the next eight years.

The World Peace Brigade eventually faded away because of internal problems, but in 1972-74, some WPB veterans revived and further developed the concept through the Cyprus Resettlement Project. The project aimed at involving both Turk and Greek Cypriots in rebuilding homes for Turk Cypriot refugees, as a step toward reconciling the two. The activists managed to secure the cooperation of leaders from both sides, and became the first group to get representatives of both to sit at the same table for talks. Intercommunal teams had actually begun rebuilding a few homes, when the project was cut short by the invasion of the Turkish army.

After the Cyprus project, the idea of international peace brigades remained mostly in limbo for the better part of a decade. But the recent spate of world crises, starting with Iran and Afghanistan, has set the idea once more moving through the minds of many. Projects and proposals for peace-brigade-type organizations have emerged independently from many sources. Already, ad hoc brigades have made their way to Iran, the Middle East, and Central America.

One of the most forward-looking of the current efforts is Peace Brigades International, formed in September, 1981 at an international conference on Grindstone Island in Ontario, Canada. Partly inspired by a call from Vinoba Bhave for a new World Peace Brigade, its chief figures include two veterans of WPB, Charles Walker and Narayan Desai, former head of Shanti Sena. PBI's main aim is to develop the capability to launch international peace brigades. It also hopes to promote, support, and coordinate local peace brigades, based in communities, states or provinces, and nations.

PBI sees its international brigades employing methods similar to those used by Shanti Sena in urban riots: mediation, investigation and observation, monitoring of truce lines, reconciliation work between communities, relief work, and if necessary, forming human buffers between attacking forces. To gain recognized authority, as well as access to leaders and conflict areas, the brigades would normally operate by arrangement with an international political body (such as the U.N., O.A.S., etc.), or with one or more national governments.

Generally, the brigades would be nonpartisan, trying to gain the cooperation of each combatant. But to overcome resistance to peacemaking efforts, they might resort to marches, fasts, or civil disobedience. They might also sound an international alarm or interpose themselves to prevent incidents of clearly one-sided aggression.

Another current effort is Peaceworkers, founded and directed by Raymond Magee, co-founder of PBI, and one of the originators of the "peace corps" concept. Peaceworkers aims at convincing the U.N. to develop its own peacemaking force on the peace brigade model. Magee believes that unarmed, trained civilians will in some ways be more effective than the U.N.'s present peacekeeping forces. Peaceworkers is now collecting signatures of prospective volunteers for such a peace force.

Still another effort is the World Peace Army, based in New York. While PBI and Peaceworkers hope to enlist the cooperation of governments and international bodies, WPA leans toward opposing them, saying that national governments themselves are responsible for war. WPA will likely involve itself in a mixture of partisan and nonpartisan actions, much as did the original World Peace Brigade.

Hopefully efforts such as these will help provide the practical alternatives that will someday make war obsolete.

Addresses

For general information on Peace Brigades International, write

Box 199
Cheyney, PA 19319 USA

Piet Dijkstra
Westerweg 2
1862 CE Bergen, NH
Netherlands

Narayan Desai
Institute for Total
  Revolution
Vedchhi
Dt. Surat, Gujarat
India
(address in capitals)

PBI is currently exploring the possibility of a peace brigade to Central America. For information on this project, or in regard to local peace brigades in the West, write

P.O. Box 1222
Walla Walla, WA 99362 USA

Addresses for other organizations mentioned in this article are

Peaceworkers
3149 Plymouth
Lafayette, CA 94549 USA

World Peace Army
15 Rutherford Place
New York, NY 10003 USA

Reading

Liberation Without Violence, A. Paul Hare and Herbert Blumberg, ed., Rex Collings, London, 1977. Detailed accounts of peace brigade and other nonviolent actions by Shanti Sena, the World Peace Brigade.

A Search for Peace and Justice: Reflections of Michael Scott, Hare and Blumberg, ed., Rex Collings, London, 1980. Includes some of the same actions as *Liberation Without Violence*, from the perspective of a major participant.

A World Peace Guard: An Unarmed Agency for Peacekeeping, Charles C. Walker, Gandhi Peace Foundation, 221 Deen Dayal Upadhyaya Marg, New Delhi 110002, India, 1981. Practical examination of the peace brigade concept, with proposals for future application. Available from PBI's main U.S. office (address given above), or from the Gandhi Peace Foundation.

America Without Violence, Michael Nagler, Island Press, Star Route 1, Box 38, Covelo, CA 95428, USA, 1982. Includes discussions of peace brigades and nonviolent civilian defense.

Acknowledgments

For permission to reprint the selections in this volume, grateful acknowledgment is made to those named below. Effort has been made to obtain appropriate permission to reproduce the copyrighted materials included in this book. If notified of errors or omissions, the editor and the publisher will make the necessary corrections in future editions.

Thanks to: American Friends Service Committee for "If We Could Talk with Ronald" and other literature; The American Railroad Foundation for their "Defense" advertisement; Anthony Storr for an excerpt from *Human Aggression*, copyright © 1968 by Anthony Storr (New York: Atheneum, 1968), reprinted with the permission of Atheneum Publishers; Steve Brodner/INX for his illustration; William M. Brown for excerpts from *The Nuclear Crisis of 1979*; CCCO/An Agency for Military and Draft Counseling, 2208 South Street, Philadelphia, PA 19146 for "The Great Fear Returns," "Once Upon a Time," "First Publicly Funded Military High School to Open," "Saying No and Saying Yes," and "How to Get into the Schools"; The Campaign Against the Arms Trade for "The Global Trade in Arms"; Robert Canfield and the *Washington University Magazine* for the article about Afghanistan; the *Chicago Tribune* and Dick Locher for the cartoon "It kills all the people, but leaves the caves intact," copyrighted 1981, *Chicago Tribune*; *The Christian Science Monitor* for "If We Could Talk with Leonid," reprinted by permission from *The Christian Science Monitor*, © 1980 The Christian Science Monitor Publishing Society, all rights reserved; *Christianity and Crisis* for the article by Molly Rush, © 1980 by Christianity and Crisis, Inc.; the Coalition for a New Foreign and Military Policy for "What Do We Really Need for National Security" and the "Hey Wimp!" cartoon; *Columbia College Today* for "The Manhasset Project" by Frederic David Schwarz, reprinted by permission of *Columbia College Today*, Spring/Summer 1981, © 1981, *Columbia College Today*; *Commonweal* for Thomas Powers' "The Bomb Bibliography," June 4, 1982, "On Nuclear Disbelief," January 15, 1982 and for "Zero in Moscow," May 7, 1982; *Confrontation, A Literary Journal* of LIU for portions of the Howard H. Hiatt, John M. Swomley, Bob Seeley and Murray Polner essays in the supplement, "Contemporary American Pacifism," Winter 1981, *Confrontation*; Fran Donelan for her study of "Careers in Peacemaking"; Doubleday & Company for excerpts from *How to Control the Military* by John Kenneth Galbraith, copyright © 1969, reprinted by permission of Doubleday & Company, Inc.; Fritz Eichenberg for his illustrations, "War & Peace Under the Cross," "The Riddle of the Peaceable Kingdom," and "The Complaint of Peace," courtesy © Fritz Eichenberg; The Federation of American Scientists and Jeremy Stone for various articles; *Fellowship* for "Disregarded History";

Francis A. Fitzgerald for permission to reprint illustrations; Frontlash for its Solidarity advertisement; The Fund for Peace for its advertisement; Bob Gale/INX for his illustration; Chellis Glendenning for "Telling Our Nuclear Stories"; *Greenpeace Examiner* for "Undersea Draftees" and "Canadian Uranium: Fueling the Arms Race"; the Herald Press for *How to Teach Peace to Children* by J. Lorne Peachey, copyright 1981 by Herald Press, Scottdale, PA 15683; *The Jerusalem Post* for "Stoking the Fires of War"; George F. Kennan for his speech, "A Proposal for Disarmament"; Tuli Kupferberg and Vanity Press for illustrations; *Maryknoll* magazine for "Merchants of Death," August 1979; NARMIC, National Action Research on the Military/Industrial Complex, 1501 Cherry Street, Philadelphia, PA 19102 for "Top 100 Defense Contractors," "Militarizing Central America," "How to Research Your Local War Industry" and other literature; *National Review*, 150 E. 35th St., New York, NY 10016, for permission to reprint the cartoons, "Brezhnev" and "Ban the Bomb"; Nej til Atomvaben Ad Group for its advertisement on nuclear disarmament; *The New Republic* for Ronald Steel's "The Absent Danger," reprinted by permission of *The New Republic*, © 1980 The New Republic, Inc.; *New York Review of Books* for permission to reprint drawings by David Levine, copyright © 1963-1982, Nyrev, Inc.; *The Objector* CCCO/Western Regional Office, 1251 Second Ave., San Francisco, CA 94122 for article on the South and the military; George Ott and *Newsday* for August 31, 1981 article on the true extent of the military threat from the USSR; *Peace News*, 8 Elm Ave., Nottingham, England for "Global Overkill"; Paul Peter Piech for illustrations; *Publishers Weekly* for "Checklist of Nuclear Books," reprinted from the March 26, 1982 issue of *Publishers Weekly*, published by R.R. Bowker Co., a Xerox company, copyright © 1982 by Xerox Corporation; M.L. Rosenthal for his poem, "To the Rulers," from *Poems, 1964-1980*, copyright © 1981 Oxford University Press, 1982; Josephine Rubin for "Women's Peace Resources"; *Science for the People* for "New War Plans for U.S. Hospitals," July/August 1981, 897 Main Street, Cambridge, MA 02139, $12/year; Mark Shepard for "Peace Brigades"; Layle Silbert for her photographs; Ruth Sivard and World Priorities for "Boomerang," an excerpt from *World Military and Social Expenditures*, © 1980 World Priorities and Ruth Sivard; Muriel Thiessen Stackley for her poetry; Lawrence Suid for his list of war and war-related films; Paul Tick for his photograph, "Stop War"; Institute for World Order, 777 U.N. Plaza, New York, NY 10017 for Robert C. Johansen article in *Transition*, vol. 4, no. 3, November 1979; Aileen Lacks and *The Vermont Vanguard Press* for "Children Ask for a Nuke Free Life"; War Resisters League for articles by Barbara Deming and Ira Sandperl; Charles C. Walker for "A World Peace Guard"; *World Goodwill Newsletter* for "Transition Activities," January-February-March 1982; and World Peacemakers for "Basic Ideas for a Strategy for Stopping the Arms Race."

NOTES

NOTES

NOTES

NOTES

NOTES